If you're serious about exam success, it's time to *Concentrate!*

Each guide in the **Concentrate** series is the result of a close collaboration with law students and examiners and careful and thorough research into effective revision techniques. We have worked with over 90 law students on every aspect of the series, from the covers to the text design, features and content. You told us what you wanted and we listened. Every guide – as well as being written by subject experts with teaching and examining experience – has been peer reviewed to ensure written style is as clear as possible and that content is rigorous but not oversimplified.

online resource centre

Additional **valuable online resources** accompany the *Concentrate* series. These include exam and revision guidelines, also available as a podcast. Resources for individual books include a **diagnostic test**, **understanding your marks**, **interactive flashcard glossaries**, and **flashcard cases** so you can test yourself, and specific multiple choice questions with instant feedback.

www.oxfordtextbooks.co.uk/orc/concentrate/

The Concentrate series launched with the publication of Criminal Law, Employment Law, Equity & Trusts, EU Law, Land Law and Public Law. Visit the website for updates on forthcoming titles, students' personal revision tips, and competitions

www.oxfordtextbooks.co.uk/law/concentrate/

D0755521

Land Law
Concentrate

Victoria Sayles

Associate Principal Lecturer, BPP

OXFORD
UNIVERSITY PRESS

OXFORD
UNIVERSITY PRESS

Great Clarendon Street, Oxford OX2 6DP

Oxford University Press is a department of the University of Oxford.
It furthers the University's objective of excellence in research, scholarship,
and education by publishing worldwide in

Oxford New York

Auckland Cape Town Dar es Salaam Hong Kong Karachi
Kuala Lumpur Madrid Melbourne Mexico City Nairobi
New Delhi Shanghai Taipei Toronto

With offices in

Argentina Austria Brazil Chile Czech Republic France Greece
Guatemala Hungary Italy Japan Poland Portugal Singapore
South Korea Switzerland Thailand Turkey Ukraine Vietnam

Oxford is a registered trade mark of Oxford University Press
in the UK and in certain other countries

Published in the United States
by Oxford University Press Inc., New York

© Oxford University Press, 2009

British Library Cataloguing in Publication Data

Data available

Library of Congress Cataloging in Publication Data

Sayles, Victoria.
  Land law concentrate / Victoria Sayles.—1st ed.
    p. cm.
  Includes index.
  ISBN 978-0-19-954459-2
  1. Real property—England. 2. Real property—Wales. I. Title.
  KD829.S29 2009
  346.4204'3—dc22 2008041396

Typeset by Newgen Imaging Systems (P) Ltd., Chennai, India
Printed in Great Britain
on acid-free paper by
Ashford Colour Press Ltd, Gosport, Hampshire

ISBN 978-0-19-954459-2

10 9 8 7 6 5 4 3 2 1

Contents

1   Introduction: proprietary rights   1

2   The distinction between legal and equitable
    interests   14

3   Registered land   28

4   Unregistered land   48

5   The freehold estate   60

6   The leasehold estate   72

7   Covenants in leases   93

8   Adverse possession   112

9   Trusts of land   131

10 Co-ownership   149

11 Licences   172

12 Easements and profits   186

13 Freehold covenants   208

14 Mortgages   230

Outline answers   A1
Glossary   A8
Table of cases   A11
Table of statutes   A17
Index   A21

#1

Introduction: proprietary rights

Issues discussed in this chapter may be examined as self-contained topics, specifically those relating to the definition of land. Typical problem questions may involve:

- assessing how far a person's rights over a piece of land extend, where, for example, there has been an invasion of airspace or removal of vegetation;
- assessing whether a purchaser can insist upon the return of numerous items removed from a property between exchange of contracts and completion of sale (ie whether the items removed were fixtures or chattels);
- assessing who has superior rights over items found on land.

(Note that these issues may also form part of another question. Take guidance from your own course as to where these issues may appear in a question.)

Depending upon the nature of your course, you may be required to explore the concepts of proprietary and personal rights and their distinguishing characteristics. Otherwise, much of the information contained in this chapter may be treated as foundation material: not specifically examinable by itself, but information which you must understand in order to comprehend how land law works.

Key facts

- Proprietary rights govern your ability to use and enjoy both land you physically possess and land physically possessed by others.

- Proprietary rights are rights in the land itself which makes them capable of enduring changes of ownership to the land.

- Whilst technically all land is owned by the Crown, holding an estate in land, and in particular a freehold estate that gives you rights to possess, enjoy, and use the land forever, is tantamount to actual ownership.

- Holding an estate in land gives you rights to possess, enjoy and use the land beyond just the physical surface area of that land.

- Apart from an estate in land, the other type of proprietary right that exists is an interest in land.

- Whilst an estate gives you a slice of time during which you are entitled to use and enjoy land you physically possess, an interest gives you rights to use and enjoy land physically possessed by another.

- Proprietary rights can be either legal or equitable in status.

Chapter overview

Proprietary rights: rights governing people's ability to use and enjoy land

Key characteristic: the potential to endure changes of ownership to the land over which they are exercised

Reasons for such durability include:
- the uniqueness of land
- to maintain marketability of land

Reason why some rights exercised over land do not have proprietary status: to ensure land does not become inalienable

Land is defined in **s 205 LPA 1925** and includes:
- physical surface area and below, subject to statutory exceptions
- lower, but not upper airspace: *(Bernstein of Leigh (Baron) v Skyviews & General Ltd* [1978]
- buildings and fixtures on the land, but not chattels

All land is technically owned by the Crown

Derives from the 'doctrine of tenures'

A person claiming land ownership merely enjoys a proprietary right over the land, perhaps so extensive it is tantamount to absolute ownership

Two key types of proprietary rights:

Estates: determine the extent to which a person may possess and enjoy his 'own' land, typically to the exclusion of all others. The two most significant are freehold and leasehold

Interests: determine extent to which a person may use and enjoy the land of another, falling short of exclusive possession

Status of proprietary rights:

Legal
- if fall into s 1(1) or (2) **LPA 1925**; and
- certain formalities are met when created

Otherwise equitable (provided certain formalities are met)

Introduction: proprietary rights

Property law concerns the regulation and management of people's enjoyment and relationships with particular things. The extent of the ability to enjoy and use property, and rights and remedies stemming from this, differ depending upon the nature of the property in question.

Where the property in question is land, rights governing people's ability to use and enjoy the land are known as **proprietary rights**. These rights can be extensive, such as an ability to use and possess land to the exclusion of everyone else (tantamount to ownership) or they can be narrow, such as a right to fish. They can relate to what you can, or cannot, do over land that you physically possess, for example the ability to carry on a business on the land. They can also relate to what you can do over land physically possessed by another, for example a right of way or an ability to restrict building. One piece of land may be subject to numerous proprietary rights: a right for a person to physically possess it; a right for a person to walk over it; a right for a person to restrict building on it etc.

Proprietary rights are distinctive. They are seen as rights in the land itself. This means that not only can you enforce your right against the person who originally granted it to you, you can also, in certain circumstances, enforce it against any other person who may come to the land over which the right is exercised. It is this durability of proprietary rights that makes them so special.

Why have rights relating to land been given this durability? Land is a unique commodity; no one piece of land is the same. This sets it apart from other types of property. It is also generally expensive. As a result, people who enjoy rights over a piece of land want the assurance that such rights are not be destroyed simply because the land changes ownership. Without such assurance, land could lose its marketability and become economically stagnant. Consequently, it could lose its value. For example, a piece of land that is landlocked is an unattractive economic investment. A person might be more willing to invest in such a piece of land if they could also be granted a right of access to it over the land of another. However, such an investment would still remain unlikely unless the purchaser had the assurance that use of the access route would endure any changes to the ownership of the land over which it is exercised. Without such an assurance, and therefore with the risk that future owners of the land might deny them the access, they probably would not invest in the landlocked property. The land would effectively become inalienable.

However, a balance must be sought. If a piece of land became too bogged down with proprietary rights exercised over it, with such rights able to survive changes of ownership, this itself might make the land unattractive and thus eventually inalienable. This is why some rights, although exercised in relation to land, have not been given proprietary status. The classic example of such a right is a licence, which effectively legalizes what would otherwise amount to a trespass. This remains, in the eyes of most, a **personal right** and therefore can only be enforced against the person who granted it to you. It is not a right in the land itself. Perhaps this is wise when you consider the number of licences people grant over their land to others and how quickly, therefore, land would become burdened.

✅ *Looking for extra marks?*

A proprietary right is considered to be a right *in rem*. It is enforceable against the property itself ie the land. Where a holder of a proprietary right is denied that right, he is entitled to seek action to recover the actual land / use of the land, rather than be limited to recovering its value or damages to compensate loss of use. Personal rights are right *in personam*. They are enforceable not against the actual property but against the person who granted the right in the first place. If revoked, even if wrongly so, the holder of the personal right may be entitled to damages but cannot insist upon recovering possession or use of the property itself. It is this fundamental difference which explains potential durability of proprietary rights which personal rights do not enjoy.

Revision tip

Some licences have been found to be enforceable against third parties and thus appear to have proprietary status. This is considered in more detail in chapter 11. Be prepared to make this link if required to examine the characteristics of proprietary, as opposed to, personal rights.

'Ownership' of 'land'

Technically, all land is owned by the Crown (see below as to how this came about). The most you could have over a piece of land is a proprietary right to physically possess, use, enjoy, and deal with the land to the exclusion of anyone else. This is known as having an estate in the land of which there are two key types: the freehold estate and the leasehold estate. The most extensive of these estates is the freehold (the reasons for which are outlined below). A person holding a freehold estate is, in practical terms, seen as the owner of the land. Their rights and relationship to the land that they physically possess are indistinguishable from that of an absolute owner.

Whilst estates are discussed in more detail below (and indeed in chapters 5 and 6), it is important that you first understand what is meant by 'land'. If someone holds a freehold estate, giving them rights to possess and enjoy the land tantamount to absolute ownership, how far do those rights extend? This will, of course, depend upon how land is defined.

Your starting point is the **Law of Property Act 1925, s 205(1)(ix)** which gives land a statutory definition. Case law has further helped to clarify what is meant by land.

In summary, where a person has a right to possess and enjoy a piece of land by virtue of holding a freehold estate, tantamount to making him the owner of the land, his rights extend to:

- the physical surface area of the land;
- the *lower* airspace above the physical surface area necessary for his ordinary use and enjoyment of that land. Any invasion of this lower airspace is *prima facie* actionable as a trespass: *Anchor Brewhouse Developments v Berkley House (Docklands Developments) Ltd* (1987), with a remedy of an injunction where damages would

not be adequate. This is qualified by statute, for example the Civil Aviation Act 1982, which allows for aircraft to pass over land at a reasonable height, without amounting to an actionable trespass. A landowner has no claim to trespass where there is interference with his *upper* airspace, ie that airspace not necessary for his ordinary use and enjoyment of the land: *Bernstein of Leigh (Baron) v Skyviews & General Ltd* [1978]. To allow otherwise would create absurdities and stifle the ability of the general public to take advantage of developments in science regarding airspace (for example satellites);

- the ground below the surface area, including mines and minerals, although this is qualified by various statutes, for example the Coal Industry Act 1994 which vests ownership of coal in the Coal Authority;

- buildings or parts of buildings found on the land, whether the division is vertical or horizontal;

- wild plants growing on the land. Commercially grown plants are not considered part of the land and belong to those who planted them;

- dead wild animals killed on the land, irrespective of who killed them. Living wild animals do not belong to anyone, although a landowner has a right to kill them whilst they are on his land, subject to any statutory protection they might enjoy;

- the soil over which water flows. Where two plots of land are separated by a river, each plot owner owns the soil up to the middle of the river. As regards any fish that may be found in these waters, where the water is non-tidal the owner of the land has exclusive fishing rights, subject to him having granted this right to others. Where the water is tidal, the public has the right to fish up to the point of ebb and flow of the tide;

- some items found on the land. Whether the landowner's rights extend to such items depends upon the answer to a series of questions, as outlined in Figure 1.1. (see page 8);

- **incorporeal hereditaments**. These are those intangible rights that benefit the land in question, for example a right of way or an ability to restrict the neighbouring landowner from building on his land;

- **fixtures** found on the land. Where a **chattel** has become attached to the land, or a building on it, it can become part of the land itself changing from being a mere chattel to a fixture. Whether this is the case will depend upon the *degree of annexation* the object has to the land, or building on it, and the *purpose of its annexation: Holland v Hodgson* (1872). The label that parties give to the object is not conclusive of its status: *Melluish v BMI (No 3) Ltd* [1996].

  - The degree of annexation test dictates that the greater the degree of annexation, the more likely the object is a fixture. Therefore, absence of any annexation at all would generally be decisive in making the object a chattel, unless the object is one that, by reason of its own weight, does not require any annexation: *Elitestone Ltd v Morris* [1997]. However, this test must now be used in conjunction with the *purpose of annexation* test, which today is the dominant test out of the two: *Hamp v Bygrave* (1983).

– The purpose of annexation test dictates that in deciding whether an object has become a fixture, you must consider the purpose for which the object has been annexed to the land. If the annexation is so that the chattel can be enjoyed as a chattel, it will remain a chattel: *Leigh v Taylor* [1902]. Where the purpose of the annexation is to make an improvement to the property itself, the chattel will become a fixture: *D'Eyncourt v Gregory* (1866). The purpose of annexation must be judged objectively (*Dean v Andrews* [1986]), although subjective intentions of the person who annexed the object may be persuasive.

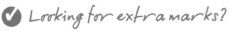 Looking for extra marks?

In the case of *Botham v TSB Bank plc* [1997] it became clear that in making a decision as to whether an object is a fixture, and thus part of the land, a court takes into account a number of factors. These include:

- the degree of physical attachment;
- the purpose of any attachment;
- whether the object is part of the overall design of the building;
- the moveability of the object: where it is intended to be moved regularly, the object may more likely be deemed a chattel;
- the lifespan of the object: if it is limited and likely to need replacing relatively regularly, this may make it more likely to be a chattel;
- the damage caused to the land, or building, when moved: the greater the amount of damage that might be caused, the more likely the object may be seen as a fixture;
- the type of person who installed / attached the object to the land. Installation by a builder may make the object a fixture; installation by a contractor, a mere chattel.

Such factors should be considered together and an overall view taken as to where the balance lies in whether the object is a fixture or a chattel.

Revision tip

An examiner would want to see good use of case law to enhance your arguments as to whether an item is a fixture or a chattel. Draw appropriate comparisons and use the legal reasoning to demonstrate you understand the factors that influence a court.

The history behind land ownership: the doctrine of tenures

✳✳✳✳✳✳✳✳✳✳

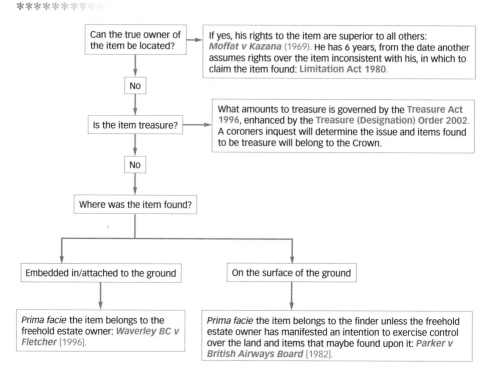

Figure 1.1

The history behind land ownership: the doctrine of tenures

Technically, as mentioned above, all land is owned by the Crown. This stems from the Norman Conquest in 1066 when the King, William the Conqueror, declared himself as owner of all the land in England. A system of landholding developed whereby the King would allow people to use and occupy his land in return for the performance of certain services. Ownership of the land was never actually transferred to such persons. Such holders of the land were known as tenants and they in turn would allow others to use and occupy their land in return for services to them. This was known as *subinfeudation*. A feudal system of land ownership thus arose. The nature of the services provided by the tenant to his immediate lord differed depending upon the nature of the **tenure** in question.

Free tenure

The services to be provided to the immediate lord were fixed and certain in nature.

- *Chivalry* – included performing services for the King of an honourable nature, for example carrying his banner (*grand sergeantry*) or providing the immediate lord with horses and men to fight for a certain number of days per year (*knight service*).

- *Socage* – included providing the King with services of a non-personal nature, for example feeding his dogs (*petty sergeantry*) and, most common of all tenures, providing the immediate lord with services of an agricultural nature, for example ploughing his fields for a certain number of days per year (*common socage*).

- *Spiritual* – where ecclesiastical bodies were required to pray for their immediate lord in return for their ability to use and occupy the land.

Unfree tenure

The services to be provided to the immediate lord were not fixed as to their nature and duration.

- *Villeinage* – strictly speaking, this was not a form of tenure at all. Persons were merely allowed to occupy land at the will of their immediate lord, who could evict them at any time, in return for unpredictable services. This later became known as *copyhold*.

- *Customary* – where the tenant held the land according to the custom of the manor but not at the will of his immediate lord.

Under this system of tenure, the immediate lord was also entitled to '*incidents of tenure*'. These differed depending upon the nature of the tenure in question but included;

- *Relief* – money payments to the immediate lord when the tenant died.

- *Aids* – money payments to the immediate lord when required to pay ransomes.

Today, the doctrine of tenures holds little significance. Since 1926, there has been only one form of tenure: *free and common socage* or *freehold* as it is now known. The tenure exists in name only. The freehold tenant need not provide an immediate lord with services; neither is the lord entitled to incidents of tenure. Indeed, almost all freehold tenants hold the land directly from the Crown, the feudal pyramid of land holding having disappeared. What it does demonstrate is the fact that today ownership of land is still, in theory, held by the Crown. Someone who claims ownership of land, rather than being the absolute owner of it, actually merely enjoys a proprietary right over the land that is so extensive it is tantamount to actual ownership.

Proprietary rights under the microscope

There are two key ways in which proprietary rights may be classified:

Estates or interests

An estate is a more extensive proprietary right than an interest. There are two main estates in land that are of significance today: the freehold estate and the leasehold estate. Whilst both these estates are discussed in more detail in their relevant chapter (chapters 5 and 6 respectively), the following key points about estates can be made here:

- Holding an estate in a piece of land gives you a 'slice of time' during which you are entitled to possess and enjoy that land.

- The 'slice of time' given to you is determined by the type of estate that you hold:

  - With a freehold estate (known technically as the fee simple absolute in possession), the slice of time is perpetual. It will only come to an end if the estate holder dies with no heirs. (If this occurs, the estate will revert to the Crown *bona vacantia*. This is the most obvious indication today that land is still owned by the Crown.) This is why someone who holds a legal freehold estate sees themselves as tantamount to the actual owner of the land.

  - With a leasehold estate (known technically as term of years absolute), the slice of time is fixed and the estate will come to an end when the time expires. It is for this reason that it is the smaller of the two estates. (The holder of a leasehold estate is also subject to more restrictions as to what they can or cannot do over the land than a holder of a freehold estate. This is another reason why it is seen as the inferior estate of the two.)

The system of holding land by virtue of an estate can create a hierarchy of estates over one piece of land. For example, one piece of land could be subject to a freehold estate and one or more leasehold estates. By dealing with land in these 'slices of time' it is possible for people to use land to make money; carving estates out of their own and selling them to others to raise capital. (The precise status of an estate, where others exist in the same piece of land, is dealt with in detail in chapter 5.)

Apart from estates, the other type of proprietary right someone could hold over a piece of land is an **interest**. Whilst an estate determines the extent to which you can possess and enjoy your 'own' land, interests concern rights you have over the land of others. Although interests may take on a possessory character, possession will be restricted so that the estate holder of the land can still use and enjoy the land for himself. It is for this reason that interests are more limited in what they allow the holder to do than estates. Having said this, they are no less important in the role they play in governing people's relationship to land.

Legal or equitable

All proprietary rights will have either legal or equitable status. The types of proprietary right that can be legal, where certain formalities have been met, are found in a closed list in s 1 LPA 1925. Where such formalities are not met, the right may only exist in equity, but this again will be dependent upon satisfaction of certain formalities, all of which is discussed in more detail in the following chapter. (An example of a right that can have legal or equitable status is an easement. The conditions that determine its status are explained in chapter 12.)

Despite being limited to those found in the **s 1 LPA 1925** list, legal rights are not insignificant. Those that are listed commonly arise over land and they include the most extensive of the two types of proprietary rights: freehold and leasehold estates.

Other types of proprietary rights can only ever exist in equity, since their recognition as proprietary rights stemmed from equity's intervention in resolving the inadequacies of common law when dealing with disputes over land. A classic example, and one discussed in more detail in chapter 13, is the restrictive covenant.

Revision tip

The status of a proprietary right as either legal or equitable is discussed in more detail in chapter 2 and again in relation to specific rights in the relevant chapters. Be sure you understand how status is determined.

 Key cases

Case	Facts	Principle
Bernstein of Leigh (Baron) v Skyviews & General Ltd [1978] QB 479	Flying a plane over land in order to take aerial photographs did not amount to a trespass of that land.	An owner of an estate in land has rights that extend only as far as the *lower* airspace above the physical surface area of the land necessary for the ordinary use and enjoyment of that land.
Botham v TSB Bank plc [1997] 73 P&CRD 1	The plaintiff owned a flat which was mortgaged. When he fell into arrears with the mortgage repayments, the bank sought possession and sold the property. A question arose as to whether some of the contents of the flat were fixtures, and thus part of the security for the debt.	In deciding the issue of whether an item is a fixture or chattel, look beyond the two key tests of degree and purpose of annexation (as discussed above).
D'Eyncourt v Gregory (1866) LR 3 Eq 382	Despite being free-standing, marble statues of lions, garden seats and ornaments were held to be fixtures, and thus part of the land.	Where evidence is produced that objects have been positioned so as to improve the overall architectural design of a property, those objects may become fixtures, even where there is no degree of annexation.

Case	Facts	Principle
Elitestone Ltd v Morris [1997] 1 WLR 687	Wooden bungalows, not themselves attached to the land, rested on concrete pillars that were attached. The bungalows were deemed to be fixtures.	Even where there is no physical attachment to the land, an object could be a fixture where it is deemed to be used in situ and could not be removed without physical destruction.
Leigh v Taylor [1902] AC 157	Tapestries attached to a wall of a building were held to be chattels.	Although physical attachment of an object to the land might suggest that object has become a fixture, this may not be the case where such attachment is purely so that the object can be enjoyed.
Parker v British Airways Board [1982] QB 1004	The plaintiff, a passenger at Heathrow airport, found a gold bracelet on the floor of the executive lounge. He handed it in to an employee of the defendant requesting it be returned to him should no-one claim the item. No-one claimed the bracelet but the defendant sold it and retained the proceeds. It was held that the plaintiff was entitled to damages.	The rights of the finder of an object found on the surface of the ground, can only be displaced by the owner of the land where the object was found if the latter manifested an intention to control the land and items found on it.
Waverley BC v Fletcher [1996] QB 334	The defendant, lawfully in a public park, unlawfully used a metal detector to detect a gold brooch buried in the ground. It was held that the council's rights to the brooch were superior to the finder's.	Where an object is found in or attached to land, the owner of that land has better title to that object than the finder.

 Exam questions

Problem question

Tim purchased the freehold estate of a property known as Nector House two weeks ago. Upon moving into the property he noticed that a water fountain had been removed from the garden and a stained glass window had been removed from the dining room and replaced with normal glass. Two days ago, a postman picked up a valuable emerald necklace from under a bush as he walked up the garden path to the door of Nector House. The true owner of the necklace cannot be found and the postman has told Tim he is keeping it for himself. Tim has also discovered that branches from his neighbour's willow tree hang over his land.

Advise Tim whether:

1. he can insist upon the return of the water fountain and the stained glass window;
2. he can require the postman to return the emerald necklace to him; and
3. he can cut off the overhanging branches from his neighbour's willow tree and use them to make a basket.

An outline answer is available at the end of the book

Essay question

'Cuius est solum eius est usque ad coelum et ad inferos': he who owns land owns everything up to the sky and down to the centre of the earth.

To what extent is this Latin phrase misleading today?

An outline answer is available online at www.oxfordtextbooks.co.uk/orc/concentrate/

#2

The distinction between legal and equitable interests

The examination

The material covered in this chapter is unlikely to appear in a self-contained problem question. Rather it is pervasive material that forms the foundation upon which land law is built. Your understanding of this material is therefore essential to your overall understanding of land law. You will see that much of the material on formalities, and the creation of legal and equitable interests in land, is repeated elsewhere in this book. Chapters devoted to specific interests repeat rules outlined below and expand upon these where necessary. The enforcement of interests against third parties in both registered and unregistered land, discussed in chapters 3 and 4 respectively, requires a consideration of the exact status of an interest when ascertaining which rules to apply.

An essay question may focus on just the material covered in this chapter but it is more likely to be combined with principles discussed elsewhere, for example the issue of notice and what role it has to play today (link with chapters 3 and 4).

Key facts

- The intervention of equity in land law can be seen in two key areas: the development of new equitable interests in land, and the availability of equitable remedies to enforce interests in land.

- Following the intervention of equity, interests in land may now have either legal or equitable status.

- To be a legal interest in land, the interest must be one listed under s 1(2) Law of Property Act 1925 and certain formalities must be met in its creation, notably being granted by deed (s 52 LPA 1925). Where these formalities are not met, the interest may have equitable status instead, but only where equity can find a specifically enforceable valid contract to create the interest.

- All other interests in land can only ever be equitable (s 1(3) LPA 1925). To achieve equitable status, formalities in creation of the interest must be met and these formalities will differ depending upon the type of interest.

- The status of an interest in land as either legal or equitable traditionally determined the rules of enforcement of that interest against third parties: legal interests bound all third parties, whereas equitable interests would only bind third parties who were not *bona fide purchasers for value of a legal estate without notice*.

- Today enforcement of interests in land against third parties is determined less by its status as legal or equitable, and more upon concepts of registration.

- However, traditional rules of enforcement still play a minor role in unregistered land.

Chapter overview

The intervention of equity

The impact that equity has had on the development of land law cannot be underestimated and is something that you must appreciate and understand.

As the English Legal System developed, it soon became clear that the courts of *law*, enforcing common law, were ill equipped at resolving disputes between holders of estates and interests in land. Not only was there the problem that the writ procedure followed in these courts was complicated and burdened by excessive formality and thus delay, the common law itself was failing to recognize rights of individuals in relation to land where it would be fair and just to do so. Furthermore, where the common law did recognize individuals as having proprietary rights, and such rights had been infringed, the common law remedy of damages often proved inadequate.

The development of the law of equity has helped, in some measure, to resolve these inadequacies.

The recognition of equitable interests in land

Whilst certain proprietary rights are recognized as existing at law, equity established the existence of some new proprietary rights based upon a desire to do justice and act on enforcing obligations of conscience.

The beneficial interest under a trust

It became quite common practice, for a variety of reasons, for land to be transferred to one person for the benefit of another. For example, during the Crusades, knights who left the country to fight abroad, wanted to make provision for their families during the time of their absence and in the event that they did not return alive. They would do this by transferring their estate in land to another, not so that the transferee enjoyed the land for himself; rather so that he looked after it on behalf of the transferor's family. However, in the event that the transferor died, at law the family he left behind had no entitlement to the land. Legal title, and thus ownership of the land, was held by the transferee and the common law did not recognize the family as having any rights in the land that they could enforce.

Equity considered this to be unfair and unjust. The transferee had been given the land to look after for the family. It was not intended that he benefited from the land. Indeed, it would be unconscionable for him to do so and unconscionable for him to ignore the rights of the family upon whose behalf it was intended he should hold the land. Equity intervened to give recognition to the family's rights. It did so by recognizing a new way in which property could be held: by way of a **trust**. Whilst legal title would rest with the transferee, known as the **trustee**, equitable title would rest with the family, the **beneficiaries** under the trust. It is the equitable title to the land, the beneficial interest under the trust, which gives a person the right to use, enjoy, and benefit from the land. It is, in essence, the true ownership of land. Legal title which vests with the trustee, merely bestows upon the trustee administrative and managerial responsibilities in respect of the land; with such responsibilities being exercised in the interest of the beneficiaries. (The beneficial interest under a trust is discussed in more detail in chapters 9 and 10.)

Equitable right to redeem

A mortgage arises in situations where money lent by a lender is secured on property owned by the borrower. The conditions and dates for repayment will be provided for in a contract. Should the borrower fail, for whatever reason, to meet these terms, the lender can obtain a court order to seize the property serving as security, sell it, and repay the loan out of the sale proceeds.

At common law, where the borrower failed to repay the debt on the date specified in the contract, they lost the property which served as security; ownership of that property transferring to the lender. Equity considered this unfair and unjust and created the equitable right to redeem, which enables borrowers to redeem the loan (ie pay back the debt and any interest that might have accrued) even after the legal date specified in the contract has passed. (This equitable right is discussed in more detail in chapter 14.)

Restrictive covenants

Restrictions on what an estate owner can do over the land he possesses often arise in situations where one landowner (X) is selling off part of his land to another (Y). Since the land retained by X will often be in close proximity to that which he is selling, he may wish to impose restrictions as to what can or cannot be done on the land sold so as to maintain the value and enjoyment of the land retained. Such restrictions would be incorporated into a contract and thus, in the event of a breach by Y, would be enforced using principles of contract law. A problem occurred at common law where the land burdened by the restrictions was later sold on to another (A). Since A was not a party to the original contract, the restrictions could not, in principle, be imposed upon him, even in circumstances where he had knowledge of the restriction prior to the purchase and paid a reduced price for the land as a result. Equally, if X sold the land benefiting from the restrictions on to another (B), B would not be able to enforce the restrictions in the event of a breach, since he was not a party to the original contract. The inadequacy at common law in enforcing the restrictions beyond the original contracting parties was resolved by the intervention of equity. Equity recognized such restrictions as creating equitable interests in land, provided certain formalities were met. By giving them proprietary status, enforcement of the restrictions could, in certain circumstances, endure changes to the ownership of the land both benefited and burdened by them. (These interests in land are discussed in more detail in chapter 13.)

Estate contracts

Where a person enters into a contract to grant another an estate over a piece of land, and that contract is breached by the grantor failing to transfer the estate in land to the grantee as agreed, the grantee, at common law, can obtain the remedy of damages. This remedy is available as a result of the infringement of the personal rights that the contract creates between the parties.

Whilst damages might provide adequate remedy for breaches of other types of contracts, equity considers the remedy to be inadequate where the contract has land as its subject matter. This is because of the fact that all land is unique. Rather equity would be prepared to award the remedy of specific performance and thus compel the grantor to transfer the estate in land as he had agreed to do in the contract.

It is the availability and indeed the expectation that specific performance will be awarded that leads to the view in equity that the grantee has an interest in the land at the time of the contract. Although at law, ownership of the estate remains with the grantor at this time, since equity views as done that which ought to be done (ie that the contract should be performed), the grantee is seen as the equitable owner of the estate at the moment a valid contract is made. The equitable proprietary interest he holds is known as an estate contract.

You must remember, however, that such an equitable interest will only arise in circumstances where an order for specific performance is available. Where circumstances are such that equity would not exercise its discretion to make such an order, no equitable proprietary interest will arise.

This type of proprietary interest is discussed in more detail in both chapters 5 and 6.

Equitable remedies

As well as recognizing new proprietary rights, equity also developed new equitable remedies. This was in response to the inadequacy of the common law remedy of damages. Such inadequacy has already been seen in relation to breaches of land contracts (see above).

Types

There are two principal equitable remedies:

Specific performance

An order of specific performance requires someone to do something, for example to perform a contract to transfer an estate in land.

Injunction

Whilst different types of injunctions exist, in general terms they forbid someone from doing something, for example forbidding a person from building a fence to obstruct a right of way.

Common characteristics

- Failure to comply with an order for either remedy results in being found in contempt of court.

- Where common law remedies are available as of right once the wrong has been proven, equitable remedies are awarded at the discretion of the court. The intervention of equity is conscience driven and is underlined by certain maxims, for example, he who comes to equity must come with clean hands; the person seeking the equitable remedy must not have disqualified himself from obtaining it by acting in a grossly unconscionable manner: *Coatsworth v Johnson* (1885).

Identifying the status of a proprietary interest

Revision tip

Link to chapter 1 and ensure that you understand the difference between the two key types of proprietary rights: estates and interests. The following considers interests in more detail. (Estates are considered in more detail in chapters 5 and 6.)

You should now understand that interests in land can have either legal or equitable status. Whilst the significance of the actual status of an interest is discussed below, first you must be able to distinguish whether an interest in land is legal or equitable.

Legal interests

The list

The types of interest in land that have the capacity to be legal are limited to those listed under **s 1(2) LPA 1925**:

s 1(2)(a)   an easement, right, or privilege but only if it is equivalent in duration to one of the two legal estates in land ie it is to last forever (equivalent to a legal freehold), or it has a fixed and certain duration (equivalent to a leasehold). An easement granted for the duration of someone's life could therefore never have legal status. (Easements and *profits à prendre* are discussed in more detail in chapter 12.);

s 1(2)(b)   a **rentcharge** in possession issuing out of or charged on land being either perpetual or for a term of years absolute. (This is similar to rent paid in respect of a lease but here it relates to a freehold estate.);

s 1(2)(c)   a charge by way of a legal mortgage. (Mortgages are discussed in more detail in chapter 14.);

s 1(2)(d)   …any other similar charge on land which is not created by an instrument; and

s 1(2)(e)   rights of entry. These are rights normally reserved by a landlord to re-enter leased property and forfeit the lease where the tenant is in breach of covenant (discussed in more detail in chapter 6).

Out of the five listed above, perhaps the most important today are those listed in paragraphs **(a)**, **(c)**, and **(e)**.

An interest not listed under s 1(2) LPA 1925 can never be legal. But remember, just because an interest is listed under this section does not mean that it will always be legal; rather that it has the capacity to be so. Whether in fact it is legal will depend upon whether certain formalities have been satisfied.

The formalities

- The person granting the interest must have the capacity to grant legal interests in land. For example, an owner of an equitable lease would not be able to grant legal easements. You cannot grant more than you have yourself.

- The interest must, in principle, be granted by **deed**: s 52 LPA 1925. The requirements for a valid deed created on/after 31 July 1990 are laid down in **s 1 Law of Property (Miscellaneous Provisions) Act 1989** (deeds created before this date had to be signed, sealed, and delivered):

---

s 1 LP(MP)A 1989

The document must:

- be clear on its face that it is a deed;
- be signed by the grantor;
- be witnessed; and
- be delivered.

✔ Looking for extra marks?

A deed may be signed by another person at the direction of the grantor. This will be in circumstances where the grantor is unable to sign for himself. When the grantor signs there need only be one witness, but where someone signs on his behalf there must be two witnesses. The witness(es) must attest the document, which requires that they also sign the document. A deed is delivered by showing that the grantor intends to be bound by the document. His signature and the dating of the document will evidence this intention.

- There is an additional requirement of registration in some circumstances, where the interest is being created over registered land. Where:
  - an easement equivalent in duration to a legal estate is being expressly granted/reserved; or
  - a legal charge is being granted; or
  - a rentcharge or right of entry is being expressly granted/reserved,

  the disposition must be registered. The interest will not operate at law until this has been done: s 27 **Land Registration Act 2002** (see chapter 3).

Identifying the status of a proprietary interest

✳✳✳✳✳✳✳✳✳

Unless all the above requirements have been satisfied, the interest will not be legal. At best, it could only be equitable but this would be dependent upon meeting the requirements in equity, discussed below.

Equitable interests

These include:

Failed attempts to grant legal interests

As discussed above, an interest which has legal capacity needs to satisfy certain formalities before it can become legal. Where such formalities are not met, the interest cannot have legal status. However, equity may be willing to recognize the existence of the interest. It will do so by recognizing the failed attempt to grant a legal interest (for lack of formalities) as a contract to create that interest. To do this there must be:

- a valid contract ie one compliant with **s 2 LP(MP)A 1989**:

---

s 2 LP(MP)A 1989

The contract must be:

- in writing;
- contain all the terms; and
- be signed by both parties.

(Subject to exemptions under s 2(5), notably contracts to create short leases.)

(These formalities are discussed in more detail in chapter 5.)

- The contract must be one that is capable of specific performance ie one upon which equity would exercise its discretion to grant such an order (see discussion above under equitable remedies).
- By applying the maxim that equity views as done that which ought to be done (ie that contract should be performed), an equitable interest arises.

Where there is no specifically enforceable valid contract, no equitable interest will arise.

✅ Looking for extra marks?

Whilst the statement above is generally true, in some circumstances equity may intervene to give a person equitable rights even where no specifically enforceable contract exists. This intervention is based upon the finding of an estoppel and is discussed further in chapter 5.

Agreements to grant interests in land

Rather than actually granting someone an interest in land, the grantor may agree to do this some time in the future. Where this agreement is contained in a valid contract, capable of specific performance, equity will recognize the grantee as having an equitable interest in the land, by applying the maxim discussed above. This can be seen, for example, in agreements to grant leases and agreements to transfer a freehold estate, both of which are discussed in more detail in chapters 5 and 6 respectively.

Interests that can only ever be equitable

Estates or interests that are not listed in either **s 1(1)** or **s 1(2) LPA 1925** could never have legal status. These include such interests as life estates (discussed in chapter 5), restrictive covenants (discussed in chapter 13), and beneficial interests behind a trust (discussed in chapters 9 and 10). Such interests could only ever be equitable in status: **s 1(3) LPA 1925**. Whether they have acquired equitable status will depend upon whether formalities required in equity have been met. These formalities differ depending upon the nature of the interest in question (and are discussed in more detail in the relevant chapters of this book). Where the formalities are not met, the right over land has failed to gain proprietary status at all and will thus remain a mere personal right between the creating parties.

Summary

In determining whether an interest is legal or equitable, remember the questions in Figure 2.1:

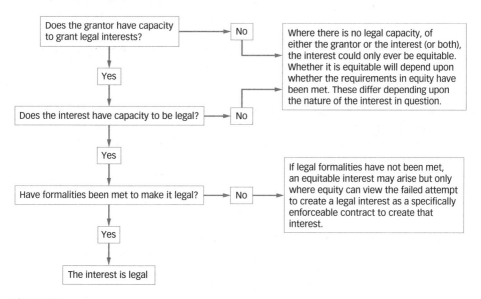

Figure 2.1

Significance of the distinction between legal and equitable interests

Revision tip

Link to material covered in chapters 3 and 4 on the enforcement of interests against third parties where the status of an interest is one of the factors in determining which rules of enforcement to apply.

Remedies

Where a legal interest is infringed, a remedy is available as of right. At common law, the remedy is damages, although equity may provide an equitable remedy where damages are seen as being inadequate.

Where an equitable interest has been infringed, only equitable remedies are available and whether such remedies are awarded will depend upon the discretion of the court (see above).

Enforcement

As you know from the discussion in chapter 1, one of the special features of proprietary rights is their ability, in certain circumstances, to be enforceable not only against the person who granted the right, but also against any other person who may come to the land over which the right exists (the burdened land).

The question of whether an interest is binding on a third party, for example a purchaser of the burdened land, traditionally rested upon the nature of the interest:

Legal interests

These were considered binding on the whole world. Anyone who came to the burdened land would have to respect the existence of the legal interest and thus would be bound by it. So, for example, if a purchaser bought a piece of land over which there existed a legal right of way (an easement), the purchaser would be bound by the right of way and would have to allow the person holding that interest to use that right, even though the purchaser was not a party to its original creation.

Equitable interests

Rather than being automatically binding upon anyone, equitable interests would only bind a person if he was not a *bona fide purchaser of a legal estate for value without notice*. If he was that type of purchaser, he would take the land free from the equitable interest. What would he need to establish to prove that he was that type of purchaser? He would need to be:

1. acting *bona fide* ie in good faith, honestly and without any fraudulent intent; and

Distinction between legal and equitable interests

✳✳✳✳✳✳✳✳✳✳✳

2. a **purchaser** ie someone acquiring the land through the act of another rather than automatically through an operation of law. (Examples of people who acquire land through an operation of law include trustees in bankruptcy (see chapter 10) and adverse possessors (see chapter 8); and

3. a purchaser *for value* ie providing some sort of consideration for the land. (An example of someone who provides no value would be someone who was gifted the land.); and

4. a purchaser *of a legal estate*. This includes someone purchasing a legal freehold or leasehold estate but also a mortgage (s 87 LPA 1925); and

5. purchasing the land *without notice of the interest*. A purchaser will be deemed to have notice of an interest if:

    - He has **actual notice** of the interest. This is where the purchaser has actual knowledge of the existence of the interest at the time of purchase; or

    - He has **constructive notice** of the interest. A purchaser is deemed to have knowledge of all things he could have acquired actual notice of, had he made those enquiries and inspections which he ought reasonably to have done. What type of enquiries is a purchaser expected to make?

        - A purchaser has a duty to investigate the title. This will involve looking at the title deeds back to the root of title which is set at 15 years: s 23 LPA 1969 (see chapter 4).

        - A purchaser also has a duty to inspect the land and make suitable enquiries of any person discovered in occupation of that land: *Hunt v Luck* [1901]. The extent of the enquiries that should be made when inspecting was discussed in *Kingsnorth Trust Ltd v Tizard* [1986].

....

Kingsnorth Trust Ltd v Tizard [1986] 1 WLR 783

A mortgagee's agent was held to have constructive notice of a wife's equitable interest in a property that was being mortgaged by the husband and which was in his sole name. The agent, when inspecting the property, discovered that the husband was married but separated, despite having stated on his mortgage application form that he was single. This should have led the agent to make further enquiries as to the whereabouts of the wife and any interest she may have in the property. Failure to make such enquiries, deemed reasonable, gave the agent constructive notice of the wife's equitable interest.

....

- He has **imputed notice** of the interest. A purchaser is deemed to have knowledge of all the things about which his agents working on the land transaction have actual or constructive notice. In *Kingsnorth Finance v Tizard* [1986], the mortgagee acquired imputed notice of its agent's constructive notice of the wife's equitable interest.

Only where the purchaser of the burdened land could establish all five components listed above would he take the land free from any equitable interests that might exist over it. Once this occurred, the equitable interest lost its ability to bind any future third parties who came to that land: *Wilkes v Spooner* [1911].

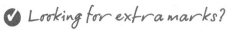 Looking for extra marks?

It has been argued that if a purchaser has notice of an interest, he is not acting in good faith and thus the requirement of good faith merely duplicates the requirement of acting without notice. However, Lord Wilberforce in the case of *Midland Bank Trust Co Ltd v Green* [1981] (discussed in chapter 4) made it clear that the two requirements are separate from one another and that one could be satisfied whilst the other is not, although it is difficult to point to circumstances where this may be the case.

Relevance of the distinction today

It soon became clear that the rules discussed above regarding the enforcement of interests in land against third parties, dependent upon whether the interest was legal or equitable, were imperfect. Attempts to improve upon the rules of enforcement by introducing systems of registration are discussed in more detail in the next two chapters. That is not to say that the system of enforcement outlined above has no role to play today. It does play a small part in the system of enforcement of interests that exist over unregistered land.

Revision tip

Make sure you link the discussion above on the doctrine of notice to the role it plays in unregistered land, discussed in chapter 4.

 Key cases

Case	Facts	Principle
Coatsworth v Johnson (1885) 55 LJQB 220	Claimant sought specific performance of an agreement for a lease which was declined since the claimant was himself in breach of one of the covenants in the lease to which the agreement related.	A court will not exercise its discretion and grant specific performance in favour of a claimant who himself has acted unconscionably and not come to the court with clean hands.

Case	Facts	Principle
Hunt v Luck [1901] 1 Ch 45	The vendor sold land occupied by his tenant. The purchaser was held to have constructive notice of the tenant's rights.	A purchaser must make enquiries as to the rights of persons who are not the vendor and who are in occupation of the land being purchased. Failure to do so fixes the purchaser with constructive notice of any rights those persons in occupation may have in the land.
Kingsnorth Trust Ltd v Tizard [1986] 1 WLR 783	Mr Tizard sought to obtain a mortgage over a house which was in his sole name. In his mortgage application form he stated he was single but when the mortgagee's surveyor went to inspect the property, his true status as married but separated became known. No enquiries were made about any rights his wife might have in the house and consequently the surveyor and mortgagee were deemed to have notice of the wife's beneficial interest in the property.	Where it is reasonable to expect a purchaser to make further enquiries about any rights a person may have in the land being purchased, failure to do so will give the purchaser notice of any such rights.
Wilkes v Spooner [1911] 2 KB 473	A purchaser of a legal estate took free from an existing equitable interest over the land as he was a *bona fide* purchaser for value of a legal estate without notice. His successor also took free from the equitable interest despite having notice of it.	Once an equitable interest has been destroyed by virtue of a transfer of the land over which it exists, to a purchaser acting in good faith with no notice of its existence, that equitable interest cannot be revived upon a subsequent transfer of the land.

(?) Exam questions

Essay question

An interest in land may have legal or equitable status. How does one determine the status of an interest in land and what is the significance of this distinction?

An outline answer is available online at www.oxfordtextbooks.co.uk/orc/concentrate/

#3
Registered land

The examination

This is a topic area that may be examined in a self-contained question or as part of a question concerning another topic area. It may be combined with unregistered land or issues of adverse possession. It can also appear in questions concerning a particular interest in land, for example an easements question or a restrictive covenants question, where the interest exists over registered land and issues of enforcement against a purchaser of that land arise.

Problem questions typically focus upon rules of enforcement of interests over registered land. For example, you may be told about various types of interests that exist over a piece of registered land. (Sometimes those interests will be clearly identified; other times you may have to work out what they are for yourself.) That land will then pass to a purchaser and you will be required to work out whether those interests will be binding upon that purchaser.

Essay questions sometimes demand drawing comparisons between the registered and unregistered land systems. You may be required to consider how, if at all, the three principles underpinning registered land are met. Frequently, attention is focused upon overriding interests and in particular how they appear to undermine the perceived objectives behind the introduction of a registered land system.

Key facts

- Registered land is land where title has been registered at the Land Registry. The objective behind registered land is to create a register which accurately reflects the state of registered property, both in terms of its current owner and any third party proprietary interests affecting it. In theory, a purchaser need look no further than the register when making enquiries about a piece of registered land. (In reality, the presence of overriding interests which bind a purchaser despite appearing nowhere on the register, means that a purchaser must look beyond the register.)

- Unregistered land can be brought into the registered land system either by the owner voluntarily applying to be registered or compulsorily upon the occurrence of certain events, notably sale of the freehold, the grant of a lease of more than seven years, or the grant of a protected first legal mortgage. Failure to register title when required can lead to the loss of legal title to that land (ss 4, 6, and 7 LRA 2002).

- Once registered, subsequent disposals of the freehold; or leasehold of more than seven years in duration, must be completed by registration to confer legal title (s 27 LRA 2002).

- When registering title to land, the specific class of title registered will reflect the strength of that title; with the strongest and most common class registered being absolute title.

- In principle, third party proprietary interests will only affect a purchaser of registered land where they have been entered on the register, typically as a notice but sometimes (where a beneficial interest under a trust) as a restriction.

- However, where interests have not been correctly entered on the register they may still bind a purchaser of registered land if they meet the requirements of an overriding interest under Sch 3 para 2.

- In any case, certain interests are not required to be entered on the register at all and yet are still deemed to be binding upon a purchaser of registered land, notably overriding interests under Sch 3 paras 1 and 3.

Chapter overview

Introduction

There exist today two types of land: registered and unregistered, each with its own rules concerning the transfer of land from one person to another and the enforcement of third party proprietary interests affecting the land.

The Land Registration Act 1925, which first introduced the system of **registered land**, was reviewed and repealed by the LRA 2002, which came into force on 13 October 2003.

 Looking for extra marks?

The LRA 2002 has maintained the basic structure of registered land introduced by the LRA 1925. However, under the new Act:

- more titles to land must now be registered;
- more interests must now be entered on to the register to be protected, consequently reducing the number of interests that automatically bind without being entered on the register (overriding interests);
- the way in which property can be acquired through adverse possession has been fundamentally watered down (see chapter 8);
- a system has been put in place which paves the way for electronic conveyancing.

The objective intended to be met by the introduction of a registered land system was essentially to simplify the process by which land is transferred from one party to another.

- In the unregistered land system, which you will see in the following chapter, a vendor has to prove his **title** ie his ownership of the land he wishes to sell. This is achieved by a time consuming and often mistake-ridden process of looking at the past title deeds to the land to see how it has been devolved and to trace ownership of the land into the hands of the vendor. With the introduction of registered conveyancing, ownership of land (or title to land) is registered at the Land Registry on a register which effectively acts as a public record of land ownership. The state guarantees the accuracy of the register in terms of who owns the land. (This is known as the *insurance principle* and indeed the state would compensate anyone who suffered a loss due to any errors present in the register: s 103 LRA 2002.) A purchaser, therefore, need not be concerned to look any further than the register to be sure that the vendor is entitled to deal with the land.

- Unlike unregistered land (discussed fully in the following chapter), the purchaser of registered land, in principle at least, need only search the register itself to discover any third party proprietary interests affecting the land that could be binding upon him. (According to the *mirror principle*, the register should be an accurate reflection not only as to who owns the land, but also any third party interests affecting it. In fact, this principle is tainted by the fact that certain third party interests, known technically as 'interests which override either first registration or registered dispositions' ('**overriding interests**' for short) are binding on a purchaser of registered land despite not being entered on the register. It is for this reason that a purchaser of registered land must conduct further enquiries beyond just looking at the register to discover third party interests.)

(Remember that there is a third principle behind title registration, known as the *curtain principle* whereby purchasers are not required to look behind the register. This particularly relates to trust property and the **overreaching** process (discussed below) by which a purchaser can take land free from any beneficial trust interests.)

Revision Tip

Exam questions sometimes focus upon whether the three principles outlined above are upheld. Give thought to this when looking at the rules of registered land discussed below.

It has always been the intention that all land in England and Wales becomes registered land and, indeed since the introduction of compulsory registration in 1990 (discussed below) which has been further extended by the **LRA 2002**, a majority of titles are now registered. However, there still remain titles that are not registered, which is why you need to be familiar with both systems of land.

The register

The register of title is a largely computerized, public (see **s 66 LRA 2002**) record maintained by the registrar at the Land Registry (**s 1 LRA 2002**). The register is divided into three parts:

1. **The Property Register**: this describes the land, the nature of the estate(s) registered, and any third party interests benefiting the land, for example a right of way.

2. **The Proprietorship Register**: this names the **registered proprietor**, states the title that has been registered (see below), and contains any **restrictions** which limit the way in which the registered proprietor can deal with the land (see below).

3. **The Charges Register**: this contains **notices** relating to any interests that burden the land, for example restrictive covenants, mortgages etc. (discussed below).

Registration of title

Some estates and interests are 'substantively registered' so that they acquire their own title number and file. These are:

- the freehold estate;
- the leasehold estate where there are more than seven years left to run;
- a rentcharge (the **Rentcharges Act 1977** prevents the creation of new rentcharges);

- a franchise; and

- a *profit à prendre* in gross (see chapter 12)

(s 2 LRA 2002)

Registration for the first time

Registration of title for the very first time can take place in the following circumstances:

- A person can voluntarily apply to the registrar to be registered as the proprietor of any one of the above interests, and financial incentives exist to encourage this: **s 3 LRA 2002**.

- In respect of a freehold estate, and a leasehold estate with more than seven years unexpired, certain events will trigger the need to compulsorily register title. Such events are now specified under **s 4 LRA 2002** and include:

  - the transfer (for consideration, by way of a gift, in pursuance of a court order, or by personal representatives upon death) of an unregistered legal estate be it freehold (the fee simple absolute in possession: see chapter 5) or leasehold with more than seven years left to run;

  - the grant of a lease of more than seven years (for consideration, by way of a gift or in pursuance of a court order);

  - the grant of a lease of any duration to take effect in possession after the end of a period of three months beginning with the date of a the grant (known as a **reversionary lease**);

  (The occurrence of these events triggers the need to register title to the estate that has been transferred / granted.)

  - the creation of a protected first legal mortgage, defined in **s 4(8) LRA 2002**.

  (This event triggers the need to register the estate charged by the mortgage.)

- The duty to register title upon the occurrence of one of the above events generally falls on the transferee or, in the case of the creation of a protected first legal mortgage, generally the mortgagor: **s 6 LRA 2002**.

- Registration should be applied for within two months beginning with the date of the triggering event (subject to any extension granted by the registrar).

- Upon receiving an application for registration, the registrar will make various enquiries so as to determine the class of title to register (see below) and there currently appears no direct means for appealing his decision.

- Persons with interests in the land who may be affected by first registration have the ability, in certain circumstances, to lodge a caution against first registration. This effectively means that when the registrar receives an application for first registration, he must notify the cautioner who then has 15 working days within which to object to the application. Where objections are made within this time frame that are not unwarranted, the matter must be referred to an adjudicator: s 71 LRA 2002.

- The consequences of failing to register title when required within the time frame are laid down in s 7 LRA 2002:

  - where the event triggering registration was the transfer of a freehold, or leasehold with more than seven years unexpired, title to the legal estate will revert to the transferor, who will hold it on bare trust for the transferee;

  - where the event triggering registration was the grant of a lease or first legal mortgage, the effect of non-registration is to treat what has happened as a contract for valuable consideration to grant that particular interest.

Late registration will be accepted with costs being the responsibility of the person who failed to register on time.

Registration on subsequent transactions

Once title has been registered, a subsequent transfer of that registered estate and the grant of a lease of more than seven years in duration out of a registered estate, must be completed by registration, so that the transferee/grantee is registered as proprietor: s 27(2) LRA 2002.

Failure to register such transactions means that the transfer will not operate at law (s 27(1) LRA 2002), the transferor retaining legal title.

The new registered proprietor will take the estate subject only to those interests entered on the register and interests which override the register, as defined in Sch 3 (discussed below).

Classes of title that can be registered

When title is registered at the Land Registry, for the first time or following subsequent dealings with the registered estate, it is important to show the strength of that title ie the validity of the claim to be registered as proprietor. The register must accurately reflect the state of title (ownership), especially since it will compensate anyone who suffers a loss due to errors present on the register (the insurance principle discussed above). The different classes of title that may be registered are laid down in ss 9 and 10 LRA 2002, with consequences noted in ss 11 and 12. The most significant of these classes is:

- *absolute title* This is the strongest title a person can be registered with. It indicates that that person has a better right than anyone else to the land and is usually only registered by the registrar in circumstances where he is happy that the title is secure and cannot be challenged.

A person registered with absolute title takes the land subject only to those interests entered on the register and those interests that override the register (defined under Sch 1: see below). Where registration of title is for the first time ie where unregistered land is being brought into the registered land system, those interests entered on the register will comprise those interests protected by registration of land charges under the Land Charges Act 1972 (see chapter 4). (Where the registered proprietor is a trustee, he will also take the land subject to the provisions of the trust; where he is a lessee, he will also take the land subject to the provisions in the lease.) Where the title registered is of a leasehold estate, registration with absolute title guarantees that the lease has been validly granted.

A person may also be registered with:

- *possessory title* where registration is based upon possession of the land, typically as an adverse possessor, rather than the provision of any title deeds, which the adverse possessor is unlikely to have. The registrar merely guarantees title as far as dealings post first registration are concerned; or

- *qualified title*, registered where there is a defect with the title, for example a lost deed, or where the registrar has a reservation about the title that cannot be ignored; or

- *good leasehold title*, in respect of leasehold estates, where the registrar is happy with the title granted to the tenant under the lease but not as to the title of the lessor.

Upgrading title

By virtue of s 62 LRA 2002, there is the possibility of upgrading a less than absolute title to absolute status, either by the registrar upon his own initiative, or upon an application typically made by the registered proprietor.

Third party proprietary interests affecting the land

When a person is registered as proprietor of a piece of land, in the circumstances outlined above, you have already seen that they take the land subject to:

- any interests entered on the register relating to the estate they have just acquired. (Where registration is for the first time, and therefore at the time of acquisition the estate was unregistered, these will be those interests registered as land charges under the LCA 1972 – see chapter 4); and

- any interests which override the register (outlined in Sch 1 where registration is for the first time, and Sch 3 where registration is to complete a subsequent transaction of an already registered estate.)

Third party proprietary interests affecting the land

✱✱✱✱✱✱✱✱✱✱

Interests entered on the register

These consist of those proprietary interests which, in principle at least, should have been entered on the register concerning the land to which they relate, in order to bind a purchaser of that land. The idea then is that a purchaser can inspect the register and discover any proprietary interests that both burden and benefit the land he intends to purchase. At the same time, holders of such proprietary interests have the certainty that by entering their interest on the register, they have protected that interest and made it enforceable against anyone who may come to the land.

The entry made to protect such interests can be either:

- a notice; or
- a restriction,

depending upon the type of interest.

Interests entered as a notice: by the registrar

It is important for you to remember that in certain cases, when creating an interest that has legal capacity (**s 1(2) Law of Property Act 1925** and discussed in chapter 2) over registered land, the creation of the interest must be completed by a process of registration (not to be confused with the process of registering title, discussed above). The most significant of these are:

- expressly created easements equivalent in duration to one of the legal estates; and
- the grant of a legal charge.

Until registration takes place, the interest will not take effect at law, but merely in equity provided the formalities required in equity are present. (This process is discussed more fully in the relevant chapters which discuss the above interests.)

For now, what you must realize is that when the registrar receives an application to register one of these interests, and the registration process is carried out, the registrar must enter a notice on the charges section of the register relating to the land burdened by the interest (discussed more fully below), so as to protect that interest and make it enforceable against anyone else who may come to the land (**s 38 LRA 2002**).

(A registrar will make a similar entry upon receipt of an application to register the grant of a lease of more than seven years to run created out of an already registered estate.)

Third party proprietary interests affecting the land

Also remember that interests which override the register (discussed below) may be entered on the register by the registrar: **s 37 LRA 2002**. Where he makes such an entry, the interest concerned can no longer have overriding status.

Interests entered as a notice: by the holder of the interest (the person benefiting from the interest)

Rather than list those interests that can be entered on the register by the holder, **s 33 LRA 2002** lists those interests that cannot be protected in this way, which include:

- interests under a trust (protected by entry of a restriction: see below);
- leases of three years or less taking effect in possession (see chapter 6); and
- restrictive covenants between a landlord and tenant (discussed in chapter 7).

What types of interests are, therefore, protected in this way?

They include:

Figure 3.1

Interest	Description
Estate contracts	Includes contracts to buy freehold estates (see chapter 5), contracts to buy leasehold estates ie equitable leases (see chapter 6), options to purchase, and rights of pre-emption.
Restrictive covenants between freehold estate owners	Defined and discussed in chapter 13.
Equitable easements	Defined and discussed in chapter 12.
Rights to occupy the family home under the **Family Law Act 1996**	A spouse (and also now civil partners under the **Civil Partnership Act 2004**) has a right to occupy the family home which, if entered on the register, is enforceable against anyone coming to the land.
Estoppel rights	Examples identified in chapter 11.

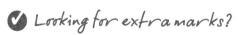 Looking for extra marks?

A right of pre-emption is an interest in land as soon as it is created: s 115 LRA 2002. This differs from rights of pre-emption created over unregistered land, whose status is governed by the decision in *Pritchard v Briggs* [1980] discussed in chapter 4.

Third party proprietary interests affecting the land
****

Where will the notice appear on the register?

Notices are entered on the charges section of the register relating to the land affected by the interest: **s 32 LRA 2002**.

What are the consequences of entering, or failing to enter, a notice?

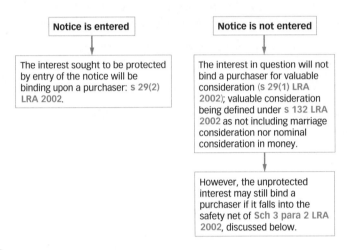

Notice is entered	Notice is not entered
The interest sought to be protected by entry of the notice will be binding upon a purchaser: **s 29(2) LRA 2002**.	The interest in question will not bind a purchaser for valuable consideration (**s 29(1) LRA 2002**); valuable consideration being defined under **s 132 LRA 2002** as not including marriage consideration nor nominal consideration in money.
	However, the unprotected interest may still bind a purchaser if it falls into the safety net of **Sch 3 para 2 LRA 2002**, discussed below.

Figure 3.2

Remember, that entering a notice on the register in respect of an interest does not by itself mean that the interest is valid. Rather, that if it is, entry will have made it enforceable against a purchaser.

✅ *Looking for extra marks?*

In the case of *Peffer v Rigg* [1977] it was declared that a purchaser could only take free of any interest which had not been protected by entry on the register, if he acted in good faith. Notice of the unprotected interest may negate any good faith that the purchaser has. This decision has been criticized and indeed the Law Commission made it clear that neither actual notice of the unprotected interest nor bad faith would have any effect on the consequences of failing to enter an interest on the register in the appropriate way. However, the existence of any fraud may require equity to intervene, since no-one should be allowed to benefit from a fraud. See for example *Lyus v Prowsa Developments Ltd* [1982]. How to determine a fraud from fair play is difficult and often the courts cannot agree (see for example the contrasting views of the Court of Appeal and House of Lords in *Midland Bank Trust Co Ltd v Green* [1981], discussed in the following chapter).

Interests entered as a restriction

What type of interest is dealt with by entry of a restriction?

The most important type of interest dealt with in this way is the beneficial interest under a trust.

Revision tip

An exam question may not expressly tell you property is held under a trust. You may have to work this out based upon facts provided. A knowledge of circumstances as to when a trust may be implied is required (link to chapter 9).

Where will the restriction appear on the register?

It will appear on the proprietorship section of the register relating to the land affected by the interest: **s 40 LRA 2002**.

What does the restriction do?

Rather than identify the nature of the interest to which it relates, the restriction limits the way in which the registered proprietor can deal with the property. It will lay down a specific procedure which must be followed when disposing of the property. Unless the procedure is followed, the registrar will not register the disponee of the property.

Where the restriction relates to a beneficial interest under a trust, it indicates that the property can only be disposed of where purchase monies are paid to at least two trustees (or a trust corporation). In other words, it stipulates that the disposal of the land complies with the mechanics of overreaching.

Overreaching: What is it and how does it work?

It is a mechanism by which a purchaser of trust land can take the land free from the beneficial interests under that trust. Whilst it can apply to other types of interests, it can only apply to those that are capable of existing without being attached to the land, and predominantly to beneficial interests under a trust, such interests being capable of existing in money as well as over land.

To overreach an interest, the purchaser must pay the purchase monies to at least two trustees or a trust corporation: **ss 2** and **27 LPA 1925**. In doing so, the interest is effectively detached from the land, so that the purchaser may take free from it. What is important for you to remember, however, is that the interest is not destroyed by this process. Rather, it is transferred from existing over land to existing in the purchase monies paid. Depending upon the terms of the trust, the trustees will then either distribute the money amongst the beneficiaries or will reinvest.

Third party proprietary interests affecting the land

✱✱✱✱✱✱✱✱✱✱

City of London Building Society v Flegg [1988] AC 54

Property was held by a married couple on trust for themselves and the wife's parents, the latter having contributed towards the purchase price for the property. The couple mortgaged the property to the building society. They squandered the mortgage advance and were adjudicated bankrupt. In seeking possession, it was held that the building society was not bound by the parent's beneficial interests under the trust. These interests had been overreached when the property had been mortgaged, by virtue of advancing the mortgage monies to two trustees ie the married couple.

Where overreaching was achieved in the case above, the case below is an example of where the requirements necessary for overreaching were not met:

William's & Glyn's Bank Ltd v Boland [1981] AC 487, HL

A husband was the sole registered proprietor of a property, held on trust for himself and his wife, the latter having contributed towards the purchase price. He mortgaged the property, defaulted on mortgage payments, and the bank sought possession. The bank was held bound by the wife's beneficial interest under the trust. It had only paid the mortgage monies over to one trustee, ie the husband and thus had not overreached the beneficial interest. The interest bound the bank by virtue of amounting to an overriding interest (see below).

What are the consequences of entering, or failing to enter, a restriction which relates to a beneficial interest under a trust?

Figure 3.3

Why bother to enter a restriction if it means that your beneficial interest is going to be detached from the land and thus you may lose having somewhere to live?

The whole point of entering a restriction is to protect your interest. Where a restriction is entered and followed, although the process of overreaching that occurs means that your interest is detached from the land, and thus you may lose having somewhere to live, it is not destroyed. You still have a beneficial interest under a trust, it just now happens to exist over money. Such money may be reinvested in property so that you obtain somewhere to live once more, though this will depend upon the terms of the trust.

If no restriction is entered, and therefore no overreaching takes place to detach your interest from the land, your interest will only bind that purchaser where you can establish the requirements under **Sch 3 para 2 LRA 2002**, discussed below. Where you cannot meet these requirements, your interest will not bind that purchaser. Effectively, it has been destroyed by the purchase. You no longer have any interest at all.

Interests which override the register

These consist of third party interests affecting a piece of land. Unlike the third party interests that must be entered on the register to be binding upon a purchaser, interests in this category will bind a purchaser despite not appearing anywhere on the register. This category of interest therefore goes against the fundamental *mirror principle*, discussed above, that the register should accurately reflect not only who owns the land but any third party interests affecting it.

 Looking for extra marks?

Despite this imperfection with the registered land system, the LRA 2002 did not take the opportunity to rid the registered land system of such interests, although it has reduced their number. The reason for the continued existence of such interests may be because, for many of them, it would be unreasonable for the holder of the interest to take steps to protect the interest by entering it on the register. In addition, interests falling into this category can often be evidenced in other ways, for example through common usage ascertainable by making a physical inspection of the land itself.

A report by the Law Commission, made prior to the introduction of the LRA 2002, also noted that the wholesale abolition of such interests, without compensation payments to those affected, might contravene Art 1 of the First Protocol of the European Convention on Human Rights 1950, incorporated into English law by s 1 Human Rights Act 1998.

Interests which override upon first registration

When title to land is being registered for the first time, bringing the land into the registered system, interests listed under **Sch 1** will override registration, including:

* legal leases of seven years or less in duration (**para 1**);

Third party proprietary interests affecting the land

- interests of persons in actual occupation (para 2) (discussed below); and
- legal easements or profits (para 3).

Interests which override subsequent transactions of already registered land

Since the majority of dispositions concern land that is already registered, interests that override under Sch 3 LRA 2002 are by far the most significant. Such interests are divided into three categories:

Sch 3 para 1

Legal leases of seven years or less fall into this category and will automatically bind a purchaser of the land, without the need for any further conditions to be met.

(Remember, legal leases over seven years must have been substantively registered to make them legal. Consequently, they will automatically be entered on the register of the freehold land to which they relate (s 38 LRA 2002), so a purchaser of that land will be bound by them. Equitable leases must have been entered on the register as a notice by the holder of the interest in order to be binding upon a purchaser (s 32 LRA 2002 and see above), although where the holder has failed to do so, he may be able to enforce the interest against the purchaser where he can establish the requirements under Sch 3 para 2.)

Sch 3 para 2

An interest will be binding upon a purchaser under this provision where the holder of the interest can establish:

- the interest he holds is a proprietary one, be it legal or equitable (and not excluded from this provision by the LRA 2002) ; and
- the interest existed at the time of the **disposition**; and
- they were in actual occupation of the land to which the interest relates and either:
  - the occupation would be obvious upon reasonably careful inspection of the land; or
  - even if not obvious, the purchaser had actual knowledge of the interest.

This is provided they did not fail to disclose the interest if enquiry had been made of them.

Remember, on this last point, a purchaser should make enquiry of the actual holder of the interest. It is not enough to make enquiries of the registered owner: *Hodgson v Marks* [1971].

Where the holder can establish the above requirements, the interest he holds will only be binding to the extent of the land he actually occupies and no more (reversing the decision of *Ferrishurst Ltd v Wallcite Ltd* [1999]).

 Looking for extra marks?

Where enquiries are made of the holder of the interest and he fails to disclose his interest, this will only prevent him from enforcing his interest under Sch 3 para 2, where it would have been *reasonable*

for him to disclose. So, for example, a person who contributes to a purchase price of a property may not realize that this gives them a beneficial interest under a trust. In such circumstances, it may not be reasonable to expect the holder of the beneficial interest to disclose it when asked. How can you disclose something you yourself do not know about? If this was the case, the holder of such an interest would not be prevented from relying upon Sch 3 para 2.

What is meant by 'actual occupation'?

This requires some physical presence on the land which itself has a degree of permanence and continuity. Temporary absences, even at the exact time of the disposition, may not prevent a finding of actual occupation, so long as the reason for such absence can be justified and is not too long.

Chhokar v Chhokar [1984] FLR 313, CA

A property was in the sole registered name of a husband who held it on trust for himself and his wife. Whilst the wife was in hospital having a baby, the husband transferred the property to an acquaintance. Upon returning from hospital, the wife found that the locks to the property had been changed. The wife was found to be in actual occupation of the property at the time of the transfer despite being in hospital at the exact time. Her absence from the property was only temporary and her furniture and belongings continued to be present at the property during this absence. Clearly her intention was to return to the property.

What amounts to being in actual occupation will differ depending upon the precise nature of the property. Actual occupation of a semi-derelict house, for example, may not require a finding that a person is living in the property since the state of the property may not make this feasible. In such circumstances, it may be enough just to find a regular presence of builders at the property, employed and supervised by the person claiming to be in actual occupation: *Lloyds Bank plc v Rosset* [1991].

Can you establish actual occupation via the occupation of the land by another?

No, unless you can establish that that other is occupying the property on your behalf as your agent.

Strand Securities v Caswell [1965] Ch 958, CA

A stepfather was unable to prove his own actual occupation of a property by producing evidence that his stepdaughter lived at the property rent free. Although he himself used the property as a convenient base when in London, this was infrequent and he in no way treated the property as his home. The stepdaughter lived there for own purposes, and certainly she was not there as his agent.

Had she been in occupation of the property as a caretaker, the outcome may have been different: *Abbey National BS v Cann* [1991].

Third party proprietary interests affecting the land

✱✱✱✱✱✱✱✱✱✱

Remember also, that where the holder of an interest is a parent, they will not be able to establish actual occupation based upon occupation by their children, since children are deemed to shadow the occupation of their parents: *Hypo-Mortgage Services v Robinson* [1997].

When must actual occupation be established?

It must exist at the time of the transfer of the land rather than the date of registration of the transfer ie when the transfer deed is executed.

Abbey National BS v Cann [1991] 1 AC 56, HL

A property was purchased with the aid of a mortgage by Cann, who was going to occupy it along with his mother. On the day of purchase, and thus when the charge in favour of the building society was being created, the mother was out of the country, although 35 minutes before completion, removal men started moving her belongings into the property. The charge was not completed by registration until a month later, by which time the mother was in physical occupation of the property. When her son defaulted on the mortgage payments, and the building society sought possession, it was held that the mother was unable to enforce her interest in the property as an overriding interest under the Sch 3 para 2 equivalent that existed under the LRA 1925, which was in force at the time. Despite her being in actual occupation at the time of registration, the relevant time was held to be the date of transfer. To allow otherwise would be unfair to a purchaser who, having inspected the land and finding no-one present, would then be held bound by an interest held by someone who took occupation of the land between transfer and registration. Her acts of moving in at the date of transfer were deemed merely preparatory steps towards actual occupation; not actual occupation itself.

(Remember, that when electronic conveyancing is established, transfer and registration will occur simultaneously; thus the problem envisaged above will be eradicated.)

Revision tip

A proliferation of case law exists on the issue of actual occupation. This is therefore often a good issue for discussion in an exam question, so be prepared to compare, contrast, and apply case law decisions.

Sch 3 para 3

Impliedly created legal easements (discussed in more detail in chapter 12) will bind a purchaser under this provision provided either:

- the person to whom the disposition is made actually knows about their existence; or
- the interest would be obvious upon reasonably careful inspection of the land; or
- the interest has been exercised in the year immediately preceding the disposition.

(Remember, expressly created legal easements and profits require registration to complete their creation. Consequently, they will automatically be entered on the register of the land which they burden to bind purchasers: **s 38 LRA 2002**. Equitable easements and profits must be entered on the register by the holder of the interest in order to be enforceable against purchasers: **s 32 LRA 2002**.)

Revision tip

Be sure you understand how to identify different types of interests and the formalities for their creation. An examiner may not always tell you the nature of the interest or whether it is legal or equitable (in cases where it could be either).

Transitional provisions

These provisions relate to interests created before the **LRA 2002** came into force and which had overriding status under the old **LRA 1925** rules. According to **Sch 12 LRA 2002**, some of these maintain their overriding status, in particular:

- legal leases of 21 years or less;
- legal easements and profits;
- rights of persons in actual occupation **or** in receipt of rent and profits from the land.

Altering the register

Section 65 and **Sch 4 LRA 2002** lay down the provisions for making alterations to the register.

Indemnities

Provisions for compensating persons who suffer a loss as a result of mistakes in the register are governed by **s 103** and **Sch 8 LRA 2002**.

 Key cases

Case	Facts	Principle
Abbey National BS v Cann [1991] 1 AC 56, HL	A mother was found not to be in actual occupation of a property, and thus have an overriding interest binding upon the building society, despite having moved some of her furniture into the property before completion took place and despite physically occupying the property at the time of registration.	The relevant time to establish actual occupation for the purpose of Sch 3 para 2 is the time of completion. Actual occupation will not be established upon mere preparatory acts to occupy.

Case	Facts	Principle
Chhokar v Chhokar [1984] FLR 313, CA	A wife's beneficial interest under a trust was found to be binding on a purchaser of the property. Having paid purchase monies to just one trustee (the husband) no overreaching had taken place. The unoverreached interest, coupled with the fact that the wife was found to be in actual occupation at the time of purchase, despite being in hospital having a baby, gave her a binding overriding interest.	Temporary absence from the property will not prevent a finding of actual occupation for the purpose of Sch 3 para 2 provided there is some physical evidence of occupation present coupled with an intention from the temporarily absent occupier to return.
City of London Building Society v Flegg [1988] AC 54	A building society was found not to be bound by beneficial interests under a trust when seeking possession of the property. It had successfully overreached the beneficial interests when it advanced the mortgage monies to the legal owners (a married couple).	Successful overreaching requires payment of monies to at least two trustees. Once overreached, beneficial interests will not bind a purchaser, regardless of any actual occupation of the beneficiaries and any notice the purchaser may have of those interests.
Strand Securities v Caswell [1965] Ch 958, CA	A father failed to establish that he was in actual occupation of a property by showing that his stepdaughter lived at the property.	Actual occupation for the purpose of Sch 3 para 2 cannot be established through occupation of another unless it can be shown that that other is your agent.
William's & Glyn's Bank Ltd v Boland [1981] AC 487, HL	A bank was found to be bound by a wife's beneficial interest under a trust. Having advanced the mortgage monies to just one legal owner (the husband) it had not successfully overreached the beneficial interest and this, coupled with the fact that the wife was in actual occupation of the property, gave her an overriding interest binding upon the bank.	Successful overreaching requires payment of monies to at least two trustees. Where a beneficial interest has not been overreached, and the interest holder is in actual occupation of the land, it will bind a purchaser as an overriding interest.

 (?) Exam questions

Problem question

Rory has just inherited a large piece of registered farmland from his uncle Stan. He has been approached by Natural Farming Ltd who wish to purchase the land for £300,000 so that they may use the land to expand their farming business. Rory is happy to sell but has been approached by several people who oppose the sale, namely:

1. his Auntie Vera, who claims to have an interest in the property by virtue of providing over half of the purchase monies when she and Uncle Stan purchased the land in 2005.

2. Malcolm, who leases part of the land for his own farming business. When asked by Rory whether he had any documentation to confirm this, he produced a document headed a deed and signed by both parties, witnessed and dated October 2006, which purported to grant him a 25 years lease and which detailed the terms of that lease.

3. Peter, a neighbour, who has been using a short cut across the land to the main road. When asked by Rory whether he had any documentation to confirm this, he produced a valid deed that granted him a right of way across the land for the duration of his lifetime.

4. Larry, a homeless person, who Uncle Stan allowed to sleep in one of the disused barns on the land, for free when he needed to.

Are any of these rights binding upon Rory now that he has inherited the land from Uncle Stan and would any of these rights be binding upon Natural Farming Ltd if it went ahead with a purchase of the land?

An outline answer is available at the end of the book

Essay question

The continued existence of overriding interests means that the objectives behind establishing a registered land system can never be met and the system itself can never be as efficient, certain, and just as was intended.

Discuss.

An outline answer is available online at www.oxfordtextbooks.co.uk/orc/concentrate/

#4
Unregistered land

This is a topic area that may be examined in a self-contained question or as part of a question concerning another topic area. Frequently, it is combined with registered land. It can also appear in questions concerning a particular interest in land, for example an easements question or a restrictive covenants question, where the interest exists over unregistered land and issues arise regarding the ability to enforce that interest against a purchaser of that land.

Problem questions typically focus upon rules of enforcement of interests over unregistered land. For example, you may be told about various types of interests that exist over a piece of unregistered land. (Sometimes those interests will be clearly identified; other times you may have to work out what they are for yourself.) That land will then pass to a purchaser and you will be required to work out whether those interests will be binding upon that purchaser. Often, you will be asked to consider how your answer would differ had the land been registered land at the time of purchase. Sometimes, issues concerning incorrect searches against the Land Charges Register may also appear.

Essay questions may require you to analyse how, if at all, the mode of enforcement of third party interests in unregistered land improved upon the system that existed before the Land Charges Act was passed. Alternatively, you may be asked to compare and contrast the rules and principles of unregistered land with those of the registered land system.

Key facts

- Unregistered land is land where title has not been registered at the Land Registry. Proof of ownership therefore comes from an examination of title deeds relating to that land.

- Identification of any third party proprietary interests burdening a piece of unregistered land cannot be discovered by a search of the land register. Rather, an examination of the title documents and various registers, the most important of which is the Land Charges Register, is required to discover their existence.

- A search of the Land Charges Register is made against the names of previous owners of the land, not the property address. A purchaser is bound by all land charges he did not discover, either by failing to search against all relevant names, or searching against incorrect names.

- Legal interests over unregistered land bind the world, with the exception of the *puisne* mortgage, which requires registration as a land charge to be binding.

- Interests covered by the Land Charges Act 1972 must be registered as the appropriate land charge to bind a purchaser.

- Failure to register such an interest appropriately means that the interest will not bind certain types of purchasers of the land.

- A purchaser can take free of a beneficial interest under a trust in unregistered land where he successfully overreaches that interest.

- Where a purchaser has failed to overreach a beneficial interest under a trust, enforcement of that interest against him depends upon the doctrine of notice.

- Enforcement of pre 1926 restrictive covenants and equitable easements, and interests arising by estoppel, is also governed by the doctrine of notice.

Chapter overview

Unregistered land: land where title is not registered at the Land Registry

When acquiring unregistered land, the purchaser must examine title deeds to establish good root of title ie proof of ownership. Legal title will pass upon execution of a valid conveyance

Whether a person acquiring unregistered land will be bound by interests over it depends upon the nature of the interest:

Legal interests: binding...

Equitable interests:

Except *puisne* mortgage...apply

Registrable as a land charge under Land Charges Act 1972

Capable of overreaching (essentially beneficial interest under a trust)

Governed by the doctrine of notice

Appropriate search of Land Charges Register must be conducted

Not binding if overreached ie met requirements under ss 2 and 27 LPA 1925

Binding if registered: s 198 LPA 1925

Otherwise...

Otherwise, will not bind certain types of purchaser (exact consequences depends upon nature of interest concerned): governed by s 4 LCA 1972

Introduction

Where title to land has not been registered ie a person's ownership of land has not been entered on the official register at the Land Registry, the land is known as **unregistered land**. Although the events that trigger the requirement to register title, as discussed in the previous chapter, are numerous, there still remains a percentage of land in England and Wales that is unregistered and it is for this reason that you need to be familiar with the rules that govern ownership of this type of land.

Revision tip

Be sure you understand the key differences between the rules and principles which govern unregistered and registered land as this can be a key focus of an exam question (link to chapter 3).

Conveyancing procedure

Whilst the procedure for buying land is outlined in detail in chapter 5, it is important to remind yourself of the following key differences when buying unregistered, as opposed to registered, land:

- Since title to the land has not been entered on an official register, which a purchaser can take as being an accurate record of ownership (see chapter 3), a purchaser of unregistered land must instead require the vendor to prove his title ie his ownership of the land. This is done by the time-consuming examination of title deeds relating to that land. These title deeds will show how the land has devolved in the past and hopefully establish that the vendor has the right to sell it. Such an examination must go back at least 15 years since the last dealing with the property (s 23 Law of Property Act 1969) so that the purchaser can establish what is known as a 'good root of title'.

- When a purchaser wishes to determine the proprietary interests that burden the unregistered land he is proposing to buy, he will not be able to go to the land register to find out about such interests. Instead, he will have to make enquiries elsewhere, discussed below.

- When purchasing unregistered land, legal title will pass upon execution of a valid deed (unlike registered land where legal title will not pass until title has been registered with the new owner: see chapter 3).

- The deed used to convey legal title of unregistered land is known as a 'conveyance' (whereas in registered land it is known as a 'transfer deed': see chapter 3).

Enforcement of third party proprietary interests exercised over the land

Where a person is purchasing a piece of unregistered land, over which various legal and equitable third party proprietary interests exist, the purchaser will wish to know whether such interests will be binding and enforceable upon him. Likewise, the holders of these interests will wish to know whether they can enforce their interests against the new owner of the land. They may wish to know whether there is anything they must do to make their interests enforceable against that new owner.

In registered land, enforceability of such interests, in principle at least, depends upon whether they have been entered on the land register (with the exception of overriding interests: see the previous chapter). Where the land in question is unregistered, enforcement of these interests is governed by different rules. The appropriate rules to apply largely depend upon whether the interest is legal or equitable in nature: see Figure 4.1.

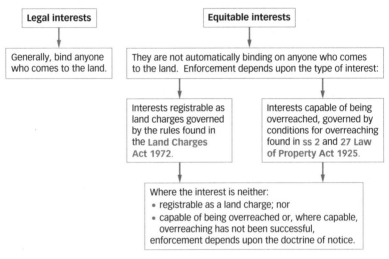

Figure 4.1

Revision tip

An exam question may not specifically identify whether an interest is legal or equitable. You must therefore know the rules regarding the formalities for creating interests (link to chapter 2).

Legal interests

Short of obtaining a waiver or release from the holder of the interest, there is little that the purchaser can do to avoid being bound by legal interests over unregistered land.

This may not be as harsh as it sounds. Generally, legal interests are created by deed and such documents should be kept with the title deeds so that a purchaser may discover their existence prior to making the decision to buy the land. Of course, there are exceptions; for example legal easements created impliedly by necessity (discussed in chapter 12). However, such rights may be (although not always) discoverable by the purchaser making a physical inspection of the land itself.

There is one exception of a legal interest that is not automatically binding upon a purchaser and that is the *puisne* **mortgage**, a legal mortgage of unregistered land that is not secured by the deposit of title deeds (usually a second or subsequent mortgage). Enforcement of this type of interest in fact depends upon registration as a land charge (see below).

Equitable interests

Interests registrable as land charges under the Land Charges Act 1972

The basic principles

Interests that fall into this category must be registered as the appropriate land charge under the LCA 1972 in order to be enforceable against anyone who comes to the land over which they exist. Registration of the interest constitutes actual notice of that interest (s 198 LPA 1925 and explained in chapter 2). Consequently, that interest will bind anyone who comes to the land.

Where the interest has not been registered in the appropriate way, it will be void against certain types of purchaser's, whether the purchaser has knowledge of the existence of the interest or not. Notice is not relevant in the land charges system: s 199(1) LPA 1925; *Hollington Brothers Ltd v Rhodes* [1951].

✅ Looking for extra marks?

There may be a strong argument today to claim that where a purchaser takes title to land expressly subject to the rights of another, this will give rise to a constructive trust or that maybe such rights should be enforceable under the Contracts (Rights of Third Parties) Act 1999.

Which interests fall into this category and what type of land charge must they be registered as?

The types of interests that must be registered as land charges, and the specific land charge they must be registered as, are laid down in s 2 LCA 1972. The interests in Figure 4.2 are the ones you should know.

✅ Looking for extra marks?

According to the decision in *Pritchard v Briggs* [1980] a right of pre-emption is not an interest in unregistered land upon creation. It only becomes an equitable proprietary interest upon the vendor making the decision to sell. A decision to sell will activate any registration of a right of pre-emption as a class c(iv) land charge, which, up until that time, remains dormant.

How does the holder of the interest register it as a land charge?

Application to register the interest as a land charge will be made to the Land Charges Department of the Land Registry at Plymouth. The interest should be registered as a land

Enforcement of third party proprietary interests

✳✳✳✳✳✳✳✳✳

Figure 4.2

Type of interest	Description	Land Charge
Puisne mortgages	A legal mortgage where the mortgagee does not take possession of the title deeds. This is because the mortgage is a second or subsequent mortgage over the property and the title deeds are with the first mortgagee.	Class C(i)
Estate contract	Includes contracts to buy freehold estates (see chapter 5), contracts to buy leasehold estates ie equitable leases (see chapter 6), options to purchase and rights of pre-emption (see chapter 5).	Class C(iv)
Restrictive covenants between freeholders created on/after 1 January 1926	Defined and discussed in chapter 13.	Class D(ii)
Equitable easements created on/after 1 January 1926	Defined and discussed in chapter 12.	Class D(iii)
Rights to occupy the family home under the Family Law Act 1996	A spouse (and also now civil partners under the Civil Partnership Act 2004) has a right to occupy the family home which, if registered as a land charge, is enforceable against anyone coming to the land. Although a statutory right, rather than a proprietary interest, enforcement is governed by the LCA 1972.	Class F

charge against the name of the estate owner at the time the interest is created and over whose estate the interest is to be exercised: s 3(1) LCA 1972. This is the name of the owner as it appears in the title deeds. The entry on the Land Charges Register will record the nature of the interest to be protected and the name of the person who claims to hold that interest.

How does the purchaser acquire knowledge of those interests registered as land charges?

The purchaser should conduct a search of the Land Charges Register to discover any land charges that have been registered and thus uncover any interests exercised over the land about to be purchased which will be binding upon him. This is typically conducted between exchange of contracts and completion (discussed in chapter 5). Where binding land charges are discovered after the purchaser has entered into a valid contract to purchase, s 24 LPA 1969 entitles the purchaser to withdraw from the contract, provided he did not know about the existence of the land charge at the time of entering into it.

The search should be made against the names of the previous owners of the land, against whom land charges may have been registered. This has proven to be a major problem with the land charges system as purchasers may not always know the names against which they should be making their searches, especially the names of owners who owned the land many years ago and who therefore may not be uncovered when looking at the title deeds to acquire a good root of title, which requires just a minimum of 15 years investigation of title. Regardless of this fact, a purchaser would still be bound by land charges he had not been able to discover. To partly address this problem, s 25 LPA 1969 provides a scheme whereby the purchaser can claim compensation for the existence of undiscoverable yet binding land charges, on condition that:

- he investigated good root of title and searched against the names of the estate owners revealed in this investigation; and
- he had no actual knowledge of the existence of the land charge(s) in question.

In addition, errors may be made where searches are made against incorrect names. Where this is the case, the land charge registered against the correct name is binding. What if it is not the search that is against the incorrect name, but the registration of the interest itself?

....

Diligent Finance Co Ltd v Alleyne [1972] 23 P&CR 346

A wife registered her Class F right to occupy the matrimonial home against the name of her husband, whom she knew as Erskine Alleyne. In fact, his full name was Erskine Owen Alleyne. When a finance company searched against the full correct version of his name, no land charge was uncovered. The company was therefore not bound by the incorrectly registered Class F land charge.

....

Where searches are made against the correct names, the purchaser acquires 15 working days' immunity so that any interests registered within this time will not bind him.

What are the consequences of failing to register an interest as a land charge?

These differ depending upon the type of interest and thus category of land charge that should have been registered: see Figure 4.3.

Revision tip

Be sure you understand the precise effect an unregistered interest will have upon different types of purchasers. Look out, in exam questions, for people who inherit or who are gifted the property.

When thinking about these consequences outlined above, remember the following:

- Once an interest is void for non-registration, it cannot be revived upon a subsequent purchase of the land, even if the later purchaser is not one for value.
- A 'purchaser' for the purposes of s 4 LCA 1972, is any person who, for valuable consideration, takes any interest in land or a charge on the land: s 17(1) LCA 1972.

Enforcement of third party proprietary interests

✱✱✱✱✱✱✱✱✱✱

Figure 4.3

- A purchaser 'for money or money's worth' under s 4(6) LCA 1972 is one who provides their valuable consideration either in the form of actual money or, alternatively, something that can be computed in financial terms, for example shares. It does not include someone who provided marriage as consideration, although marriage is itself recognized as valuable consideration elsewhere in land law (s 205(xxxi) LPA 1925) and indeed would be considered appropriate value for the purpose of s 4(5) and (8) above.

- As long as the consideration provided by the purchaser is valuable (and in addition, where the land charge is one governed by s 4(6) LCA 1972, provided in the form of money or money's worth), the court will not enquire into the adequacy of the consideration provided.

- The fact that the purchaser has knowledge of the existence of the unregistered interest prior to the purchase will not mean that he will be bound by that interest. Notice has no role to play under the LCA 1972 and there is no requirement that the purchaser must be acting in good faith.

These last two points were confirmed in the key case of *Midland Bank Trust Co Ltd v Green* [1981]:

....

Midland Bank Trust Co Ltd v Green [1981] AC 513

A father gave his son an option to purchase the family farm. This estate contract was not registered by the son as a Class C(iv) land charge. The father later sold the farm to his wife for £500. Despite this being considerably less than the value of the land, and the wife having knowledge of the unregistered estate contract when she made the purchase, she was held to take free from that unregistered interest. Since the interest had not been appropriately registered, it would not bind her. The fact that she knew that the interest existed was deemed irrelevant. The court also felt it inappropriate to consider the adequacy of the consideration provided.

✅ Looking for extra marks?

When the case was heard by the Court of Appeal, Lord Denning felt that the £500 provided by the wife for the purchase was a 'gross undervalue'. Lord Everleigh said that the transaction was more akin to a gift of land coupled with a token £500 to meet the requirements under s 4 LCA 1972. The dealing between the father and his wife was deemed fraudulent and dishonest. However, Lord Wilberforce in the House of Lords disagreed, stating that it would be difficult to hold £500 as a nominal sum of money. In any case provided the consideration was real, there would be no enquiry into whether the consideration was adequate; an expression he termed as one of transparent difficulty. On the issue of the wife not acting in good faith because she knew about the son's unregistered estate contract, Lord Wilberforce noted that the LCA 1972 did not include the words 'good faith' when describing a purchaser. He considered this omission a deliberate one and indeed thought that if acting in good faith had been a requirement of the purchaser, it would effectively be reintroducing an element of notice, which the LCA 1972 was aiming to avoid.

Interests capable of being overreached

The main equitable interest that is capable of being overreached is the beneficial interest under a trust (discussed in chapters 9 and 10). Such interests are not capable of being registered as land charges. Instead their enforcement against a purchaser of unregistered land primarily depends upon application of the conditions for overreaching laid down in ss 2 and 27 LPA 1925, already discussed in the previous chapter. These conditions operate exactly the same in unregistered land.

Figure 4.4

Interests subject to the doctrine of notice

Although one of the principle objectives of the land charges registration system was to make the enforcement of proprietary interests dependent upon registration, for a minority of interests, the doctrine of notice still determines the enforcement of that interest against a purchaser of unregistered land. The main interests that are still governed by this doctrine are:

- overreachable interests that have not been successfully overreached; and
- restrictive covenants entered into between freeholders of land and created before 1 January 1926; and
- equitable easements created before 1 January 1926; and
- interests arising by estoppel.

How does the doctrine of notice work?

An interest will only bind a person if he is not a *bona fide purchaser of a legal estate for value without notice*. These conditions are considered in more detail in chapter 2. Perhaps the most important is that in order not to be bound by an interest a purchaser must have no notice of that interest be that actual, constructive, or imputed notice (again, explained in chapter 2). But remember, *without notice* is merely one of the requirements a purchaser must satisfy if he is not to be bound by an interest governed by this doctrine. The others stated above must also be met.

Revision tip

An exam question may require you to show how the doctrine of notice operates (link to chapter 2). It may also require you to assess its role in unregistered land today, so link with discussions in *Midland Bank Trust Co Ltd v Green* [1981].

 (✱) Key cases

Case	Facts	Principle
Diligent Finance Co Ltd v Alleyne [1972] 23 P&CR 346	A wife failed to register her Class F land charge against her husband's full name. The right was subsequently not binding upon a finance company who had correctly searched the register against the full name.	A land charge registered against the incorrect name, will not bind a purchaser who searches the register against the correct name.
Hollington Brothers Ltd v Rhodes [1951] 2 All ER 487	An equitable lease which had not been registered as an appropriate land charge, did not bind a purchaser of the reversion, despite the sale being expressly subject to the lease with a purchase price that reflected this fact.	An interest must be registered as a land charge, where appropriate, to bind a purchaser. Notice is irrelevant under the LCA 1972.

Case	Facts	Principle
Midland Bank Trust Co Ltd v Green [1981] AC 513	An estate contract which had not been registered as a Class C(iv) land charge was not binding upon a purchaser who knew about it and who provided consideration that appeared to be undervalue.	A court is not to enquire about the adequacy of consideration provided by a purchaser in respect of application of the LCA 1972 rules. The knowledge of the purchaser is irrelevant.

 (?) Exam questions

Problem question

Josh has just purchased Willow House, a detached property with a garage and large garden. Title to the property is unregistered.

When the vendor, Guy, originally purchased the house, his wife, Marian, contributed a quarter of the purchase price, although the legal title was conveyed to Guy alone. Marian works in Italy and has to spend most of the week there, returning to stay in Willow House just at weekends. She does, however, leave many of her personal belongings in Willow House to make travelling between the countries easier. When a survey of the property was conducted prior to the purchase, it was on a weekday so Marian was out of the country. The surveyor noticed female belongings in the house and photos of Guy with a lady but made no enquiries as to who the lady was or who the female possessions belonged to. The surveyor did not mention anything about this to Josh.

Whilst Guy owned Willow House, he allowed Susie, the neighbour, to use a short cut across the garden of Willow House to get to the main road. Susie has a valid deed detailing this arrangement. Guy also allowed the garage to be leased to his friend Pete. This arrangement was drawn up in document signed by both Guy and Pete, and gave Pete exclusive use of the garage for ten years.

Advise Josh as to whether Marian, Susie, and Pete have any rights that are enforceable against him.

How, if at all, would your answer differ, if Josh had been gifted Willow House rather than purchased it?

An outline answer is available at the end of the book

Essay question

What were the perceived problems with the doctrine of notice? How did the land charges system seek to address these problems and was it successful in doing so?

An outline answer is available online at www.oxfordtextbooks.co.uk/orc/concentrate/

#5
The freehold estate

The examination

How the material covered in this chapter appears in an exam paper will, to a large extent, be dependent upon individual approaches taken by different teaching institutions (and it is for this reason that no specimen exam questions have been provided at the end of this chapter). You must be guided by the tutorials and lectures that you have attended to ascertain where such material may appear within the exam and to what degree. For example, some institutions may not cover material concerning the characteristics of a freehold estate in any depth; others may, perhaps linking it to the concept of settled land and the creation of trusts (discussed in chapter 9). The material covered in relation to the creation of a freehold estate, the formalities and principles as to when equitable and legal ownership is established, applies elsewhere and you must be able to identify scenarios where such material is relevant for discussion.

Key facts

- The freehold estate is the largest of the two estates in land that has legal capacity and a person who holds a freehold estate over land is tantamount to being the owner of that land (although technically ownership rests with the Crown).

- The legal freehold estate is technically known as the *fee simple absolute in possession* and the characteristics of a legal freehold estate can be found from interpreting this technical definition.

- A contract for the transfer of a freehold estate must meet the requirements under s 2 Law of Property (Miscellaneous Provisions) Act 1989.

- Where the contract is to be varied, s 2 LP(MP)A 1989 must be complied with when the variation is of a material term.

- A valid and specifically enforceable contract for the transfer of a freehold estate will give the purchaser an equitable interest in the land to be purchased, known as an estate contract.

- Legal title to the land will not pass to the purchaser until completion, which involves execution of a valid deed (s 52 Law of Property Act 1925, s 1 LP(MP)A 1989) and registration of title.

- The exact moment when legal title passes differs depending upon whether the land being purchased is registered (where title passes upon registration of title) or unregistered land (where title passes upon execution of a valid deed).

Chapter overview

Introduction

The **freehold estate** is one of the recognized estates in land capable of being legal: s 1(1)(a) LPA 1925. It is the largest of the two estates that have legal capability, the other being the leasehold estate (see chapter 6).

The characteristics of a freehold estate

Whilst there is more than one type of freehold estate, the largest, and the only one that has legal capability, is the **fee simple absolute in possession**. This is usually what people mean when they say they hold the freehold estate.

A person who holds this estate over a piece of land is entitled to use and possess that land forever, or at least until he dies with no heirs, at which point the estate will come to an end and the land will revert to the Crown *bona vacantia*. The extent of that person's rights to possess and use the land are virtually unlimited, subject only to certain statutory limitations and the rights of lesser estate holders, whose estates have been carved out of that freehold estate.

It is for these reasons that holding the fee simple absolute in possession is the nearest thing to absolute ownership of the land. The continuing technical ownership by the Crown (as discussed in chapter 1) can only be seen should the estate holder die without heirs.

The characteristics of this freehold estate can be identified by looking at the meaning of fee simple absolute in possession:

1. **It is an inheritable estate (*fee*)**
   This differs from:
   - a *life estate* which is not inheritable as it comes to an end upon the death of the grantee; and
   - an *estate pur autre vie*; again not inheritable as it comes to an end upon the death of someone other than the grantee.

   Both the *life estate* and the *estate pur autre vie* are types of freehold estates but neither have legal capability under s 1(1) LPA 1925 and can only exist in equity behind a trust.

2. **The estate is inheritable by anyone (*simple*)**
   This differs from a *fee tail* estate where inheritability is curtailed to direct lineal descendants and sometimes only to those of a certain gender, for example *fee tail male*. Although another type of freehold estate, since 1 January 1997, when the **Trusts of Land and Appointment of Trustees Act 1996** came into force, it is no longer possible to create this estate of limited inheritance.

3. **The estate is perpetual and not liable to end prematurely upon the occurrence of a specified event (*absolute*)**

This differs from:

- A *determinable fee simple*: this is a fee simple estate that will be held until it is terminated automatically upon the occurrence of a specified event. For example, if Blackacre is granted to X until he qualifies as a solicitor, the fee simple he holds is not *absolute* and will terminate upon his qualification, if and when it occurs. Such fee simple estates can be ascertained by looking for words which limit the grant, for example 'whilst', 'until', 'during'.

- A *fee simple on condition subsequent*: this is where the fee simple is granted but is subject to a clause that if a particular condition is met in the future, the estate may be forfeited from the grantee. For example, Blackacre is granted to X on condition that he does not qualify as a solicitor. Such fee simple estates can be ascertained from wording in the grant that indicates the estate will last forever unless a condition limiting its duration is met, for example 'unless', 'provided that', 'on condition that'. It is normal when granting this type of fee simple that a right of entry is reserved for the grantor, entitling him to forfeit the estate in the event that the condition is fulfilled.

- A *fee simple on condition precedent*: this is where a fee simple is granted but which will only commence when a certain event has occurred; for example, granting Blackacre to X and his heirs when he reaches 21 years of age.

✅ Looking for extra marks?

What are the differences between a *determinable fee simple* and a *fee simple on condition subsequent?*

- A *determinable fee simple* terminates automatically when the determining event occurs, with the fee simple reverting back to the grantor. When the condition which allows for the estate to be forfeited is met in a *fee simple on condition precedent*, the fee simple remains vested in the grantee until such time as the grantor chooses to exercise his right to forfeit.

- A *determinable fee simple* can only ever exist in equity behind a trust. A *fee simple on condition subsequent* ranks as a legal estate. A fee simple subject to a right of entry is absolute according to the Law of Property Amendment Act 1926, thus falling within s 1(1)(a) LPA 1925.

The courts have a greater tendency to strike out undesirable *conditions subsequent* than equivalent clauses in *determinable fee simples*. Whilst striking out the latter destroys the grant of the fee simple in its entirety, striking out the former, whilst it gets rid of the offending condition, will not destroy the grant of the fee simple which takes effect as a *fee simple absolute*.

4. **The estate is one that gives the estate holder the present right to enjoy and possess (*in possession*)**
   According to **s 205(1)(xix) LPA 1925** possession need not be physical. It can include being in receipt of rent or profits or having a right to receive the same. This is how a person can still hold the freehold estate even when a leasehold estate has been carved out of it and physical possession is with the tenant.

The characteristics of a freehold estate

✱✱✱✱✱✱✱✱✱✱

Are all freehold estates in possession?

No. The freehold estate may be:

- *in reversion*: this is where the freehold owner carves out a lesser estate, for example a life estate, from the fee simple estate, but makes no express provision as to what should happen once the lesser estate expires. Whilst the lesser estate exists, the fee simple owner has parted with his present right to use and possess the land so he no longer holds the fee simple *in possession*. However, such rights to use and possess the land will revert to him (or his heirs) once the lesser estate expires. Hence, during the existence of the lesser estate, the fee simple is being held *in reversion*.

- *in remainder*: this is where the fee simple owner carves out a lesser estate from the fee simple estate and grants it to another to use at some point in the future. This lesser estate is then known as one that is *in remainder* ie it gives the grantee a present right but to future use and enjoyment of the land.

  For example, X holds the fee simple and leaves it in his will to his wife for life and thereafter to his son. The son's interest is held by him *in remainder*. He has to wait for the expiry of his mother's life interest before he has the right to use and enjoy the land.

Estates held *in reversion* or *in remainder* can only exist in equity behind a trust. Only fee simple estates held *in possession* have legal capability: s 1 LPA 1925.

The commonhold

This is a form of freehold estate that was introduced by the Commonhold and Leasehold Reform Act 2002. Key points to note are:

- The **commonhold** is intended to benefit blocks of flats and apartments where rights to possess and enjoy are usually based upon leasehold estates.

- It allows occupants, known as 'unit holders', to own the freehold of their flat/apartment.

- The freehold of the shared common parts within the building is held by a 'commonhold association', a private limited company that assumes responsibility for the management and upkeep of these shared common parts.

- Each unit holder becomes a member of the commonhold association. Collectively, they have the ability to control and manage the building in accordance with the 'commonhold community statement', which specifies the rights and duties of the commonhold association and unit holders.

Currently, few commonhold estates have been established, since the requirements to do so are difficult to meet. Applications to register land as commonhold must be accompanied by the consent of certain persons with an interest in the building, notably the registered freehold owner, leasehold owners and mortgagees, amongst others. Getting the consent of all such interested persons is not always easy. And remember, commonhold is not compulsory so developers of new blocks of flats still have a choice as to whether to create commonhold or leasehold estates.

✅ *Looking for extra marks?*

Why create a commonhold rather than a long leasehold estate?

- Whilst the owner of a lease, even where the term of that lease is very long, essentially owns a wasting asset, the owner of a commonhold, a type of freehold estate, does not.

- Duties imposed upon unit holders by the commonhold community statement will equally apply to incoming unit holders as outgoing ones, thus erasing problems of enforcing freehold covenants on the transfer of land (see chapter 13).

Formalities for transfer of a freehold estate

Since the freehold estate is such a valuable asset, its transfer from one party to another will involve a series of stages. The ultimate aim of the purchaser will be to acquire legal freehold title. The exact moment when this will be achieved differs depending upon whether the freehold title being transferred is registered title or not at the time of purchase. If it is not, one of the consequences of the transfer will be to bring the title into the registered system (see below and chapter 3).

Pre contract stage

This will involve numerous enquiries being made by the purchaser about the freehold title he wishes to purchase, and negotiations between the vendor and the purchaser, regarding such things as price, inclusion of chattels in the sale, time frame for the completion of the sale etc. The Housing Act 2004, which came into effect in 2007, now requires the vendor to produce a Home Information Pack. The intention is that such packs will reduce the extent of enquiries the purchaser should himself undertake prior to purchase, thus reducing his pre-purchase costs.

Contract stage

Transfer of the equitable interest

The completion of a valid contract for the transfer of a freehold estate creates personal rights between the vendor and the purchaser. Should either party breach the contract, the party who suffers from that breach could seek contractual damages.

However, the valid contract may also give the purchaser a proprietary interest in the estate he is purchasing, such interest being equitable in nature. How?

- Equity considers the remedy of damages inadequate where the contract breached has land as its subject matter. As no one piece of land is the same, monetary damages may not compensate for the breach of a land contract.

Formalities for transfer of a freehold estate

✳✳✳✳✳✳✳✳✳✳✳

- Equity will normally, therefore, give the purchaser the remedy of specific performance where there is a breach of such a contract (subject to discretion).
- Since equity views as done that which ought to be done, once a valid contract is made, equity views it as having been performed. The purchaser is therefore seen, in equity, as being the owner of the land, assuming specific performance is available to him and the court exercises its discretion in his favour. The equitable interest in the land has passed to him upon completion of a valid contract: *Sookraj v Samaroo* [2004].
- This equitable interest is known as an **estate contract**.

Legal title remains with the vendor, who effectively holds it on trust for the purchaser until such time as the sale is completed (see below). Remember, however, that this trust relationship does not reflect a usual trust: the vendor remains in possession of the property and can exclude the purchaser, although he must keep the land in the same condition as it was when the valid contract was made.

Revision tip

Remember that a person may acquire an equitable proprietary interest upon the completion of any valid contract relating to the creation/transfer of other estates or interests in land which is capable of specific performance. See chapter 6 and the discussion of the case of *Walsh v Lonsdale* (1882).

Formalities

All contracts must meet basic contractual formalities ie offer and acceptance, consideration, intention etc. However, where the contract has land as its subject matter, such as one for the transfer of a freehold estate, additional requirements must be met. These differ depending upon the date of creation of the contract.

Created Pre 27/09/89	Created On / After 27/09/89

Contracts must comply with **s 40 LPA** 1925 ie
 	
- in writing (containing the essential terms and signed by the party against whom it is sought to be enforced); or
- oral with either
  - written evidence signed by the party against whom it is sought to be enforced; or
  - part performance.
	Contracts must comply with **s 2 LP(MP)A** 1989 ie
	
	- in writing;
	- containing all the terms; and
	- signed by both parties
	
	unless they fall into the exceptions in **s 2(5)** LP(MP)A 1989, in which case compliance with these three requirements is not necessary eg contracts to create leases of three years or less in duration.

Section 2 LP(MP)A 1989 analysed

A contract which fails to satisfy all three requirements under s 2 will be deemed void.

In writing

This can include typing, printing, and emailing (*J Pereira Fernades SA v Mehta* (2006)).

Containing all the terms

What terms?

The four 'P's:

- Parties, for example vendor and purchaser;
- Price, whether specifically or the mechanism by which it is to be calculated;
- Property ie land and estate, for example freehold;
- other Provisions. These include those terms that have been expressly agreed upon between the parties. Otherwise, standard terms and conditions will be implied, without the need for their express insertion.

Where?

The terms should be found either:

- in one document; or
- two identical documents where they are to be exchanged; or
- by reference to another document (s 2(2)).

Omissions

Where an essential term of the contract has been omitted, this would make the contract void. However:

- if you can establish that the omission is a mistake and that both parties had orally agreed to the omitted term but that the written document failed to reflect this, the court may allow rectification to correct the inaccurate written record: s 2(4) LP(MP)A 1989 and *Wright v Robert Leonard Developments Ltd* [1994];
- alternatively, you could try and argue that the omitted term is not part of the sale contract; rather that it is collateral to that contract: *Record v Bell* [1991]. If this argument succeeded the sale contract would not be void for failing to contain all the terms. It is for the court to decide whether the omitted term was part of the sale contract or not: *Grossman v Hooper* [2001]. In this case it was declared that the idea of collateral contracts was not a helpful notion.

Formalities for transfer of a freehold estate

✳✳✳✳✳✳✳✳✳✳

Signed by both parties

Where the terms are incorporated by reference to another document, it is the incorporating document that must be signed by both parties.

This requirement must be interpreted in accordance with its ordinary meaning. Printing a name on the document will therefore not suffice: *Firstpost Homes Ltd v Johnson* [1995]. The introduction of e-conveyancing will allow for electronic signatures: **Electronic Communications Act 2000.**

Varying the contract terms

To do so may require you to comply with certain formalities but whether this will be the case depends upon the nature of the term that you are seeking to vary: *McClausland v Duncan Lawrie Ltd* (1997).

Varying a Material Term	Varying an Immaterial Term
The variation must comply with **s 2 LP(MP) A 1989.** If it does not comply then: • the variation will be invalid; • the original terms of the contract will stand unless the oral variation is so fundamental that it amounts to a wholly new agreement, with the original agreement considered rescinded (*British & Benningtons Ltd v NW Cachar Tea Co* (1923)).	No need to comply with **s 2 LP(MP)A 1989.**

Can contracts arise through correspondence?

The decision in *Hooper v Sherman* [1994], which allowed for a contract to arise from two letters, was not followed in the case of *Commission for the New Towns v Cooper (GB) Ltd* [1995]. Since no one letter contained all the terms and was signed by both parties, there was no document compliant with s 2 and thus no contract had arisen. This decision would seem to be the current position on this issue.

✅ Looking for extra marks?

Options to purchase are a specific type of land contract involving two key stages:

• the vendor grants the option to the purchaser, whereby the former agrees to keep open a specified offer to sell the freehold estate to the purchaser for a specified period;

- the purchaser may accept that offer at any time during the specified period on the terms as outlined in the option.

According to *Spiro v Glencrown Properties Ltd* [1991], it is the initial grant of the option that must comply with s 2, whilst the exercise of it need not. Since the exercise of the option is a unilateral act by the purchaser, to enforce s 2 compliance at this stage would be nonsensical. To require both parties to sign the exercise of the option, as s 2 requires, would destroy the whole purpose of an option. The purpose of s 2 is to record the mutual consent of the parties. Only the grant of the option depends upon this mutual consent.

Estoppel intervention

In some circumstances, equity may intervene to give a purchaser equitable rights even where no document compliant with **s 2 LP(MP)A 1989** exists.

- -

Yaxley v Gotts [2000] Ch 162

The claimant had reached an oral agreement with the father of the defendant that, if the latter bought a house and the claimant conducted substantial building works to convert the house into flats, he (the claimant) would be given the ground floor flats. In fact, the defendant bought the house. Unaware of this fact, the claimant carried out the works to the value of £9,000 and when the defendant sought to evict the claimant, the latter claimed an interest in the property. Since the claimant had relied and acted upon the oral agreement to his detriment, the court was willing to recognize that in equity the claimant had an interest in the land. The defendant was estopped from asserting the true legal position that no valid contract existed.

- -

Completion stage

Transfer of the legal interest

Completion is where legal title to the freehold estate will pass from the vendor to the purchaser. The exact time that this occurs will differ depending upon whether the title being purchased is registered or unregistered at the date of purchase.

Formalities

Deed

To pass legal freehold title, there must be a valid deed: **s 52 LPA 1925**. The current requirements for a valid deed are laid down in **s 1(2) LP(MP)A 1989**, as discussed in chapter 2.

> *Revision tip*
>
> Remember not to confuse the formalities for a valid deed with those for a valid contract. For example, whilst a contract must be signed by both parties, a deed need only be signed by the person granting the interest.

Key cases

✳✳✳✳✳✳✳✳✳✳

Registration

Title will then have to be registered. This may be for the first time. Whether it is or not will determine when legal title actually passes to the purchaser.

Revision tip

Link to chapter 3 where the requirement to register a transfer of a freehold estate is considered in more detail.

Figure 5.1

 Key cases

Case	Facts	Principle
Commission for the New Towns v Cooper (GB) Ltd [1995] Ch 259	Faxes were exchanged amounting to an offer an acceptance regarding the sale of land. The exchange did not create a valid land contract.	For a valid contract in land to exist, there must be one document containing all the terms and signed by both parties.

Case	Facts	Principle
Firstpost Homes Ltd v Johnson [1995] 1 WLR 1567	A letter regarding the sale of land, and which enclosed a plan identifying the land, was held not to constitute a valid contract under s 2 LP(MP)A 1989, as it had not been signed by both parties. Although both the letter and the plan had been signed by the vendor, the purchaser had only signed the plan. The typing of his name on the letter was not enough to constitute his signature.	Where a document is required to be signed by someone, that must take the ordinary meaning, ie that person actually writing his name on the document with his own hand.
McClausland v Duncan Lawrie Ltd [1997] 1 WLR 38	A completion date set for a Sunday was changed in an exchange of letters that did not comply with s 2 LP(MP)A 1989. The variation of the completion date was thus ineffective and the original agreement stood.	When seeking to vary a material term of the contract, the variation itself must comply with s 2 LP(MP)A 1989.
Record v Bell [1991] 1 WLR 853	A contract for the purchase of a property was conditional upon the vendor producing evidence of proof of title. This condition was agreed in a separate letter and not in the contract of sale. When the purchaser failed to complete the purchase he claimed there was no valid contract containing all the terms. This argument was rejected. The court identified two separate contracts: one for the sale of the property and a second collateral contract regarding proof of title	Whilst a land contract must contain all terms to be valid, it is possible for the courts to interpret an apparent omission as a separate collateral contract, thus not invalidating the existence of a land contract.
Wright v Robert Leonard Developments Ltd [1994] NPC 49	An agreement related to the sale of a flat and furnishings, although the latter were not contained in the contract but in a separate schedule to which the contract made no reference. Upon removing the furnishings, the vendor's defence was that there existed no valid contract containing all the terms expressly agreed between the parties, since the written agreement failed to incorporate the furnishings. This was rejected. Convincing evidence existed to establish that the parties had agreed upon the inclusion of the furnishings in the sale and thus the contract, once rectified, was enforced.	If a contract appears invalid for not containing all the terms expressly agreed between the parties, where there is convincing evidence that the parties had agreed upon the omitted term, the court may order rectification of the contract, thus making it valid.
Yaxley v Gotts [2000] Ch 162	The claimant had reached an oral agreement with the father of the defendant that, if the latter bought a house and the claimant conducted substantial building works to convert the house into flats, he would be given the ground floor flats. In fact, the defendant bought the house. Unaware of this fact, the claimant carried out the works to the value of £9,000 and when the defendant sought to evict the claimant, the latter claimed an interest in the property. The court recognized the claimant had an interest in the property.	A person may be estopped from asserting the true legal position where it would be unconscionable to do so: where another has relied and acted upon a promise to their detriment.

#6
The leasehold estate

The topic of leases is a vast one and material on this topic has been divided into two separate chapters in this book. How much of this material is relevant to you will depend upon the course that you have studied. You must also be guided by your tutorials and lectures as to how this material may be combined in an exam question as different teaching institutions adopt different approaches. For example, the issue of forfeiture, dealt with in this chapter, may be combined with an issue of breach of covenant, dealt with in the following chapter.

On the material covered within this chapter, typical problem questions require you to assess the status of occupants in a property: whether they occupy on the basis of a lease or licence. Sound knowledge of the principles used to distinguish the two is vital and good use of case law is key to doing well. As a general guide:

- Explain the key differences between a lease and a licence and the significance of these differences in terms of the issue you are being asked to consider.

- Assess whether the occupants enjoy exclusive possession. If no, occupancy can only be based upon a licence. If yes, remember to check that the occupants don't fall into the exceptions where a finding of exclusive occupation may not give rise to a lease.

- Where multiple occupiers, check for the four unities where seeking to establish a joint tenancy, rather than occupants holding individual leases.

- Assess whether there is certainty of term.

- Where a lease, assess the status of that lease by looking at compliance with formalities.

You may also have to assess whether any lease you find will bind a purchaser of the freehold.

As for essay questions, these too could focus on the distinction between a lease and a licence. Sometimes examiners require you to consider the differences between equitable and legal leases, both in terms of their creation and operation.

Key facts

- A lease is one of the estates in land capable of being legal: s 1(1)(b) LPA 1925.

- Without both certainty of term and exclusive possession there can be no lease (*Street v Mountford* [1985]), although the presence of both does not necessarily mean that a lease exists. Exclusive occupation could be based upon a licence (*Facchini v Bryson* [1952]).

- In addition to certainty of term and exclusive possession, a joint tenancy requires the four unities (*AG Securities Ltd v Vaughan* [1990]).

- Formalities for the creation of a legal lease differ depending upon the duration of the lease.

- Where these formalities have not been met, an equitable lease may exist instead, provided there is a valid contract capable of specific performance (*Walsh v Lonsdale* (1882)).

- An equitable lease is not as good as the legal equivalent. For example, the recognition of an equitable lease depends upon court discretion; a legal lease does not.

- The most common types of leases are fixed term and periodic.

- The process of terminating a lease by forfeiture differs depending upon the type of covenant breached. In each case, whether the property is residential or commercial will dictate the actual procedure to follow and may influence the tenant (and any sub-tenant's) ability to seek relief.

Chapter overview

The leasehold estate: term of years absolute: Capable of being legal: **s 1(1)(b) LPA 1925**

Proprietary interest or mere contractual arrangement? *Bruton v London & Quadrant Housing Trust* [2000]

Essential characteristics of a lease: *Street v Mountford* [1985]:
- certainty of term: *Lace v Chantler* [1944]; and
- exclusive possession
- rent not essential: *Asburn Anstalt v Arnold* [1989]

Disguising a lease as a licence: attempts to exclude exclusive possession

Exceptions where presence of exclusive occupation does not necessitate the finding of a lease: *Facchini v Bryson* [1952]

Joint tenancies: the requirement of the four unities: *AG Securities v Vaughan* [1990]

Types of leases

Formalities for the creation of leases:

Agreement to grant a lease:
- where formalities are met, equitable lease arises (*Walsh v Lonsdale* (1882))

Grant of a lease:
- Difference in formalities required depending upon whether lease granted is over 3 years in duration or less than 3 years in duration
- registration required where lease granted is over 7 years in duration (**LRA 2002**)

Meet formalities: legal lease arises

Fail to meet formalities: at best an equitable lease, if meet formalities in equity. Otherwise, possible periodic tenancy will be implied.

Formalities for the assignment of a lease: differ depending upon whether a legal or equitable lease

Termination of leases

Forfeiture for:
- non-payment of rent;
- breaches of all other covenants

Introduction

A **leasehold estate**, one of the recognized estates in land capable of being legal (s 1(1)(b) **Law of Property Act 1925**), is inferior to the freehold estate because:

1. it endures for a smaller 'slice of time' than the freehold estate; the former having a fixed and certain duration, where the latter is perpetual in duration, only coming to an end when there are no heirs to inherit it (see chapter 5); and

2. the possessory rights enjoyed by the holder of a leasehold estate (the tenant) are more limited than those enjoyed by a freehold estate owner, since a leasehold estate is subject to limitations placed upon it by the superior estate holder (the landlord).

The leasehold estate is technically known as a **term of years absolute**, but is more commonly referred to as a **lease** or tenancy. These terms are often used interchangeably but in the case of *Bruton v London & Quadrant Housing Trust* [2000], a distinction was made between a 'term of years', which confers a proprietary estate, and a 'lease', which is a mere contractual agreement (see further discussion below).

The essential characteristics of a lease

According to Lord Templeman in the case of *Street v Mountford* [1985], there are three essential characteristics of a lease, without which a lease could not exist:

- certainty of term; and
- exclusive possession; and
- rent.

Certainty of term

There must be:

- a fixed and certain maximum duration: *Lace v Chantler* [1944]. Provided the maximum duration is known when the lease is granted, it is irrelevant that the lease may, in fact, terminate earlier due, for example, to the presence of a break clause within the terms of the lease. It would also be irrelevant that the possession within this known duration is discontinuous, for example due to a time-share arrangement: *Cottage Holiday Associates v Customs & Excise Commissioners* [1983]; and

- a certain start date. This may be express or by reference to something which itself has sufficient certainty at the time the lease is granted. Where nothing is specified it is assumed the lease commences upon the tenant taking possession.

The term itself can '*include a term of less than a year or for a year or years and a fraction of a year or from year to year*': s 205(1)(xxvii) LPA 1925.

The essential characteristics of a lease

✳✳✳✳✳✳✳✳✳✳

What if the term appears uncertain?

In some circumstances, the court may be willing to resolve the uncertainty by implying a periodic tenancy (see below for further discussion as to what this is). This is possible where:

- the tenant has taken possession; and
- has started paying rent by reference to a period.

(*Prudential Assurance v London Residuary Body* [1992])

What period will be implied?

The period implied will be calculated on the basis upon which the rent itself has been calculated, irrespective of how it is being paid: *Martin v Smith* (1874). For example, where rent is £5,000 per annum payable monthly, a yearly periodic tenancy may be implied.

How does this resolve the issue of uncertainty?

The law regards a periodic tenancy as a lease for a period (the fixed and certain term), followed by another lease for that period and so on until the lease is terminated in the appropriate way.

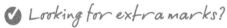 ✔ *Looking for extra marks?*

It is important to recognize that the court's ability to imply a periodic tenancy will not be exercised automatically. This was illustrated in the case of *Javad v Aqil* [1991], where the court refused to imply a periodic tenancy as the parties were still in negotiations over the terms of the lease and thus clearly had not reached an intention that a lease be granted.

Exclusive possession

This is the ability to exclude all others from the property, including the landlord. Where there is no exclusive possession, there can be no lease. Possession of the land will be based instead upon a **licence** ie personal permission that creates no proprietary interest over that land. Exclusive possession is thus a key factor when distinguishing between a lease and a licence.

Attempts to disguise the creation of a lease as a licence

In the past, landlords have been keen to declare occupants of their land licencees rather than tenants, so as to avoid numerous statutory benefits that tenants enjoy but which are not conferred upon licencees. Security of tenure is one such benefit landlords have been keen to avoid. It effectively enables a tenant to remain in occupation of the land even after the expiration of his lease. The courts have been eager to detect sham or pretence agreements, whereby landlords try to disguise the creation of a lease as a licence, thus attempting to avoid the application of security of tenure legislation and the associated benefits that operate in favour of a tenant. In many cases, the attempt to disguise a lease as a licence has focused upon the issue of exclusive possession. Landlords have tried to create agreements between themselves and their tenants which appear to prevent exclusive possession from arising, subsequently preventing possession of the land being based upon a lease. The role of the court has been to ascertain when such agreements are a pretence.

In deciding this issue, the courts must go beyond the form of the agreement, and rather look to the substance of the transaction: *Street v Mountford* [1985]. By looking at the reality of the arrangement, a court will then be better placed to assess whether the wording of the agreement, and the clauses that have been inserted, accurately reflect the nature of the arrangement or, whether they have been inserted merely to act as a smoke screen to disguise as a licence what is, in reality, a lease.

Looking for extra marks?

The courts' willingness to strike down pretence clauses has been criticised by some as ignoring the subjective intentions of the parties involved and the idea that parties are free to contract upon whatever terms they wish. Certainly, in the case of residential property there is a tendency to give less weight to freedom of contract in situations where people are desperate to find accommodation and thus might sign up to an agreement couched in any language and with any terms, in order to obtain shelter: *AG Securities Ltd v Vaughan* [1990]. However, in cases involving commercial parties, where equality of bargaining power exists, indications are that the courts may be more prepared to accept the parties subjective intentions and give weight to the fact that the agreement has been labelled a 'licence': *National Car Parks Ltd v Trinity Development Co (Banbury) Ltd* [2002].

Attempts to exclude exclusive possession

Revision tip

Problem questions on the distinction between a lease and a licence often require you to compare and contrast case law to the facts in your exam question. Be sure to know both the key facts of each case *and* the legal reasoning behind each decision.

What factors will a court take into account when deciding whether clauses attempting to exclude exclusive possession are real or pretence?

- The relationship between prospective occupiers (where more than one).
- The course of negotiations.
- The nature and extent of the accommodation provided.
- The intended/actual mode of occupation.

(*Stribling v Wickham* (1989))

The essential characteristics of a lease

✳✳✳✳✳✳✳✳✳✳

Remember, this list is not exhaustive and other factors may be relevant depending upon the circumstances of each case.

Case law examples which demonstrate this:

. . . .

Antoniades v Villiers [1990] 1 AC 417

A clause which stated the licensor was unwilling to grant exclusive possession and able to share, or invite others to share, the property with the licencees, was held a sham. The following were some of the key factors to influence the court:

- The occupiers were a quasi matrimonial couple, who had specifically asked for a double bed and clearly intended to occupy the property as a family home, thus making it unrealistic to introduce strangers to share with them.

- The accommodation was a small one bed-roomed flat; too small for others to share with the couple. This was evidenced by the fact that when they had a friend to stay, the conditions were very cramped.

- The clause to introduce others specified no maximum number. If real, any number of persons could be introduced to share with the couple. This was clearly unrealistic.

- The clause to introduce others had never been exercised.

. . . .

. . . .

Aslan v Murphy [1990] 1 WLR 766

A 'licence agreement' that stated the licensor was unwilling to grant exclusive possession and had a right to introduce others to share was held a sham. A key influence behind the decision was the nature of the accommodation. As a basement room 4ft3″ by 12ft6″, the ability of the licensor to introduce others to share with the occupant was clearly not operational.

. . . .

Contrast the above with the following case:

. . . .

AG Securities Ltd v Vaughan [1990] 1 AC 417

A clause stating that a maximum of three other persons could be introduced to share the property with the licensee, was held to be real and reflect the reality of the arrangement. The court was influenced by the fact that:

- Each occupant signed an agreement, which incorporated a clause that a maximum of three other people could be introduced to share the house with them. This was a realistic clause in relation to the shared occupation of a four-bedroomed house.

- This clause was actually exercised, indicating that it was not a mere pretence.

- The occupants were strangers who arrived at the property willing, presumably, to share with other persons they did not know, unlike the couple in *Antoniades v Villiers* [1990].

. . . .

Exceptions

Does the presence of exclusive possession necessitate the finding of a lease?

No. There are some circumstances where, despite the existence of exclusive possession, the occupants possess the property on the basis of a licence. Such exceptions were first highlighted in the case of *Facchini v Bryson* [1952] and subsequently confirmed in *Street v Mountford* [1985]. They are situations where the factual enjoyment of exclusive occupation falls short of any conferment of a right to exclusive possession since overall control remains with the owner of the property. These exceptions include:

- occupancy based upon acts of friendship or generosity where there is no intention to create legal relations: *Marcroft Wagons Ltd v Smith* [1951];
- occupancy based upon family relationships: *David v LB Lewisham* (1977), although a family relationship between the occupant and the grantor will not automatically preclude the creation of a lease; it will depend upon the circumstances: *Nunn v Dalrymple* (1990);
- occupancy based upon service as an employee, where the provision of accommodation is for the better performance of the employee's duties: *Norris v Checksfield* [1991];
- occupancy as a lodger, where the provision of regular services, such as changing bed linen and cleaning the accommodation, prevents exclusive possession from arising: *Marchant v Charters* [1977]. This is provided that such clauses have not been inserted into the agreement to act as a smokescreen disguising the creation of a lease. In *Aslan v Murphy* [1990], the agreement stipulated that services would be provided, suggesting no exclusive possession for the occupant. The reality, however, was that in fact no services were ever provided and the clause had been inserted merely to camouflage as a licence what, in reality, was a lease.

Rent

In *Ashburn Anstalt v Arnold* [1989], it was established that rent is not essential to the finding of a lease. Indeed, the definition of a term of years absolute in s 205(1)(xxvii) LPA 1925 makes it clear that a lease can exist *'whether or not at a rent'*.

Revision tip

Where a lease is found to exist, you may be required to consider whether it is legal or equitable, which requires knowledge of formalities (see below).

Multiple occupation

Where more than one person is occupying the property on the basis of a lease, their occupation must either be on the basis of:

- each having separate leases; or
- having a joint tenancy between themselves.

Types of leases

✳✳✳✳✳✳✳✳✳✳

Individual leases

Each occupant must have exclusive possession of a defined area, over which he has the ability to exclude all others, including the other occupants of the property. This may be possible, for example, in a situation where each occupant can claim a lease over his own bedroom in the property, with a licence to share the common parts. This possibility was recognized in an *obiter* statement in *AG Securities Ltd v Vaughan* [1990].

Joint tenancy

However, in situations where the property is such that individual leases are not possible, occupants will have to claim they have a joint tenancy; that together they are seen as a single entity entitled to exclusive possession of the whole. For this to exist, certainty of term and exclusive possession is not enough. The occupants must also share the four unities as stated in *AG Securities Ltd v Vaughan* [1990].

These are:

- *possession*: all occupiers are entitled to possess the whole of the property;
- *title*: all occupiers obtain their interest in the property by virtue of the same document. Technically, this requires all occupants to sign one single agreement. However, the courts are aware that landlords sometimes ask occupants to sign separate agreements purely to try and defeat unity of title and thus prevent a joint tenancy from arising:

. . . .

Antoniades v Villiers [1990] 1 AC 417

Despite the couple signing separate agreements, the court found unity of title. The reality was that one occupant would not have signed his agreement without the other also signing hers. The agreements were thus interdependent and could therefore be seen as a single transaction.

. . . .

- *time*: occupants must obtain their interest in the property at the same time; and
- *interest*: occupants must occupy the property with the same rights and obligations, for which they are jointly liable.

. . . .

Mikeover Ltd v Brady [1989] 3 All ER 618

Each occupant was found to be liable for just his own monthly payment. Therefore, no unity of interest was found to exist and occupancy of the accommodation was based upon a licence.

. . . .

Types of leases

Fixed term tenancy

This is where a lease is granted for a fixed term at the outset, for example a ten year lease. The lease will not terminate until the end of the fixed term, subject to the presence of break clauses allowing for early termination, or a breach of covenant, which could lead to termination of the lease by forfeiture (see below).

Periodic tenancy

This is a lease that is granted initially for a certain period (for example weekly, monthly, yearly) but that period will automatically recur until the lease is brought to an end, either by serving the appropriate notice period or through procedures following a breach of covenant. Typically the notice period has to equate to the period of the lease, for example a monthly period tenancy requires one month's notice. However, a yearly periodic tenancy requires six months' notice and a periodic tenancy over a dwelling house requires a minimum of four weeks' notice (Protection From Eviction Act 1977). Notice periods can also be specified by the parties themselves.

Remember, a periodic tenancy may be implied when a person takes possession and pays rent by reference to a period in circumstances where the term would otherwise be uncertain (see earlier discussion).

Tenancy at will

This is a personal relationship between the parties whereby a person is allowed to take possession of a property as a tenant but the agreement is such that either party can terminate the tenancy at will. Should the tenant start paying rent whilst in possession, a periodic tenancy may be implied, but only where there is sufficient intention between the parties.

Tenancy at sufferance

This is where a tenant remains in possession once his lease has expired with neither the consent nor dissent of the landlord. If, and when, the landlord consents, a new tenancy will be created. However, in the meantime the possession of the property will not amount to a trespass as the initial possession was lawful.

Tenancy by estoppel

This arises in situations where the landlord has represented that he will grant a lease and the tenant has, quite reasonably, relied upon this representation to his detriment.

Formalities for creation

Capable grantor

The person purporting to grant a lease must be capable of so doing. Where there is no such capability, a licence will arise.

Formalities for creation

However, in the case of *Bruton v London & Quadrant Housing Trust* [2000], a lease was recognized as having been created even though the grantor had no proprietary estate out of which to grant the lease.

Bruton v London & Quadrant Housing Trust [2000] 1 AC 406

Lambeth London Borough Council gave a charitable housing trust a licence to use a block of flats for the purpose of providing short term accommodation for the homeless. The trust gave a licence to Mr Bruton, a homeless person, to occupy a flat in return for a weekly 'licence' fee. An issue arose as to whether Mr Bruton qualified to benefit from certain statutory obligations that a landlord has to repair, such benefits only being available under a tenancy. The House of Lords held that despite the clear labelling of his occupancy as a licence, and the fact that the trust had no proprietary interest in the property out of which to grant a term of years, Mr Bruton was a tenant. Mr Bruton did enjoy exclusive possession for a term at a rent, and thus, in the absence of any exceptional circumstances, a lease had been created in his favour.

According to Lord Hoffman in this case, 'lease' or 'tenancy' are terms used to describe a contractual relationship between parties who are landlord and tenant. Often a lease will also create a proprietary interest that is binding upon third parties, known as a 'term of years absolute'. But whether it does so will depend upon whether the landlord has an estate out of which to grant it.

✅ Looking for extra marks?

By finding that a contractual tenancy exists, Mr Bruton was entitled to enforce the statutory repair obligations against his landlord. Such a tenancy could support independent dealings with the land and allow for the parties to benefit from various types of statutory protection. However, should the relationship be challenged by a third party, it will be deemed not binding upon them. This is illustrated in the case of *London Borough Council of Islington v Green* [2005]. Upon similar facts to *Bruton*, Islington Borough Council granted a housing association a licence to use council property to provide temporary accommodation. The association granted a 'licence' in favour of Ms Green and Mr O'Shea which, as in *Bruton*, was found to actually create a tenancy between them. However, when the Council terminated the licence with the housing association, Mr O'Shea (Ms Green having already left the property) had no defence to a possession action brought by the Council. His tenancy was found not to be binding upon this third party.

Formalities for an agreement to grant a lease

In some cases, and especially for long leases, the parties may first enter into an agreement to create the lease. The formalities required differ depending upon the duration of the lease intended:

Agreement to grant a lease of over 3 years in duration	Agreement to grant a lease of 3 years or less in duration

• The agreement must amount to a valid contract in land in accordance with s 2 Law of Property (Miscellaneous Provisions) Act 1989. It must be:
 	
  – in writing;
 	
  – containing all terms; and
 	
  – signed by both parties.
	• Under s 2(5)(a) LP(MP)A 1989, a contract to grant a lease of 3 years or less in duration requires no written document and may be valid even if merely oral.

Proprietary status of an agreement to grant a lease

The valid contract, provided that it is one capable of specific performance, transfers an equitable interest in the land to the transferee (the prospective tenant). Since equity views as done that which ought to be done, equity views the contract as having already been performed. As such, in the eyes of equity, the transferee at this stage already has an equitable lease: *Walsh v Lonsdale* (1882). (This principle has already been illustrated in the discussion concerning a contract to transfer a freehold estate, which was dealt with in the previous chapter.)

Revision tip

An equitable lease is a type of estate contract. The significance of the transferee having an equitable interest at this stage becomes apparent in circumstances where the freehold estate is transferred to a third party. Link to enforcement of third party interests against purchasers: chapters 3 and 4.

Formalities for the grant of a lease

Whether there has been a prior agreement to grant a lease or not, only once a lease has actually been granted, upon satisfaction of certain formalities outlined below, will a legal leasehold estate be created in favour of the grantee.

Revision tip

Be alert, when reading an exam question, as to whether there has been merely an *agreement to grant* a lease, in which case at best only an equitable lease can exist (subject to satisfying formalities required by equity), or an actual *grant* of a lease, in which case a legal lease may exist (subject to satisfying formalities required at law).

Formalities for creation

✳✳✳✳✳✳✳✳✳✳

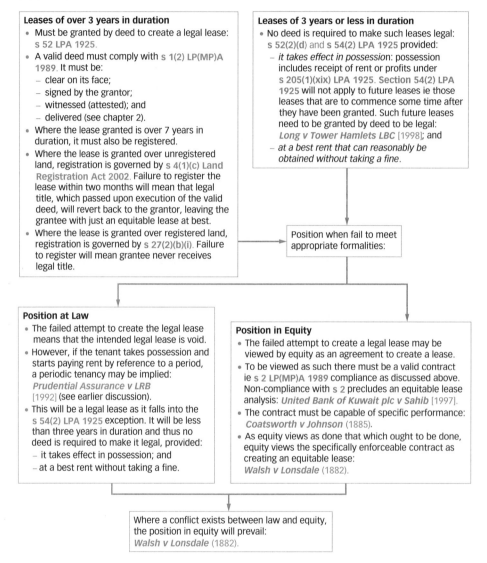

Leases of over 3 years in duration
- Must be granted by deed to create a legal lease: s 52 LPA 1925.
- A valid deed must comply with s 1(2) LP(MP)A 1989. It must be:
  - clear on its face;
  - signed by the grantor;
  - witnessed (attested); and
  - delivered (see chapter 2).
- Where the lease granted is over 7 years in duration, it must also be registered.
- Where the lease is granted over unregistered land, registration is governed by s 4(1)(c) Land Registration Act 2002. Failure to register the lease within two months will mean that legal title, which passed upon execution of the valid deed, will revert back to the grantor, leaving the grantee with just an equitable lease at best.
- Where the lease is granted over registered land, registration is governed by s 27(2)(b)(i). Failure to register will mean grantee never receives legal title.

Leases of 3 years or less in duration
- No deed is required to make such leases legal: s 52(2)(d) and s 54(2) LPA 1925 provided:
  - *it takes effect in possession*: possession includes receipt of rent or profits under s 205(1)(xix) LPA 1925. Section 54(2) LPA 1925 will not apply to future leases ie those leases that are to commence some time after they have been granted. Such future leases need to be granted by deed to be legal: *Long v Tower Hamlets LBC* [1998]; and
  - *at a best rent that can reasonably be obtained without taking a fine.*

Position when fail to meet appropriate formalities:

Position at Law
- The failed attempt to create the legal lease means that the intended legal lease is void.
- However, if the tenant takes possession and starts paying rent by reference to a period, a periodic tenancy may be implied: *Prudential Assurance v LRB* [1992] (see earlier discussion).
- This will be a legal lease as it falls into the s 54(2) LPA 1925 exception. It will be less than three years in duration and thus no deed is required to make it legal, provided:
  - it takes effect in possession; and
  - at a best rent without taking a fine.

Position in Equity
- The failed attempt to create a legal lease may be viewed by equity as an agreement to create a lease.
- To be viewed as such there must be a valid contract ie s 2 LP(MP)A 1989 compliance as discussed above. Non-compliance with s 2 precludes an equitable lease analysis: *United Bank of Kuwait plc v Sahib* [1997].
- The contract must be capable of specific performance: *Coatsworth v Johnson* (1885).
- As equity views as done that which ought to be done, equity views the specifically enforceable contract as creating an equitable lease: *Walsh v Lonsdale* (1882).

Where a conflict exists between law and equity, the position in equity will prevail: *Walsh v Lonsdale* (1882).

Figure 6.1

Is an equitable lease as good as a legal lease?

An equitable lease can, of course, be converted into a legal lease by an order of specific performance. In the meantime, equity will uphold the rights of the parties as though the legal lease had already been granted. However, this does not make an equitable lease as good as having the legal equivalent, for the following reasons:

- The existence of an equitable lease is dependent upon the contract being capable of specific performance. This will not always be the case, as shown in *Coatsworth v Johnson* (1885). Here, the court was unwilling to see the plaintiff as having an equitable lease despite having a valid contract. As the plaintiff was in breach of one of the terms of that contract, the court was unwilling to grant an order of specific performance (also discussed in chapter 2).

- Before the system of registration was introduced, it was easier to enforce legal proprietary interests against third parties than equitable ones; the latter being defeated when the land over which they were exercised fell into the hands of a *bona fide* purchaser for value of a legal estate without notice (see chapter 2). Whilst this distinction between legal and equitable proprietary interests has been eroded to some extent by the system of registration, there are still some clear examples of when legal proprietary interests are easier to enforce against third parties than equitable equivalents (see chapters 3 and 4 on enforcement of proprietary interests).

- An equitable lease is based upon the existence of a contract, which is not a conveyance. Thus on the creation of an equitable lease, the leaseholder will not receive certain benefits that he would have received had there been a conveyance. This is clearly visible when looking at the law of easements (see chapter 12).

- In leases created before 1996, the burden and benefit of tenant covenants will only pass to a successor in title where there has been a legal assignment of a legal lease. This clearly will not occur if the lease is merely equitable in nature (see chapter 7).

- A person who acquires merely an equitable lease, may be bound by other equitable interests created earlier over the property, since generally where the equities are equal, the first in time prevails: *Barclays Bank v Taylor* (1974).

Revision tip

This is a common topic for an essay question so when revising, be sure to make the links with material covered in the other chapters outlined above. Also make sure you understand the circumstances and formalities in which either equitable or legal leases arise.

Formalities for the assignment of an existing lease

The formalities required for transferring an existing lease from one party to another differ depending upon whether the lease in question is legal or equitable in nature.

Enforcement of leases against third parties

✳✳✳✳✳✳✳✳✳✳✳

Where the existing lease is legal	Where the existing lease is equitable
• The **assignment** of the lease must be by deed (s 52 LPA 1925), irrespective of the duration of the term: *Crago v Julian* [1992].	• The assignment must comply with s 53(1)(c) LPA 1925. It must be:
• A valid deed must comply with s 1 LP(MP)A 1989 (see above).	– in writing; and
• Where the lease being assigned exists over unregistered land, the assignment must be registered where the lease is for a term which, at the time of transfer, has more than seven years to run: s 4(1)(a) LRA 2002.	– signed by the person making the disposal ie the assignor.
• Where the lease being assigned exists over registered land, the assignment must be registered to convey legal title: s 27(2)(a) LRA 2002; this is irrespective of the duration of the lease term.	
• Where formalities are not complied with, the assignee may receive an equitable lease instead, but only where the failed attempt amounts to a valid agreement to assign that is capable of specific performance.	

Enforcement of leases against third parties

This is dealt with in detail in chapters 3 and 4. However, on page 87 is a brief overview as a reminder (Figure 6.2 and Figure 6.3):

Registered land

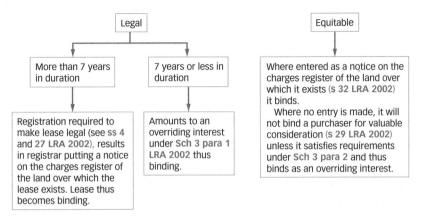

Figure 6.2

Unregistered land

Figure 6.3

Termination of leases

Expiry

A fixed term lease will come to an end upon expiry of the term for which it was granted. (It cannot be brought to an end earlier than the term envisaged in the lease unless there exists some provision in the lease to do so, ie a break clause, or there has been some breach of a covenant in the lease allowing for forfeiture (see over)).

✳✳✳✳✳✳✳✳✳✳

Notice to quit

The parties to a periodic tenancy may give a notice to quit to bring the tenancy to an end. (See above regarding specific notice periods). Where it is a joint periodic tenancy, notice to quit given by one of the joint tenants will be effective on all: *Hammersmith & Fulham LBC v Monk* [1992].

Surrender

This is where the landlord and tenant can agree that the tenant is going to give up the lease.

Merger

This occurs where the tenant obtains the freehold estate so that the freehold and leasehold estates become merged.

Repudiatory breach

In rare cases where a landlord may be in breach of his obligations, the tenant can accept the breach and walk away from the lease: *Hussein v Mehlman* [1992].

Forfeiture

This is a remedy that a landlord may use when a tenant is in breach of a covenant under a lease. It results in the lease being terminated. It is (generally) only available where there is an express forfeiture clause in the lease. Even with the presence of such a clause, a landlord loses his ability to forfeit a lease if he has waived the right ie

- he is aware of the existence of the breach, either himself or through an agent; and
- he does some unequivocal act that recognizes the continuation of the lease, for example accepting rent: *Central Estates (Belgravia) Ltd v Woolgar (No 2)* [1972].

There are two different procedures for forfeiting a lease depending upon the nature of the covenant that has been breached, both of which are complex. Key points have been outlined below. In common to both procedures, however, is that where a landlord seeks to forfeit a residential property, he must first obtain a court order: **s 2 Protection From Eviction Act 1977.** Where there is no-one lawfully residing at the property, the landlord may peaceably re-enter without first obtaining a court order.

 Looking for extra marks?

Where a landlord has a choice as to whether to obtain a court order to possess or not, he must weigh up the advantages and disadvantages. The advantages of proceeding without a court order are that it saves time and money. The disadvantage of proceeding without a court order is the risk involved. Should there be any use or a threat to use violence for the purpose of gaining entry against anyone on the premises opposed to that entry, criminal liability may result: s 6 Criminal Law Act 1977. Indeed, the courts appear to disapprove of peaceable re-entry. In *Billson v Residential Apartments Ltd* [1992] Nicholls LJ declared that it cannot be right 'to encourage law abiding citizens to embark on a course of conduct which is a sure recipe for violence'.

Forfeiture for non-payment of rent

In theory, the landlord must make a formal demand for the exact sum owed on the day it becomes due. Normally, a lease expressly waives this requirement. In any case, where there are at least six months rent arrears and insufficient goods that could be taken from the property and sold to pay off the debt under the remedy of distress, the need to make a formal demand is dispensed with: **s 210 Common Law Procedure Act 1852**.

A tenant can make an application for relief, which, if successful, will result in the forfeiture proceedings being stayed and the lease being retrospectively re-instated.

The scope for a relief application differs depending upon whether the landlord is seeking forfeiture with or without the benefit of a court order. Where forfeiting with a court order, and the tenant pays everything he owes before the hearing takes place, relief will be granted automatically. In all other cases, whether relief is granted will be subject to the discretion of the court. Applications can be submitted by the tenant up to six months after the landlord has re-entered the property.

Where a sub-tenant resides at the property, he too can submit a relief application. This generally must be submitted before the landlord has successfully re-entered the property and whether it is granted will be subject to court discretion: **s 146(4) LPA 1925**. Where an application is successful, the court can order the landlord to grant the sub-tenant a lease for a period not exceeding the remainder of the original sub-lease.

 Looking for extra marks?

When deciding whether to exercise discretion in favour of a tenant seeking relief, the general view taken by the court is that forfeiture is merely security for non payment of rent (Lord Greene MR in *Chandless-Chandless v Nicholson* [1942]). As such, where the tenant pays all outstanding sums, or provides evidence that such sums will be paid in the immediately foreseeable future, relief is likely to be granted. There are, of course, exceptions. Where the landlord has already let the property out to a third party, relief may not be granted if this would unfairly affect the innocent third party: *Stanhope v Haworth* (1886). In respect of a sub-tenant application relief may not be granted where the sub-tenant is present on the property unlawfully: *St Marylebone Property Co v Tesco Stores* (1988).

Forfeiture for all other breaches of covenants

The landlord must first serve a notice on the tenant under **s 146 LPA 1925**, specifying the breach, requiring it to be remedied (where capable) and requesting compensation (where desired). (Where forfeiting for breach of a repair covenant, the tenant may need to be notified of his rights under the **Leasehold Property (Repairs) Act 1938** (see chapter 7.)) The landlord must then wait a reasonable time to see if the notice is going to be complied with (generally three months where a remedy has been requested: *Expert Clothing Service & Sales Ltd v Hillgate House Ltd* [1986]; **14 days where the breach is irremediable:** *Scala House District Properties v Forbes* [1974].)

 Looking for extra marks?

When is a breach capable of remedy? In *Expert Clothing Service & Sales Ltd v Hillgate House* [1986], the court accepted that capability turned on whether the harm caused to the landlord by the breach is capable of remedy, rather than on whether the breach itself is capable of remedy. With this question in mind, most covenants are capable of remedy. This view has been endorsed recently in *Akici v LR Butlin* [2006].

There are exceptions however. A breach of an alienation covenant is still considered incapable of remedy: *Scala House and District Property v Forbes* [1974]. Some breaches of user covenants where the property is used for immoral purposes are also considered incapable of remedy where a stigma has attached to the property: *Rugby School (Governors) v Tannahill* [1935]. However, if the immoral user is stopped quickly enough, so that no stigma has been given the chance to attach to the property, the breach may be considered remediable: *Ropemaker Properties Ltd v Noonhaven Ltd* [1989].

As with the procedure for forfeiting for non-payment of rent, a tenant can apply for relief. Where a landlord is seeking to forfeit with the benefit of a court order, an application for relief must be submitted before the landlord has re-entered the property: **s 146(2) LPA 1925.** However, where the landlord is seeking peaceable re-entry, an application may be submitted up to a reasonable time after re-entry: *Billson v Residential Apartments Ltd* [1992]. Whether an application is successful will be subject to court discretion. (Applications may also be submitted by any sub-tenants as above).

 Key cases

Case	Facts	Principle
AG Securities v Vaughan [1990] 1 AC 417	Four separate licence agreements had been signed on different days relating to the occupancy of a four-bed flat. Each agreement stipulated for different payment amounts and each excluded exclusive possession and stipulated sharing with a maximum of three other people. Held to be licences.	Look to the nature of the accommodation and the relationship between the occupiers when considering whether a clause excluding exclusive possession is real or a sham. All four unities must exist for a joint tenancy to arise.

Case	Facts	Principle
Antoniades v Villiers [1990] 1 AC 417	A cohabiting couple signed separate but identical licence agreements contemporaneously giving them the right to occupy a small one bed flat. The agreement stipulated exclusive possession had not been granted and the licensor had the ability to invite others to share the flat. Held to be a lease.	Look to the nature of the accommodation and the relationship between the occupiers when considering whether a clause excluding exclusive possession is real or a sham. Signing separate agreements will not defeat unity of title provided the agreements can be seen as interdependent.
Aslan v Murphy [1990] 1 WLR 766	Licence agreement in respect of a tiny basement room, to which the licensor retained keys. The agreement excluded exclusive possession and required the occupant to vacate the premises for 90 minutes each day. It was held to be a lease.	Look to the nature of the accommodation when considering whether a clause excluding exclusive possession is real or a sham. There is no magic in the retention of keys. Look at the purpose for which keys have been retained.
Bruton v London & Quadrant Housing Trust [2000] 1 AC 406	A licencee of a block of flats purported to give a homeless person a licence over one of the flats. The House of Lords found the homeless person to have a 'lease' since he enjoyed exclusive possession for a term at a rent.	An apparent distinction exists between a lease, which amounts to a mere contractual arrangement, and a term of years which is a proprietary interest.
Prudential Assurance Co Ltd v London Residuary Body [1992] 2 AC 386	A 'tenancy' had been granted over a strip of land until such time as it would be required back for the purpose of widening the road. Whilst it was held that this was an uncertain term, the House of Lords upheld the finding of a periodic tenancy.	There must be certainty of term for a lease to exist. Where the term appears uncertain, if the tenant has taken possession and started paying rent by reference to a period, a court may be willing to imply a period tenancy has been created
Street v Mountford [1985] AC 809	Occupancy was based upon a 'licence agreement' which gave M, in return for a weekly 'licence fee', exclusive occupancy of a self-contained flat. Despite the agreement containing a clause stating a tenancy was not intended to arise, M was found to have a tenancy.	Where an agreement satisfies the characteristics of a lease (exclusive possession, certainty of term, at a rent) a tenancy will be found (subject to exceptions). One must look to the substance of the transaction and not just its form.
Walsh v Lonsdale (1882) 21 Ch D 9	A 7 year lease was granted to W in writing but not by deed. W went into possession and started paying rent and an issue arose which required determining whether his occupation was based upon a legal periodic tenancy or a 7 year equitable lease. He was held to occupy on the basis of the latter.	Where a valid contract to grant a lease exists that is capable of specific performance, as equity sees as done that which ought to be done, this arrangement creates an equitable lease. Where a conflict exists between law and equity, equity prevails.

Exam questions

 Exam questions

Problem question

Carrie is the freehold owner of a large house. She has converted the top floor into a self-contained flat, consisting of two bedrooms, a bathroom, kitchen, and large living room. In December last year, she placed an advertisement in a local university paper stating 'flat available for immediate occupation at £400 a month'.

Friends Raj and Sally applied. Each signed separate 'licence' agreements on the same day which contained a number of identical terms including:

1. the licensor reserves the right to increasse the number of occupants of the flat by one;
2. the licensor will provide laundry services to the licencee on a weekly basis and retains a key for this purpose;
3. the licencee shall be responsible to pay a licence of fee of £200 per month.

To date Carrie has provided no laundry services and has only used the keys to access the flat once in order to retrieve something from the loft, when she gave Raj and Sally 24 hours notice.

Advise Raj and Sally as to their legal status.

What difference would it make to your answer if Raj and Sally were strangers and they had replied to the advertisement independently of one another, signing the agreements on different days?

An outline answer is available at the end of the book

Essay question

The distinction between an equitable lease and a legal lease lies in its creation and no further. Discuss.

An outline answer is available online at www.oxfordtextbooks.co.uk/orc/concentrate/

#7

Covenants in leases

The examination

The extent to which the material covered in this chapter is relevant to you will depend upon the course that you have studied. You must be guided by your tutorials and lectures when working out how much is relevant to you and also the way in which different issues within the topic of leases will be combined in a question. Remember that material covered here may be combined with material covered in the previous chapter on leases. A problem question concerning breach of covenants, for example, may involve issues of forfeiture. You may be required to assess whether a lease exists in the first place (rather than a licence) before considering liability for apparent breach of covenants.

Essay questions on issues covered within this chapter often focus upon statutory changes that occurred in 1995 regarding enforcement of leasehold covenants. Some examiners focus upon the way in which the law balances the interests of landlords and tenants and whether the law tends to favour the rights of one above the other.

Key facts

- Leasehold covenants are promises made between a landlord and tenant. They can be express or implied; positive or negative in nature.

- An express covenant to repair should not include work that renews virtually the whole of the property in one go, brings completely new improvements to the property or requires the correction of design faults with the property unless such faults are causing physical damage to the property which itself falls within a covenant to repair.

- Certain repair obligations are impliedly imposed upon a landlord by common law and statute, notably the Landlord and Tenant Act 1985.

- Remedies available for breach of a repair obligation include forfeiture, damages and specific performance.

- Covenants not to assign or sub-let may be absolute or qualified. Where qualified a landlord must not refuse consent unreasonably: s 19(1)(a) Landlord and Tenant Act 1927.

- Covenants are enforceable between the original covenanting parties based upon the contractual relationship they share.

- The enforcement of covenants between successors in title depends upon whether the burden and/or benefit of the covenants have passed. Rules governing this differ depending upon whether the lease was created before or after 1 January 1996 when the Landlord and Tenant (Covenants) Act 1995 came into force.

Chapter overview

Introduction

Leasehold covenants are promises that are made between a landlord and his tenant, regulating the relationship between them and the way in which a leasehold estate is enjoyed. Both the landlord and the tenant will enter into a variety of covenants for the benefit of the other party.

The covenants may be either express or implied. The nature and extent of liability imposed by express covenants will be a matter of negotiation between the parties. Implied covenants, which can occasionally be expressly excluded from the lease (where it is allowed), may impose burdens on either the landlord or the tenant. An example of a landlord's implied obligation is a covenant to allow the tenant quiet enjoyment ie to allow the tenant to take exclusive possession of the property without any interference. An example of a tenant's implied obligation is a covenant not to commit waste.

Covenants, whether express or implied, may be either positive or negative. An example of a positive covenant is a covenant to repair or pay rent. An example of negative covenant is a covenant prohibiting any change of use to the property.

Covenants to repair

These may be express, burdening either the landlord or the tenant or, in some circumstances, both. For example, the landlord may promise to keep the exterior of the property in good repair whilst the tenant promises to do the same with the interior.

An implied obligation to repair can also be imposed upon a landlord (see below), but not a tenant.

Express covenants to repair

The extent of liability imposed

The following should be borne in mind when considering the scope of an express covenant to repair:

- The exact wording of the covenant may give guidance. For example, a covenant that stipulates the covenantor must *'**keep** the property in good and substantial repair'* (rather than merely *'**maintain** the property…'*) requires him to put the property into a good state of repair at the start of the lease term and maintain such a state throughout the term. This comes from the court interpretation of the word *'**keep**'* (*Credit Suisse v Beegas Nominees Ltd* [1994]). However, *'**good and substantial** repair'* imposes no heavier burden on the covenantor than a covenant merely *'to keep the property in a state of **repair**'*.

- Whilst an express covenant to repair will inevitably require some element of renewal, to replace whatever is in a state of disrepair, liability should not extend to renewal of virtually the whole of the property in one go: *Lister v Lane* [1893]. Ultimately, it is a question of degree and looking at how much of the property is to be affected by the repair required: *Ravenseft Properties Ltd v Davstone (Holdings) Ltd* [1980]. There may also be a linked issue of costs. Where the costs of the repair work required are close to the overall value of the property as existed before it fell into disrepair, the work required may fall outside the ambit of the covenant: *Brew Brothers v Snax (Ross) Ltd* [1970].

- Whilst an express covenant to repair should not impose an obligation to make new improvements to the property, for example putting in a damp proof course where none previously existed, an improvement may occur as a by product of the repair itself, for example replacing a broken boiler with a modern version: *Pembury v Lamdin* [1940].

- An express covenant to repair should not itself impose an obligation to correct design faults with the property, as originally constructed: *Post Office v Aquarius Property Ltd* [1987]. However, if that fault causes disrepair to the property which can only be fixed by correcting the design fault from which it flows, the correction of that design fault may fall within the ambit of the covenant to repair.

The standard of repair required

The standard is to be determined according to the age, character and locality of the property *at the time that the lease was granted*: *Proudfoot v Hart* (1890). The repair works should be to a standard fit for a reasonably like-minded tenant of the type likely to take a lease of that property.

When does liability arise?

Under a tenant obligation, liability arises as soon as the property falls into a state of disrepair, even where the tenant is unaware of this. Whereas, under a landlord obligation, since a landlord generally has no access to the property, liability will arise only once he has been given notice of the disrepair.

The effect of a fair wear and tear proviso

An express covenant to repair may exempt a tenant from liability for fair wear and tear. However, if this fair wear and tear leads to other disrepair to the property, which itself falls into the ambit of the express covenant to repair, and the only way to correct this consequential disrepair is to correct the fair wear and tear from which it flows, a tenant may be required to do so, despite the existence of the fair wear and tear exemption: *Regis Property Co Ltd v Dudley* [1959].

Implied covenants to repair

These burden the landlord and override any express obligations to the contrary. They include:

- Where a house is let furnished, an obligation to ensure that the house is fit for human habitation at the start of the lease term: *Smith v Marrable* (1843).

Covenants to repair
✱✱✱✱✱✱✱✱✱✱✱

✅ Looking for extra marks?

Whilst the above is a common law obligation imposed upon a landlord in respect of the condition of a dwelling, its impact is curtailed by application to furnished dwellings only. It is true to say that the courts have in the past tended to adopt a rather *laissez-faire* approach when it comes to regulating the condition of rented property, seeing it as a matter of negotiation between the parties (in the absence of any statutory control). This approach, however, assumes that equality of bargaining power will exist between the parties, which is not always the case. A change of direction from the courts can be seen in the case of *Lee v Leeds CC* [2002], where the Court of Appeal indicated that where property is let for social housing, a landlord should be obliged to take steps to ensure that it is not in such a condition that a tenant's right under Art 8 of the European Convention on Human Rights 1950 is infringed, namely respect for private family life and the home.

- In respect of leases of houses at a low rent, an obligation to keep the property in a fit state during the term of the lease: **s 8 Landlord and Tenant Act 1985**. This covers very few leases since few fall into the low rent threshold (currently £82pa in London; £52pa outside of London)

- **Sections 11 to 14 Landlord and Tenant Act 1985:**
  An obligation for the landlord to keep in repair the structure (something essential to a buildings appearance, stability, or shape: *Re Irvine's Estate v Moran* (1992)), exterior (including drains, gutters, and external pipes) and installations of a house, for the supply of water, gas, electricity, and for sanitation and heating. It does not extend to the correction of design faults with the property (*Quick v Taff-Ely BC* [1986]) unless the design fault is itself causing disrepair to the structure, exterior, or installations of the house. If the only way to fix this disrepair is to correct the design fault from which it flows, a landlord will be obliged to do so under this Act: *Staves & Staves v Leeds CC* (1990).

  The obligation only applies to leases of dwelling houses granted on/after 24 October 1961 for a term of less than seven years. The landlord's liability will only arise once he has notice of such disrepair: *O'Brien v Robinson* [1973]. Upon notice, he will be liable not only for the disrepair to the structure, exterior, or installations as appropriate, but also for any disrepair that is consequential to this, provided he has notice of such consequential damage and provided the tenant has acted promptly in notifying the landlord so as to mitigate the loss.

  In determining the standard to which the landlord is required to repair, regard must be had to the age, character and prospective life of the dwelling house and its locality.

Specific remedies for breach of repairing covenants

Forfeiture

Available to the landlord and has the effect of bringing the lease to an end.

Revision tip

Link your revision here to material on forfeiture covered in chapter 6.

Damages

Under s 18 Landlord and Tenant Act 1927, damages must not exceed the amount by which the value of the reversion in the premises is diminished owing to the existence of the breach. Damages are not recoverable where the premises are to be demolished or intended structural alterations would render the repairs valueless.

✅ *Looking for extra marks?*

Where either forfeiture or damages is sought by a landlord for breach of a tenant's repairing obligation in respect of a lease granted for more than seven years and with at least three years remaining, the Leasehold Property (Repairs) Act 1938 will apply.

Upon commencing the action, the landlord must serve notice on the tenant of the tenant's right to serve a counter notice within 28 days claiming protection from the Act. Where the tenant correctly serves the counter notice, the landlord is precluded from taking any further action without first obtaining leave from the court. Such leave will typically be given where the court considers:

- the cost of doing the repairs now will be less than if the repairs were left and done in the future; or
- there is a risk of substantial damage to the property if the repairs are not carried out immediately; or
- immediate repair is necessary in order to prevent a substantial decrease in the value of the reversion.

Specific performance

This is available to a tenant: *Jeune v Queens Cross Properties* [1974]. Where the breach is of a landlord's implied covenant to repair under ss 11–14 LTA 1985, s 17 LTA 1985 provides for the availability of this remedy.

It is more rarely given in favour of the landlord; perhaps where the lease does not provide for the alternative remedy of forfeiture: *Rainbow Estates Ltd v Tokenhold Ltd* [1999].

Covenants not to assign or sub-let the property

Where a lease is silent as to whether a tenant can assign or **sub-let** the property, a tenant may do either freely. However, most leases contain either an absolute or qualified covenant not to assign or sub-let the property.

Covenants not to assign or sub-let the property

✱✱✱✱✱✱✱✱✱✱

Absolute covenants

These prohibit any assignment or sub-letting of the property, subject only to the landlord changing his mind upon request.

Qualified covenants

These allow an assignment or sub-letting of the property but only with the landlord's consent. They are interpreted strictly by the court. A qualified covenant precluding sub-letting the whole of the property without the landlord's consent will not prohibit the sub-letting of part of that property: *Wilson v Rosenthal* (1906).

When considering the issue of consent, you must take into account the following points:

- A landlord must not unreasonably withhold consent: **s 19(1)(a) Landlord and Tenant Act 1927**, which overrides any express provision to the contrary.

  Whilst it may be unreasonable to withhold consent on the grounds of race, sex, or age discrimination (contrary to statute), no guidance as to what is unreasonable is given in the **Landlord and Tenant Act 1927**. Such guidance must be taken from case law.

  In *International Drilling Fluids Ltd v Louisville Investments (Uxbridge) Ltd* [1986], it was declared that the purpose of a qualified covenant is to protect the landlord from having his premises used/occupied by an undesirable tenant in an undesirable way. The grounds for refusal must have something to do with the relationship of landlord and tenant. So, whilst a landlord would not be entitled to refuse consent on the grounds that the proposed assignee is having an affair with his wife, it may be reasonable to withhold giving consent to a tenant already in serious breach of another covenant in the lease.

✅ Looking for extra marks?

In the case of *Ashworth Frazer Ltd v Gloucester CC* [2001] 1 WLR 2180, Lord Bingham identified three principles by which a court should be guided in determining whether a landlord's refusal is unreasonable:

1. A landlord cannot refuse consent on grounds wholly independent of the landlord and tenant relationship;

2. Whether the landlord's conduct is unreasonable is a question of fact to be decided upon the basis of the circumstances of each individual case. Just because similar reasons have been declared unreasonable in the past, does not mean that they should automatically be declared so again should they arise;

3. The landlord must show that his conduct is reasonable, not that it is right or justifiable according to some objective standard of correctness.

- In addition, you should consider:
  - the effect a refusal will have on the tenant. Where the detriment caused to the tenant far outweighs any benefit the landlord is gaining by refusing consent, such refusal may be considered unreasonable; and
  - in respect of commercial leases, whether the ground(s) given for refusal is one identified in the lease. If yes, refusal cannot be considered unreasonable: s 22 **Landlord and Tenant (Covenants) Act 1995**.
- Ultimately, the burden of proof rests with the landlord: s 1(6) **Landlord and Tenant Act 1988**.

The consequences

- Assigning or sub-letting the lease without first seeking consent, where such consent is required, will amount to a breach of the qualified covenant, even if the landlord could not have reasonably refused consent: *Eastern Telegraph Co Ltd v Dent* [1899].
- Where consent has been sought but refused, the tenant really has three options:
  - Accept the landlord's refusal and abandon any attempt to assign or sub-let.
  - Ignore the refusal and go ahead with the assignment or sub-letting anyway. Whilst the disposition itself would (usually) be effective (*Old Grovebury Manor Farm Ltd v W Seymour Plant Sales & Hire Ltd (No 2)* [1979]), it will be in breach of covenant and thus the tenant will risk proceedings for damages or, more seriously, forfeiture. Arguably, the proposed assignee or sub-tenant would not wish to go ahead with the disposition where they know it is in breach of covenant since, with such knowledge, they would be unlikely to succeed in getting relief in any subsequent forfeiture proceedings (see chapter 6).
  - Seek a court declaration that the consent is being unreasonably withheld, which will take time and money.

Enforcement of leasehold covenants

Enforcement between the original parties to the lease

Figure 7.1

Enforceability of covenants between the original parties to the lease is based upon their contractual relationship to one another; the parties have **privity of contract**.

Enforcement of leasehold covenants

****

Liability extends to all the covenants in the lease, regardless of whether they touch and concern the land or not, and such liability continues, in principle, for the entire duration of the lease term.

Enforcement between successors in title to the original parties to the lease

When either the lease or the reversionary interest is passed on to a successor in title, the question arises as to whether the benefit and burden of the covenants in the lease pass to that successor.

The answer to this question is dependent upon the date that the lease was *originally* created. Leases created on/after 1 January 1996 are governed by the rules in the **Landlord and Tenant (Covenants) Act 1995**, whilst leases created before this date are largely governed by rules found in the **Law of Property Act 1925**. However, remember that **ss 17** to **20** of the **LT(C) A 1995** apply equally to pre, as well as to post, 1996 leases.

Revision tip

The changes to the law brought about by the Landlord and Tenant (Covenants) Act 1995 is a popular area for discussion in an essay question. You should know the key changes brought about by the Act (highlighted below) and be able to reflect upon the motivation and fairness of these changes.

Assignment of the lease

Figure 7.2

When the original tenant (T) assigns his lease to his assignee (A), will the burden of covenants T entered into pass to A?

Figure 7.3

POSITION OF T–POST ASSIGNMENT	
Pre-1996 Lease	**Post-1996 Lease**
T remains liable throughout the entire duration of the lease term, as originally envisaged, on all the covenants of the lease due to privity of contract:	T will automatically be released from liability for all tenant covenants upon assignment (s 5 LT(C) A 1995), unless:

Figure 7.3 *(continued)*

POSITION OF T–POST ASSIGNMENT	
Pre-1996 Lease	**Post-1996 Lease**
Thursby v Plant [1668]. This continuing liability is reinforced by s 79 LPA 1925. T retains the right to pursue breaches committed by the landlord, whether committed before (*City & Metropolitan Properties Ltd v Greycroft Ltd* [1987]) or after (*City of London Corp v Fell* [1994]) the assignment to A took place.	1. the breach is of a purely personal covenant to him: *BHP Petroleum GB Ltd v Chesterfield Properties Ltd* [2000]; or 2. the breach was committed whilst T was the tenant: s 24 LT(C)A 1995; or 3. the assignment was an *excluded assignment* under s 11 LT(C)A 1995; typically one in breach of covenant. T's liability continues under until a non excluded assignment occurs, at which point T's liability will cease; or 4. T entered into an Authorised Guarantee Agreement under s 16 LT(C)A 1995, whereby he guarantees the performance of the covenants *by his immediate assignee* only.

In respect of either a pre-1996 lease or a post-1996 lease, remember the following two points:

- Where T retains liability, either on the basis of privity of contract under a pre-1996 lease, or, for example, an AGA under a post-1996 lease, he cannot be held liable for a breach of covenant, where such covenant had been varied after the assignment took place and the variation was such that the landlord had an absolute right to refuse: **s 18 LT(C)A 1995**.

- Where L wishes to pursue T for rent or any other fixed charge owed by A, he will first have to serve upon T a default notice, governed by **s 17 LT(C)A 1995**. The notice must be served within six months of the monies becoming due, notifying T of the amount owing and the fact that T is to be pursued for this sum. This procedure prevents L from allowing a debt to increase whilst T has no knowledge of the breach or indeed the fact that he is to be held responsible for the sums owed.

✅ *Looking for extra marks?*

Authorised Guarantee Agreements usually arise in circumstances where the tenant requires the landlord's consent to an assignment of the lease and the landlord makes his consent conditional upon the tenant entering into an AGA. Where the lease is silent, this condition must be reasonable. In commercial leases that expressly stipulate this as a condition to granting consent, there is no issue of reasonableness.

Enforcement of leasehold covenants

✳✳✳✳✳✳✳✳✳✳

What could T do if held liable for a breach committed by A?

Whether the lease was a pre-1996 or post-1996 one, the following options are available to T:

- Employ the *Moule v Garret* (1872) principle: where you are compelled to pay damages for the legal default of another, you can go against that other to recover the sums you paid.

- Recoup sums paid by utilizing an indemnity covenant. These are only exercisable against your immediate assignee. Thus if A assigned the lease to A2, who commits a breach for which T is held liable, T would utilize his indemnity covenant to recoup the money from A, who would do the same to recoup the money from A2. Where there is a complete chain of indemnity, ultimately the person left out of pocket should be the person who has committed the breach (here A2). However, if there is a break in the chain, for example A is insolvent or has disappeared, T would not be able to skip over A and try and claim monies back from A2: *Re Mirror Group (Holdings) Ltd* (1993).

  Indemnity covenants may be express or, in the case of pre-1996 leases only, implied:

  - into assignments of leases over unregistered land for valuable consideration: s 77 LPA 1925; and

  - into assignments of leases over registered land, regardless of value: Sch 12 para 20 LRA 2002.

- Where there has been full payment of monies requested in a s 17 LT(C)A 1995 default notice, request an overriding lease under s 19 LT(C)A 1995. The request must be made in writing and within 12 months of the payment being made. L would then have to grant an overriding lease, within a reasonable time. The term of the overriding lease would be equal to that of the remaining term of the lease plus three days and on essentially the same terms. The effect of the overriding lease would be to put T in the position of A's immediate landlord and thus give T landlord powers over A, including the right to forfeit the lease. T's overriding lease would then become a lease in possession which T could then assign (or sub-let) to a more attractive tenant, less likely to breach the covenants in the future. In doing so, not only does T get rid of the defaulting tenant but it also enables him to recoup some of the money he may have paid out for a breach he did not commit.

Figure 7.4

POSITION OF A–POST ASSIGNMENT	
Pre-1996 lease	**Post-1996 lease**
As A (generally) does not enjoy a privity of contract relationship with L, he will only be liable if the burden of the covenants passed to him under *Spencer's Case* (1583). To do so:	As A (generally) does not enjoy a privity of contract relationship with L he will only be liable if the burden of the covenants passed to him

Figure 7.4 *(continued)*

POSITION OF A–POST ASSIGNMENT	
Pre-1996 lease	**Post-1996 lease**
1. the covenant must *'touch and concern'* the land ie affect the landlord and tenant in their capacity as such: *Breams Property Investment Co Ltd v Stroulger* [1948]; and 2. there must be **privity of estate** ie a direct relationship of landlord and tenant must exist between the parties L and A: *Purchase v Lichfield Brewery Co* [1915]; and 3. there must have been a legal assignment of a legal lease.	under s 3 LT(C)A 1995. This will pass the burden of all tenant covenants except those expressed to be personal to the original party (s 3(6) LT(C) A 1995).

Revision tip

Link point (2) above to chapter 6 and the discussion whether an equitable lease is as good as a legal one. (Since an equitable lease does not give an estate in land, rather an equitable right to specific performance of a contract to grant a lease, the equitable tenant has no estate with which to create a privity of estate relationship.)

In respect of either a pre-1996 lease or a post-1996 lease, remember the following:

- although generally A will not enjoy a privity of contract relationship with L, it is possible for such a relationship to arise where A enters into the covenants directly with L after the assignment takes place thus creating a contractual relationship between them (as illustrated under a pre-1996 lease in the case of *Estates Gazette Ltd v Benjamin Restaurants Ltd* [1994]).

- Where the burden of the covenants has passed to A, he cannot be made liable for breaches that occurred before the assignment to him, unless such breaches are of a continuing nature (for example a breach of a covenant to repair), in which case A's liability for that breach will commence from the date of the assignment (*Grescot v Green* (1700) (pre-1996 lease); s 23 LT(C)A 1995 (post-1996 lease).

- Where a landlord has the choice as to whether to pursue T or A for the breach, he is free to choose either party, or both simultaneously, provided that he does not obtain double recovery.

Enforcement of leasehold covenants

****

When the original tenant (T) assigns his lease to his assignee (A), will the benefit of covenants T enjoyed pass to A?

Figure 7.5

POSITION OF T	
Pre-1996 lease	**Post-1996 lease**
T retains the right to pursue breaches committed by the landlord, whether committed before (*City & Metropolitan Properties Ltd v Greycroft Ltd* [1987]) or after (*City of London Corporation v Fell* [1994]).	When the benefit of covenants pass from T to A under s 3 LT(C)A 1995, T retains the right to pursue breaches committed by the landlord whilst he was tenant: s 24 LT(C)A 1995, (unless the right to do so has been expressly assigned to his successor, A: see below)
POSITION OF A	
A will only be able to pursue those breaches committed by the landlord after the assignment has occurred, provided he can establish the benefit of the covenants passed to him by meeting the *Spencer's Case* (1583) requirements.	A only acquires the right to pursue breaches that occur after the assignment to him has taken place, unless the right to pursue pre-assignment breaches has been expressly assigned to him: s 23 LT(C)A 1995.

Assignment of the reversion

Figure 7.6

When the original landlord (L) assigns his reversionary interest to his assignee (L2), will the burden of covenants L entered into pass to L2?

Figure 7.7

POSITION OF L–POST ASSIGNMENT	
Pre-1996 lease	**Post-1996 lease**
L remains liable throughout the entire duration of the lease term, as originally envisaged, on all the covenants of the lease due to privity of contract: *Stuart v Joy* [1904]. This continuing liability is reinforced by s 79 LPA 1925.	L remains liable until such time as he is released from liability under s 6 LT(C)A 1995. The procedure for seeking release is governed by s 8 LT(C)A 1995, although release is not possible where the assignment is an excluded one under s 11 LT(C)A 1995.
	Even where a release has been successfully obtained, it will not be effective in respect of:

Figure 7.7 *(continued)*

POSITION OF L–POST ASSIGNMENT	
Pre-1996 lease	**Post-1996 lease**
	1. purely personal covenants: *BHP Petroleum GB Ltd v Chesterfield Properties Ltd* [2000]; or 2. breaches that were committed by L whilst he was the landlord: s 24 LT(C)A 1995.

What could L do if held liable for a breach committed by L2?

Whether the lease was a pre-1996 or post-1996 one, the following options are available to L:

- use the *Moule v Garret* (1872) principle as discussed above; or

- recoup sums paid using indemnity covenants, as discussed above. This is only possible where they have been expressly provided for.

Figure 7.8

POSITION OF L2–POST ASSIGNMENT	
Pre-1996 lease	**Post-1996 lease**
As L2 does not enjoy a privity of contract relationship with T, he will only be liable if the burden of the covenants passed to him under s 142 LPA 1925, which passes the burden of covenants having reference to the subject matter of the lease. This means the same as 'touch and concern': *Hua Chiao Commercial Bank Ltd v Chiaphua Industries Ltd* [1987] (see above *Spencer's Case* (1583)).	As L2 does not enjoy a privity of contract relationship with T, he will only be liable if the burden of the covenants passed to him under s 3 LT(C)A 1995. This will pass the burden of all tenant covenants except those expressed to be personal to the original party (s 3(6) LT(C)A 1995).

In respect of either a pre-1996 lease or a post-1996 lease, remember the following:

- Where the burden of the covenants has passed to L2, he cannot be made liable for breaches that occurred before the assignment of the reversion to him, unless such breaches are of a continuing nature (for example a breach of a covenant to repair), in which case L2's liability for that breach will commence from the date of the assignment (*Duncliffe v Caerfelin Properties Ltd* [1989] (pre-1996 lease); s 23 LT(C)A 1995 (post-1996 lease).

Enforcement of leasehold covenants

✳✳✳✳✳✳✳✳✳✳

When the original landlord (L) assigns his reversionary interest to his assignee (L2), will the benefit of covenants L enjoyed pass to L2?

Figure 7.9

POSITION OF L	
Pre-1996 lease	**Post-1996 lease**
L loses the right to pursue any breach of tenant covenants upon assignment; even in respect of those breaches committed whilst he was the landlord. The benefit to do so passes to his successor upon assignment under s 141 LPA 1925: *Re King* [1963].	Where released from the burden of landlord covenants under s 6 LT(C)A 1995, L would also cease to be entitled to the benefit of covenants under the lease, save the right to pursue those breaches that occurred before he ceased to be so entitled: s 24(4) LT(C)A 1995, (unless that right has been expressly assigned to his successor, L2).
POSITION OF L2	
L2 will acquire upon assignment the benefit of all covenants which have reference to the subject matter of the lease (s 141 LPA 1925) including the right to pursue breaches that occurred before the assignment took place: *Arlesford Trading Co Ltd v Servansingh* [1971].	L2 will not be able to pursue breaches of tenant covenants that occurred before the assignment unless either: • the right to do so had been expressly assigned to him upon the assignment of the reversion: s 23 LT(C)A 1995; or • the breach was of a continuing nature in which case he could pursue but only as from the date of assignment.

Sub-tenants

Figure 7.10

What is the position of ST?

Figure 7.11

Pre-1996 lease	Post-1996 lease
In principle, L cannot enforce covenants directly against ST as there is neither privity of contract nor privity of estate between them: *South of England Dairies Ltd v Baker* [1906]. Instead,	ST could be held directly liable to L for a breach of a *restrictive* covenant: s 3(5) LT(C)A 1995. (Satisfaction of the other requirements under *Tulk v Moxhay* (1848) is not required.)

Figure 7.11 *(continued)*

Pre-1996 lease	Post-1996 lease
L would have to seek remedy against T, assuming ST's breach put T in breach of a covenant in his **headlease**. T might then be able to recoup his losses from ST, assuming an express indemnity covenant existed between them. However, direct enforcement between L and ST is possible where the requirements under *Tulk v Moxhay* (1848) are met. These requirements are discussed in chapter 13 and will only aid in the enforcement of restrictive covenants.	

On the issue of notice, the fourth requirement under *Tulk v Moxhay* (1848), it is generally assumed that a sub-tenant would have constructive notice of all the covenants in the headlease as it is an open contract term that a sub-tenant can look at the headlease out of which the sub-lease is created: *Hall v Ewin* (1887).

Revision tip

The case law concerning enforcement of leasehold covenants highlighted above is used to provide authority for principles of law. It is unlikely, therefore, that you need to concern yourself with revising the facts of these cases.

 Key cases

Case	Facts	Principle
Brew Brothers Ltd v Snax (Ross) Ltd [1970] 1 QB 612	Seepage from drains damaged foundations of a property, causing a wall to tilt. Repairs held outside the scope of the tenant's express covenant to repair, since would have cost the same as the value of the premises if totally rebuilt.	Where the cost of repair works amounts to a significant proportion of the value of the property itself, the works may be deemed to fall outside the ambit of a repair covenant.
Lister v Lane [1893] 2 QB 212	A tenant was held not liable to rebuild a house which had to be demolished due to its wooden foundations having rotted.	Where works would affect the whole or substantially the whole of the building, making the building different from the one demised, such works are likely to fall outside the ambit of a repair covenant.

Exam questions

✱✱✱✱✱✱✱✱✱✱

Case	Facts	Principle
Post Office v Aquarius Property Ltd [1987] 1 All ER 1055	Basement built with porous cement so basement flooded when water table rose, though this caused no physical damage to the building. Tenant not liable to correct the design fault.	Repair does not require the correction of design faults unless the design fault causes further physical damage to the property and the only way to correct this physical damage is to correct the design fault from which it flows.
Quick v Taff-Ely Borough Council [1986] QB 821	Lack of insulation around single glazed windows caused condensation resulting in damage to house contents and decoration. Landlord not liable to repair this design fault with the windows.	Repair does not require the correction of design faults unless the design fault causes further physical damage to the property and the only way to correct this physical damage is to correct the design fault from which it flows.
Ravenseft Properties Ltd v Davstone (Holdings) Ltd [1980] QB 12	Stone cladding on a block of flats cracked and was in danger of falling off the building, due to a failure to install expansion joints. Tenant was held liable under his covenant to repair. The work required repair to only a trivial part of the building in total and the improvement would not change the nature of the building.	Whether repair falls into the ambit of an express covenant to repair is a question of degree. Where it involves giving the landlord back something wholly different from that which he demised, it will fall outside the ambit.

 ⑦ Exam questions

Problem question

In January 2008, Constance, the freehold owner of a flat, granted Miriam by deed a six-year lease over the flat at a rent of £7,000 per annum. The lease contained, *inter alia*, covenants:

1. to keep the premises in good and substantial repair;
2. not to assign or sub-let the whole or any part of the premises without the consent of the landlord.

Six months later, Miriam was offered a job in France and so, with the consent of Constance, she assigned her lease to Patrick.

On a recent visit to the premises, Patrick gave Constance a letter, requesting that she consent to a sub-let of the property to his friend, George, who had just returned from a gap year in South America. Constance told Patrick that George had approached her about renting a different flat she owned. Patrick informed Constance that he had changed his mind about renting this other flat when he found out that sub-letting from Patrick would be cheaper.

On the same visit, Constance noticed that a patch of damp had appeared near to the window frame in the kitchen. Upon a closer inspection she noticed that the window frame was actually cracked. It had been letting in the rain which, she concluded, must have been the cause of the damp. When she asked Patrick whether he knew about this problem he said that he did. He had been meaning to tell her about it but kept forgetting. When she told him that it was his responsibility to do the repairs, he said he had no money but that if she allowed him to sub-let to George he would use this income to do the repairs.

Advise Constance as to her rights and remedies, if any.

What difference, if any, would it make to your answer if the lease had initially been granted to Miriam in 1994 for a term of 25 years?

An outline answer is available at the end of the book

Essay question

To what extent has the Landlord and Tenant (Covenants) Act 1995 eradicated the perceived problems that existed in relation to the enforcement of leasehold covenants prior to the Act coming into force?

An outline answer is available online at www.oxfordtextbooks.co.uk/orc/concentrate/

#8

Adverse possession

This is a relatively self-contained topic area. Problem questions will frequently require you to establish that land has been adversely possessed, by showing satisfaction of the four key requirements discussed below. You may then have to apply specific rules for establishing adverse possession. Here, it will be essential that you clarify not only the type of land in question, be it registered or unregistered land, but also the nature of the estate, whether freehold or leasehold. Dates as to when the adverse possession commenced and when the relative time period expired will also be important since these too will affect which rules to apply.

Essay questions commonly focus upon how easy/difficult it is to establish an adverse possession claim and you will frequently be required to make comparisons between the rules that operate in unregistered and registered land. You may be required to analyse changes brought about by the LRA 2002, especially looking at the motivation for such changes. This may be linked to human rights issues and a consideration of the moral and social policies that underlie the law relating to adverse possession.

Key facts

- To establish adverse possession of any type of land there must be:
  - discontinuance/dispossession of the land by the paper owner; and
  - factual possession of the land by the adverse possessor; and
  - the possession must be adverse to the paper owner; and
  - the adverse possessor must have the requisite intent to possess.

- Twelve years adverse possession of unregistered freehold estate must be completed by the adverse possessor before the paper owner's title to that land is extinguished and he becomes statute barred from seeking recovery of the land. The adverse possessor then acquires a better title to that land than the paper owner. (These rules also apply to adverse possession of a registered freehold estate where the 12 years expires before 13 October 2003 when the LRA 2002 came into force.)

- Since the LRA 2002, ten years adverse possession of registered freehold estate must be completed before the adverse possessor can apply to the Land Registry to be registered with title to that land. Applications are unsuccessful where objections, that should not be ignored, are submitted by notified interested parties, usually the paper owner. Successful applications lead to a statutory conveyance of title to the adverse possessor, who will usually be registered with absolute title.

- In order to claim a leasehold title through adverse possession, the claimant must complete a successful period of adverse possession against the leasehold estate owner. If he then wishes to claim the freehold title, a second period of adverse possession must be completed against the freehold estate owner. The required periods of adverse possession will differ depending upon whether the leasehold estate is unregistered or not.

- Whilst human rights issues have been raised about this area of law, recent European case law suggests that no human rights are violated by the existence of this law.

Chapter overview

Adverse possession requires (*Buckinghamshire CC v Moran* [1990]):

| Discontinuance (ie abandonment) by the paper owner of his land or dispossession of his land (ie driven out of his land by another) | Factual possession of the land by the adverse possessor ie exertion of physical control over the land so that he may deal with it as an occupying owner might | Possession adverse to the paper owner ie without his express or implied permission | An intention on the part of the adverse possessor to possess the land |

Adverse possession is established:

Over Unregistered Freehold Estate (and Registered Freehold Land Pre-LRA 2002)
- with at least 12 years adverse possession (s 15 LA 1980); after which
- paper owner's title to land is extinguished (s 17 LA 1980); and
- adverse possessor acquires better title to the land than the paper owner

Over Registered Freehold Estate Post-LRA 2002
- with at least 10 years adverse possession; after which
- adverse possessor may apply to the Land Registry to be registered with title to the land, and
- success will be dependent upon whether interested parties notified of the application object and whether such objections should be heeded or ignored

Unregistered Leasehold Estate:
- as above against the leasehold estate owner; after which
- adverse possessor acquires right to possess but leasehold estate owner still liable under the lease, breach of which may result in forfeiture and adverse possessor being evicted

Registered Leasehold Estate:
- as above against registered leasehold estate owner; after which
- a successful application will result in adverse possessor being registered with leasehold title and being liable under the lease

The law of adverse possession does not violate **Art 1, Protocol 1** of the **European Convention of Human Rights 1950**; decision reached by the Grand Chamber at the end of a long journey for the case of *Pye (JA) (Oxford) Ltd v Graham* [2003]

Introduction

An owner of an estate in land (hereafter known as the paper owner) is under no obligation to make use of the land over which his estate exists. Mere neglect of that land does not mean that he should lose his ownership rights over it, those rights belonging to him by virtue of being the estate owner. However, where that land is adversely possessed by another, for a certain period during which the paper owner makes no attempt to evict him, the paper owner will lose his title to the land. Through his acts of **adverse possession**, the adverse possessor acquires a better title to the land than the paper owner. This is so even if such acts stem from an initial wrong, such as a trespass.

Clearly, what this law has meant is that estate owners, in the past at least, had to be vigilant as regards land that they owned but did not currently use for themselves. If the land became adversely possessed and the estate owner did nothing about it, he would lose his title. Today, with the introduction of the Land Registration Act 2002, such vigilance is not as necessary as estate owners will be notified by the Land Registry when an adverse possessor applies to be registered as title holder of that land. This change to the law will inevitably decrease the number of successful adverse possession claims.

Nevertheless, the continued existence of this law seems inevitable and necessary to achieve certainty and finality as regards ownership claims over land. This objective has been recognized as a legitimate one by the European Court of Human Rights.

How do you establish adverse possession?

The case of *Buckinghamshire CC v Moran* [1990], highlighted the requirements necessary to establish adverse possession:

Figure 8.1

How do you establish adverse possession?
✱✱✱✱✱✱✱✱✱✱

These requirements have been confirmed in the recent important case of *Pye (JA) (Oxford) Ltd v Graham* [2003], and apply equally whether the disputed land is registered or unregistered.

> *Revision tip*
>
> Many of the fundamental principles of adverse possession are discussed in *Pye (JA) (Oxford) Ltd v Graham* [2003] so a good understanding of this case is essential.

Discontinuance or dispossession

A paper owner will have discontinued possession of the land in circumstances where he has abandoned it. This should not be assumed from the mere fact that the land is not currently being used by him (*Techbild Ltd v Chamberlain* (1969)), but could arise, for example, in circumstances where he has made it impossible for himself to use the land. In the case of *Hounslow LBC v Minchinton* (1997), this was shown by the paper owner building a fence to enclose part of his land, access to which thereafter could only be achieved by going through another's land.

A paper owner will be dispossessed of the land in circumstances where he has been driven out of that land by another. This rarely involves any dramatic event and may occur even in circumstances where the paper owner does not realize that he has been dispossessed (*Powell v McFarlane* (1977)). An example would include a person remaining on land belonging to the paper owner when a licence to do so has expired (*Pye (JA) (Oxford) Ltd v Graham* [2003]).

Factual possession by the adverse possessor

The adverse possessor must demonstrate a sufficient degree of physical control over the land in question. What is required is evidence that the adverse possessor has been able to deal with the land as an occupying owner might be expected to deal with it and that no-one else has done so (*Powell v McFarlane* (1977)).

....

Pye (JA) (Oxford) Ltd v Graham [2003] 1 AC 347

The defendants farmed a piece of grazing land belonging to the claimant upon the basis of a grazing licence. Once the licence expired, they continued to farm the land for over 12 years, during which time the land was accessed through a padlocked gate, for which the paper owner did not have a key. The defendants had shown factual possession of the land since they had used the land as their own, in a way which would be normal for an owner of that land to use it and contrary to the paper owner's wishes.

....

How do you establish adverse possession?

The degree of physical control that must have been exerted will obviously vary depending upon:

- whether possession takes place following the paper owner discontinuing his own possession or rather being dispossessed of his land (the former perhaps requiring a lesser degree of activity than the latter); and

- the type, state, and location of the land in question.

Examples have included:

- enclosing the land by the erection of fences: *George Wimpey & Co Ltd v Sohn* [1967];

- padlocking a gate which provides the only access to the land in dispute: *Buckinghamshire CC v Moran* [1990].

What is important for you to remember when assessing whether there is a sufficient degree of physical control of the land by the adverse possessor, is the following:

- The possession cannot be presumed from mere temporary or trivial acts by the adverse possessor.

....

Techbild Ltd v Chamberlain (1969) 20 P&CR 633, CA

The claimants sought to establish sufficient physical control of the land by establishing that their children played on the land whenever they wished and that their horses were tethered and exercised there. Such acts were deemed to be 'mere trivial acts of trespass' and thus insufficient to establish factual possession of the land.

....

However, remember that when assessing whether someone has taken sufficient physical control of the land, the court will look at the whole of the activity being conducted on the land. So, in some cases, although individual acts may seem trivial, when looked at together, they may be enough to establish sufficient physical possession.

- The possession must be open ie the sort of possession that the paper owner, with reasonable diligence could discover (s 32(1) Limitation Act 1980). This stems from the principle that the paper owner must have had the chance to challenge the possession before it can be allowed to evolve into an indestructible right.

- The possession should be exclusive to the person seeking to establish adverse possession.

- It is the effect of the adverse possessor's actions over the land that is important when establishing whether they have exerted a sufficient degree of physical control and not their motivation for taking such actions.

How do you establish adverse possession?

✳✳✳✳✳✳✳✳✳✳

Hounslow LBC v Minchinton (1997) 74 P&CR 221, CA

The adverse possessor had fenced part of the disputed land so as to prevent her dogs from escaping when she exercised them there. Although the motivation for her action had been to prevent her dogs from escaping, the effect of her action was to keep out the whole of the world from the land. It was the objective effect of her action, rather than her subjective motivation which, when taken into account with other things she had done on the land, deemed her to have assumed sufficient physical control of the land.

The possession must be adverse to the paper owner

This essentially means that the possession must be inconsistent with the rights of the paper owner in respect of the land in question and will be assessed objectively.

Remember the following:

- Where possession is with the permission of the paper owner, it cannot be adverse. So, in the case of *Smith v Lawson* (1997), there was no adverse possession where the defendant possessed the disputed land based upon an occupation licence for life. Of course, if the permission expires and yet possession continues, such possession could become adverse.

- The possession need not be hostile to be adverse. For example, it may follow discontinuance by the paper owner and therefore could take place even without the paper owner being aware, let alone showing signs of hostility (*Wilson v Martin's Executors* [1993]).

What if the possession is not inconsistent with the paper owner's intended future use of the land? Can it be deemed adverse?

This is looking at circumstances where the paper owner intends to use the land being possessed for a particular purpose in the future, but currently has no use for that land. Until recently, possession that was not inconsistent with the paper owner's future intended use of the land would not be classified as adverse (*Leigh v Jack* (1879)). So a paper owner who was keeping land for a particular purpose in the future, would not be dispossessed by an adverse possesor who made use of it in the meantime. Such an approach was supported by the courts using the doctrine of implied licence and thus concluding the possession not to be adverse. As Lord Denning said in the case of *Wallis's Cayton Bay v Shell-Mex and BP* [1975], by possessing land currently unoccupied but for which the paper owner has an intended use in the future, and with the knowledge that the land does not belong to him, the adverse possessor impliedly assumes the owner will permit it. The owner, by not evicting him from the land, impliedly gives that permission. Such an approach seemed to severely restrict the operation of adverse possession in cases where the paper owner had a future intended use for the land.

Today, under **LA 1980 Sch 1 para 8(4)**, a licence will no longer be automatically implied in cases where possession is not inconsistent with the paper owner's future use of the land. An implied licence will only be found where specific facts justify such a finding. Otherwise, possession may be deemed adverse even though it is not inconsistent with the paper owners intended future use of the land:

Buckinghamshire CC v Moran [1990] Ch 623, CA

The defendant adverse possessor possessed the claimant's land but only with an intention to do so until such time as the claimant went ahead with plans to build a by-pass over it. Despite this limited intention, his desire to possess the land for himself as long as he could for his own benefit was enough to establish that the possession was adverse. The defendant's knowledge of the intended future use of the land would not, by itself, prevent the possession from being adverse.

✅ Looking for extra marks?

The decision in *Moran* above has been expressly approved by the House of Lords in *Pye (JA) (Oxford) Ltd v Graham* [2003]. Possession need not be inconsistent with the future intended use of the land by the paper owner to be adverse. This seems a clear rejection of the rule in *Leigh v Jack* (above). Yet, in the High Court decision of *Beaulane Properties Ltd v Palmer* [2005] (facts similar to *Pye*), an attempt to resurrect the *Leigh v Jack* principle was made, namely that possession could be adverse only if the acts done were inconsistent with the purposes for which the paper owner intended to use the land. On the facts, there had been no adverse possession. The reason for reviving a principle previously rejected by the House of Lords was based upon issues of human rights and is discussed further below.

What if the adverse possessor is willing to pay rent when asked?

The fact that the adverse possessor would be willing to pay rent if asked by the paper owner in respect of his possession of the disputed land does not mean that his possession cannot be adverse. Of course, if he did actually pay rent to the paper owner then he would acquire the status of a tenant, possess the land with the paper owner's consent, and, therefore, not adversely to the paper owner's rights. Until this should happen, the possession could be deemed adverse. Indeed, the adverse possessor in *Pye (Oxford) Ltd v Graham* [2003] had asked for a renewal of their grazing licence which had been declined by the paper owner. Their apparent willingness to possess the land with the permission of the paper owner, did not deny them being in adverse possession of the land, where such permission was not forthcoming.

How do you establish adverse possession?

✳✳✳✳✳✳✳✳✳✳

Intention to possess

Often such intention can be found when looking at the adverse possessor's actions on the disputed land. The acts required to establish a sufficient degree of physical control on the land (discussed above) may well indicate the existence of the requisite intent to use the land 'in the way in which a full owner would and in such a way that the owner is excluded' (Lord Hutton in *Pye (Oxford) Ltd v Graham* [2003]). Such actions which may give rise to the finding of this intent could include fencing the land or putting up a sign on the land saying 'Private Property. Keep Out'. In *Buckinghamshire CC v Moran* [1990], the court acknowledged that there could be a link between actions conducted on the land and finding the necessary intent.

However, where the actions of the adverse possessor could be open to more than one interpretation, and thus his intention ambiguous, he will not be deemed to have the requisite intent. His intention must be clear for all to see, and especially the paper owner.

....

Powell v McFarlane (1977) 38 P&CR 452

The adverse possessor was a 14-year-old boy who had been grazing his cow on the disputed land. The court declined to find an intention to possess from just these actions. When taking into account his age, it was not clear that his intention was to possess the land for his own benefit for as long as he could.

....

When trying to establish the requisite intention to possess, you must remember the following:

- The adverse possessor need not have an intention to dispossess; merely an intention to possess. So he could adversely possess the land without knowing it: *Hughes v Cork* [1994].

- The adverse possessor need not have an intention to own the disputed land; merely an intention to possess it for as long as he can for his own benefit. So, in the case of *Lambeth LBC v Blackburn* [2001], where the adverse possessor's intention was to stay in the council house until evicted, intention to possess was found. This also explains how the court found the requisite intent in the case of *Buckinghamshire CC v Moran* [1990] (discussed above) even though the adverse possessor intended only to possess the property until the paper owner went ahead with plans to build a by-pass on it.

- If the adverse possessor believes that he has the consent of the paper owner to be on the land, this will defeat any claim for adverse possession.

Establishing adverse possession of unregistered land

The principle

A claim of adverse possession of unregistered land is based upon limitation of actions. In other words, where a person takes adverse possession of a piece of unregistered land, anyone who wishes to recover that land, usually the paper owner, has 12 years to do so: s 15(1) LA 1980. The clock starts ticking as soon as the adverse possession begins (ie from the time the paper owner has been dispossessed or has discontinued his possession and another has taken factual possession adversely from him, with the requisite intent). Once 12 years have expired, then any action to recover that land from the adverse possessor is statute barred.

Twelve years' adverse possession

The 12 years of adverse possession may be completed in their entirety by the successful adverse possessor. Alternatively, the 12 years may be made up of aggregating periods of adverse possession by others, being completed by that adverse possessor who successfully makes the claim.

Obviously, any successful recovery of the land before 12 years adverse possession is completed, effectively stops the clock and wipes the slate clean. Subsequent adverse possession of that land would start the clock ticking again, but from the beginning.

What is important for you to remember is that the 12 years adverse possession need not be *immediately* before any action for recovery of the land is taken. Provided a full 12 years of adverse possession can be established, even if those 12 years were completed a year ago for example, an action by the paper owner to enforce his title to the land will not succeed. Upon expiration of the 12 years, his title to the land would have been extinguished (see below). Where the paper owner has since taken back possession, it will not be until a further 12 years of his possessing the land has passed before he can be confident in his ability to defeat any claim to the land should the adverse possessor return.

The effect of a successful claim

Once 12 years of successful adverse possession have passed, the paper owner's title to the land is extinguished: s 17 LA 1980. He no longer has an ability to bring an action to recover the land. Since his title to the land is deemed extinguished, it does not transfer to the successful adverse possessor by way of a conveyance. However, the adverse possessor is deemed to have a better title to the land than the paper owner.

Remember, that the title acquired by the adverse possessor will be subject to all proprietary rights that burden the land, whether legal or equitable, registered in accordance with the **Land Charges Act 1972** or not, and irrespective of whether the successful adverse possessor had notice of those rights or not.

Subsequent dealings with the adversely possessed land

You might assume that it would be difficult for a successful adverse possessor to be able to convey the adversely possessed land on to a purchaser, without having any proof of title. A purchaser would presumably wish to establish good root of title (discussed in chapter 4) before going ahead with any purchase of the land. In actual fact, a subsequent conveyance of the land by the adverse possessor may not be that difficult to achieve. A purchaser may be happy to proceed with a conveyance of the land where the adverse possessor provides a statutory declaration of good title and title insurance. This is insurance paid for by the adverse possessor that would compensate the purchaser in the event that title was found to be defective.

Establishing adverse possession of registered land

This is now governed by the provisions in the **LRA 2002** which has fundamentally changed the way in which a claim for adverse possession can be established as regards registered land. It will apply to all adverse possession claims of registered land that commenced after the Act came into force in October 2003. (Claims that commenced prior to the Act taking effect are still governed by the rules outlined above for unregistered land.)

✔ Looking for extra marks?

What are the motivations behind implementing changes brought about to the law relating to adverse possession by the LRA 2002? These may be numerous. Some consider that there has been a general shift in public policy away from seeing land as a commodity to be used, towards seeing land as a form of investment. Landowners are no longer expected to use their land and therefore can no longer be expected to stay alert to potential adverse possession claims. For others, in a system of registered land, where title is based upon registration rather than possession, acquisition by an adverse possessor of land through possession appears to undermine the security that registration of title seeks to achieve. Whilst few would suggest abolition of adverse possession completely, restricting the ability to acquire title through adverse possession under the LRA 2002 is welcomed. Perhaps the new law also sits more comfortably with the European Convention on Human Rights 1950.

The principle

A claim of adverse possession of registered land is not, unlike unregistered land, based upon limitation of actions. There is no time limit by which the paper owner must act to evict the adverse possessor, otherwise risk having his title to the land extinguished (s 96 LRA 2002). Instead, the onus for acting lies with the adverse possessor who must take positive steps to apply to the Land Registry to be registered with title to the land that he adversely possesses. Only once such steps are taken will the paper owner have to act himself, by taking appropriate steps to try and recover the disputed land.

Ten years' adverse possession

After ten years of adversely possessing a piece of land, the adverse possessor can apply to the Land Registry to be registered with title to the land that he is adversely possessing.

Remember that:

- In establishing whether the possession is adverse or not, the rules discussed above apply equally to registered land as unregistered land: Sch 6 para 11 LRA 2002.

- The possession must be for a period of ten years immediately preceding the adverse possessor's date of application: Sch 6 para 1(1) LRA 2002.

- The estate adversely possessed need not have been registered at the Land Registry throughout the entirety of this period: Sch 6 para 1(4) LRA 2002.

- No application can be made when the current registered proprietor is unable, due to mental disability, to make decisions on the application or to communicate those decisions: Sch 6 para 8 LRA 2002.

When the Land Registry receives the adverse possessor's application to be registered as title holder, it must notify the current registered title holder of that estate, together with any other interested parties, including any chargee, for example a mortgage lender: Sch 6 para 2 LRA 2002.

These duly notified parties then have 65 working days in which to submit an objection to the adverse possessor's application.

Where the paper owner successfully objects to the adverse possessor's application but then fails to take steps to evict him, a further two years adverse possession will allow the adverse possessor to make another application (Sch 6 para 6 LRA 2002).

Establishing adverse possession of registered land

✳✳✳✳✳✳✳✳✳✳

No objection made	Objection made
Adverse possessor will be registered proprietor of the registered estate.	Adverse possessor's application to be registered proprietor of the registered estate will fail unless: • The objection made should be ignored as: – it would be unconscionable because of an estoppel for the adverse possessor to be dispossessed; or – there is some other reason as to why the adverse possessor should be registered proprietor, for example he has paid the purchase price for the land but it has not been conveyed to him: *Bridges v Mees* [1957]; or – the land concerned involves a boundary dispute and the adverse possessor reasonably believed that for the preceding 10 years the disputed land belonged to him (Sch 6 para 5 LRA 2002).

Figure 8.2

The effect of a successful claim

Where an application to be registered as title holder is successful, the applicant's name will be substituted for that of the former proprietor. The effect is to transfer the estate to the applicant.

Remember, that the title acquired by the adverse possessor will be subject to virtually all proprietary rights that burden the land. The one exception to this rule is that of registered charges that existed over the land immediately prior to the adverse possessor being registered with title. The rationale for this exception is clear. Since chargees are notified of an adverse possessor's application to be registered as title holder, they have the opportunity to raise objections to the application. Where they fail to do so, they cannot later claim to enforce their charge against the new registered owner (unless registration followed, ignoring any objections made based upon one of the three grounds stated above, in which case the registered charge can be enforced against the new registered title holder).

Subsequent dealings with the adversely possessed land

Where the adverse possessor has successfully been registered with absolute title of the land he adversely possessed, any further dealings with that land will occur in much the same way as any registered estate. The fact that it has a history of adverse possession will hold little significance.

Where the adverse possessor has not made an application to be registered as title holder, yet continues to adversely possess the land, his rights, such as they are, will bind any successor to the paper owner who provides no consideration for the transfer of the land. Where the successor provides consideration, the adverse possessor's rights may constitute an overriding interest under Sch 3 para 2 LRA 2002 provided certain conditions are met (discussed in full detail in chapter 3). Such rights could therefore be binding upon that successor. Should the adverse possessor stop possessing the land, even after he has successfully completed ten years adverse possession, he will no longer be deemed in actual occupation of the land and thus have no rights enforceable under Sch 3 para 2 LRA 2002.

Revision tip

Link the above discussion, concerning dealings with adversely possessed land, to material covered in chapter 3.

Adverse possession of a leasehold estate

By the tenant

Remember that in order to establish adverse possession, the possession must be without the permission of the paper owner. It is for this reason that a tenant cannot claim adverse possession against his landlord whilst his lease still exists. Even if, during the term of the lease, the tenant possesses more of the landlord's land than is actually demised, this will not amount to adversely possessing that land. Instead, the demised premises are seen as having been extended.

By someone other than the tenant

Here, the person possessing the land is doing so adversely to the leasehold estate owner only (ie tenant), and not to the freehold estate owner (ie landlord) who has no right to possession (generally) until the lease expires (such rights having been given to the tenant; see chapter 6 for more detail). It is not until the lease expires that adverse possession begins to run against the freehold estate owner. To achieve a better title than anyone to the land, the adverse possessor must adversely possess the land against both the leasehold and freehold estate owners. This can take some time, as seen below.

Where possession is in relation to an unregistered leasehold estate

Remember that the clock does not begin to tick against the unregistered freehold owner until the lease has expired, regardless of the fact that the adverse possessor may have already completed 12 years' adverse possession against the leasehold estate owner.

The adverse possessor completes 12 years' adverse possession against the leasehold estate owner, after which the leasehold estate owner's title is extinguished and he is statutorily barred from seeking recovery of the land: **LA 1980**.

Having extinguished the leasehold estate owner's title, there is nothing to assign to the adverse possessor. He is thus not liable (generally) on the terms of the lease. Instead, until the original lease expires, the dispossessed leasehold estate owner remains liable. Where he breaches any of the lease terms, the landlord can bring forfeiture proceedings against him. If successful, the lease will be terminated; the landlord regains his right to possess the land and can thus take action to evict the adverse possessor.

Provided there has been no such eviction of the adverse possessor, once the lease expires, a further 12 years of adverse possession against the unregistered freehold owner, will extinguish the latter's title and he will be statute barred from seeking recovery of the land.

Figure 8.3

Where possession is in relation to a registered freehold estate subject to a registered lease

The adverse possessor completes 10 years' adverse possession against the registered leasehold estate owner (ie tenant). He can now apply to the Land Registry to be registered as the title holder of the leasehold estate: **Sch 6 para 1 LRA 2002**.

Upon receiving the application, the Land Registry notifies all interested parties who are given the opportunity to submit an objection to the application (as with adverse possession of a freehold estate, discussed above).

Where the application is successful, the adverse possessor will be registered with title to the leasehold estate. In effect, there has been a statutory assignment of the lease to him thus he is liable on all the terms of the lease: **Sch 6 para 9 LRA 2002** and *Central London Commercial Estates Ltd v Kato Kagaku Ltd* [1998].

Where the adverse possessor completes a further 10 years of adverse possession against the registered freehold estate owner, he will be entitled to apply to the Land Registry to be registered with title to the freehold estate. (These applications have been discussed above.)

Figure 8.4

Human rights

Is the law of adverse possession incompatible with Art 1, Protocol 1 of the European Convention on Human Rights 1950, enacted into English law by the Human Rights Act 1998?

What does Article 1 provide?

Essentially, it entitles a person to peaceful enjoyment of his possessions save in circumstances where it is in the public interest that he be deprived of his possessions.

The debate in the case of *Pye*

The potential incompatibility of the law of adverse possession with the Convention has been raised at various stages in the case of *Pye* (facts outlined above) which finally found itself in the European Court of Human Rights.

How did it get to Europe?

Following a decision by the High Court in favour of the adverse possessor (Graham) having acquired title to land owned by Pye, an appeal to the Court of Appeal resulted in the first instance decision being reversed, on the basis that the adverse possessor failed to have the requisite intent to possess. A subsequent appeal to the House of Lords restored the order of the High Court, in favour of the adverse possessor. Having lost the appeal and failed to secure the recovery of land or, at the very least compensation for its loss, Pye applied to the European Court of Human Rights alleging that the UK law violated Art 1 of Protocol 1 of the European Convention on Human Rights 1950.

What views were expressed on this issue during its journey?

1998: The High Court

Although not a direct issue, Neuberger J started the debate by expressing the view that to allow a paper owner to be deprived of his land merely because he had been content to allow a trespasser to remain on his land for 12 years was 'illogical and disproportionate'. He did not consider that the operation of the law here was upholding any principle of justice. Any argument that the LA 1980 could be justified by the practical consideration that it promoted certainty of title was lost in the system of registered land, governed then by the Land Registration Act 1925, where title was (and indeed still is) based upon registration rather than upon physical possession.

2001: The Court of Appeal

The Court of Appeal declared that the English law relating to adverse possession was entirely compatible with the Convention. Indeed, it was the view of Mummery LJ that the operation of this law did not even engage Art 1. Rather than seek to deprive a person of his possessions, the LA 1980, upon which all adverse possession claims were based prior to the LRA 2002 coming into force, merely sought to deprive a person of his ability to take an action in court to recover property if he delayed in commencing proceedings for more than 12 years.

If he was wrong on this point, and the law did in fact engage Art 1, his view was that any deprivation of possessions which resulted from the operation of the law could be justified on the grounds of public interest, namely:

Human rights

1. the avoidance of potential injustice which could result from allowing people to commence 'stale claims';
2. the guarantee of certainty of title; and
3. the promotion of social stability by ensuring peaceful and established possession of land is not disrupted by the resurrection of old claims.

2002: The House of Lords

Although the case was heard on appeal here, the question of compatibility with the convention was not pursued although Lord Bingham and Lord Hope both considered the operation of the law relating to adverse possession in unregistered land as being unfair and producing unjust results.

2005: The European Court of Human Rights

Here, it was declared that the law of adverse possession did indeed engage Art 1. Whilst acknowledging that legislation which barred a person from commencing an action after a certain period of time did not conflict with Convention rights, the effect of the LA 1980 and the LRA 1925 was clearly to deprive a person of his possessions, namely the right to possess his land, by a process which led to extinguishment of title to land.

The Court was not convinced by any argument that the operation of the law could be justified on grounds of public interest. The balance between public interest and the rights of individuals was not fairly set. Although it recognized that 12 years was a relatively long period for a paper owner to take action to prevent losing title to his land (either by commencing court proceedings or granting a licence to the trespasser), the fact remained that under the system as it stood, the paper owner would receive no warning to alert him of the need to take such action. He would be deprived of his property merely by the expiration of 12 years and although it would be his inaction that would trigger his being deprived of property, it was the LA 1980 itself which gave such inaction this effect.

2007: The Decision of the Grand Chamber

On appeal, the Grand Chamber reversed the earlier decision of the European Court of Human Rights. The loss of registered title to land by virtue of the operation of the LA 1980 and the LRA 1925 did not violate Art 1.

The right to peaceful enjoyment of possessions under Art 1 of Protocol 1 should not impair the right of a state to enforce such laws as are deemed necessary to control the use of property in accordance with the general interest. Rather than seeing the law relating to adverse possession as means by which a person is deprived of his possessions, the Grand Chamber saw adverse possession, and the resulting deprivation of possessions, as merely a consequence of the legitimate operation of the limitation rules affecting land. It is a means by which property is controlled. The statutory provisions under the LA 1980 and LRA 1925 are not themselves intended to deprive a person of his possessions but rather are there to regulate title to land following 12 years' adverse possession and thus control the use of the property.

On the issue of whether a fair balance is struck between public interest and the rights of individuals, the Chamber declared that the extinguishment of the paper owner's title to land, and thus deprivation of his possessions, was a proportionate result which served to regulate and clarify the position between the paper owner and the adverse possessor.

✅ Looking for extra marks?

Where does this leave the decision in *Beaulane Properties Ltd v Palmer* [2005]? This case had facts similar to *Pye* but with one important difference: the expiration of 12 years adverse possession occurred after the Human Rights Act 1998 had come into force (rather than before as in *Pye*). The Deputy Judge of the High Court was therefore obliged to consider whether statutory rules on adverse possession (the LA 1980 and LRA 1925) were compatible with the Convention. He deemed them not to be. Consequently, governed by s 3 HRA 1998, he was required to see whether there existed another way to interpret these statutory rules that would be compatible. He achieved compatibility by reviving the principle from *Leigh v Jack* (1879) (see above). Following the decision of the Grand Chamber in *Pye* it is doubtful that the decision in *Beaulane* can still stand, certainly as far as issues of compatibility with the Convention go. As for the revival of the *Leigh v Jack* principle, at best this applies to only those limited number of cases where adverse possession occurred over registered land and the required time period for such possession expired between October 2000 (when the HRA 1998) came into force and October 2003 (when the LRA 2002 came into force).

✳ Key cases

Case	Facts	Principle
Buckinghamshire CC v Moran [1990] Ch 623, CA	Possession of land over which the paper owner intended to build a by-pass in the future. The adverse possessor knew this and intended to possess until such action was taken.	An adverse possessor's knowledge of the intended future use of the land will not prevent possession from being adverse. The adverse possessor must intend to possess the property for his own benefit for as long as he can.
Hounslow LBC v Minchinton (1997) 74 P&CR 221, CA	Enclosure of land by adverse possessor to prevent her dogs escaping when exercised there.	It is the objective effect of an adverse possessor's actions, rather than his subjective motivations, which must be considered when establishing a sufficient degree of physical control to amount to factual possession of land.
Powell v McFarlane (1977) 38 P&CR 452	14 year old boy grazed his cow on disputed land.	Where the actions of an adverse possessor could be open to more than one interpretation, thus his intention is ambiguous, the requisite intent cannot be found.

Exam questions

Case	Facts	Principle
Pye (JA) (Oxford) Ltd v Graham [2003] 1 AC 347	Farming of grazing land by the defendants, initially on the basis of a grazing licence, but once expired and a request for renewal refused, without such a licence. Defendant's padlocked gate giving access to the land, with no key being given to paper owner. Defendants acquired title to the land by adverse possession.	An adverse possessor must be dealing with the land in a way an occupying owner would, to the exclusion of others and contrary to the paper owner's wishes. Willingness to possess land with permission will not prevent possession from being adverse until such permission is given.
Techbild Ltd v Chamberlain (1969) 20 P&CR 633, CA	Acts relied upon by claimants to establish physical possession of land were tethering and exercising their horses on the land and allowing their children to play on the land.	Factual possession of the land will not be established by mere temporary and trivial acts of trespass.

(?) Exam questions

Problem question

Fred was the registered freehold proprietor of a large country estate (The Elms). The property consists of a large house, some fields, and a wooded area. The estate was unoccupied from 1995. At some point in the future Fred planned to turn the property into a country house hotel. In the summer of 1996 George and Hilly, who have nowhere to live, break off a padlock on the gate which provides access to the wooded area. They pitch a tent in the wood. In 1997 George and Hilly fit their own padlock to the existing gate and in 1998 they build a more permanent structure made out of corrugated iron and old packing cases. In May 1999 they are joined by their friends Ian and John. In 2004 George and Hilly are given a council flat. Ian and John remain in place. In late 2007, Fred decides not to go ahead with the development and the whole estate is sold to a chain of hotels – Town and Country Hotels Ltd. In early 2008 Ian and John are discovered by builders working on the redevelopment but they refuse to leave.

Advise Ian and John and Town and Country Hotels Ltd.

An outline answer is available at the end of the book

Essay question

The scope of adverse possession, and the ability to acquire land by stealth, has been severely curtailed by the Land Registration Act 2002, resulting in a law that can be morally justified. Discuss.

An outline answer is available online at www.oxfordtextbooks.co.uk/orc/concentrate/

#9
Trusts of land

The examination

This is an area that is closely linked with co-ownership of land (discussed in the following chapter) and also with trusts of the family home, which is not discussed in any great detail in this book but is covered in the Equity and Trusts book that accompanies this series.

Since trusts of land are a relatively new concept to land law, introduced by the Trusts of Land and Appointment of Trustees Act 1996, examiners often require an analysis of the legislative changes brought about by TLATA; why they were necessary and how trusts of land differ from their predecessor, the trust for sale. This may also incorporate a discussion on changes brought about regarding how successive interests in land are governed. Issues regarding the sale of trust property, the powers of trustees, and rights of beneficiaries may also be a focus of an exam question, with a need to contrast the position pre and post TLATA.

Key facts

- Whilst strict settlements created before TLATA 1996 and governed by the Settled Land Act 1925 can continue to exist, the creation of new successive interests must be by way of a trust of land.

- The creation of concurrent interests in land generally now occurs by way of a trust of land, governed by TLATA 1996 and replacing their forerunner, trusts for sale.

Key facts

✳✳✳✳✳✳✳✳✳

- Trusts of land may be expressly or impliedly created and where implied, may be resulting or constructive trusts.

- Whilst the key feature of a trust for sale was that trustees had a duty to sell the trust land, with a power to postpone, under a trust of land trustees have the power to sell, but need not do so.

- Key provisions of TLATA 1996 include:

  - ss 6–8: governing the extent of trustees powers over the trust property;

  - s 11: governing the circumstances in which trustees have a duty to consult beneficiaries when exercising their powers;

  - ss 12–13: governing the rights of beneficiaries to occupy the trust property; and

  - ss 14–15: governing the right of an interested party to make an application to the court for an order to resolve a dispute over trust land (see chapter 10).

Chapter overview

Successive and concurrent interests in land

Pre TLATA 1996

Successive interests in land were created when an estate owner disposed of his estate, either *inter vivos* or by will, to a number of people in succession; for example A leaves his freehold estate to B for life; remainder to C in fee simple. Both B and C acquired interests in the land: B acquired a life estate and C acquired a fee simple in remainder. Since 1925, neither of these interests could exist as legal estates in land (see s 1 Law of Property Act 1925 and chapter 5). Devices were therefore established to allow for the creation of such successive interests, namely:

- a strict **settlement**, governed by the Settled Land Act 1925; or
- a **trust for sale**, governed by the LPA 1925.

As well as the creation of successive interests, concurrent interests in land arose where more than one person was entitled to enjoy and possess the land at the same time. The creation of such concurrent interests resulted either from an express intention, where legal title to an estate was conveyed to two or more people, or it was implied from the circumstances, where equity felt the need to intervene to do justice to the parties involved; for example where land had been conveyed to just one person but contributions made by another towards the purchase price made it necessary to give recognition to that contributor's interest in the land.

Whatever the circumstances in which they arose, concurrent interests existed behind a trust for sale.

Post-TLATA 1996

Concurrent interests and, to a much lesser extent, successive interests are still created today. However, devices established for their creation have been fundamentally overhauled by TLATA 1996. Key changes include:

- an inability to create new strict settlements: s 2 TLATA 1996, although strict settlements that already existed before TLATA can continue and remain governed by SLA 1925;
- the creation of any successive interests after 1 January 1997 must now take effect as a **trust of land**, governed by TLATA 1996 (s 1 TLATA 1996);
- the creation of concurrent interests now generally exists behind a trust of land, which, to a large extent, has replaced trusts for sale.

Successive interests

Although it is not impossible to expressly create successive interests in land today, it has become rare. On grounds of public policy, it is now seen as undesirable to keep land off the market and unavailable for sale to others; a consequence of the creation of successive interests. However, successive interests may still arise. For example, where a person is given a limited right to reside in a property for his lifetime, a life interest is created in his favour, with an interest in remainder arising in favour of whoever can possess the property upon expiry of the life interest. These successive interests take effect under a trust of land, governed by TLATA 1996, and discussed in more detail below.

Successive interests created before TLATA, which took effect under a strict settlement governed by the SLA 1925, can continue to exist and it is for this reason that you need to be aware of how strict settlements operate.

Creation of strict settlements

Two documents had to be executed to create a strict settlement (s 4(1) SLA 1925):

Vesting Deed

Vests legal title in the appropriate person – generally the tenant for life (see below).

Trust Instrument

- details beneficial interests under the settlement;

- appoints persons to act as trustees of the settlement (see below);

- may expand powers under SLA 1925 conferred upon the person vested with legal title of the settled estate.

The characters

In the example where A leaves his freehold estate to B for life; remainder to C in fee simple, A, the estate owner disposing of his estate, is known as the settlor. B is known as the tenant for life. He is the person who is currently entitled to physically possess the property. C is known as the remainderman, whose right to physically possess the property lies in the future and only takes effect when B dies and his interest in the land expires.

The tenant for life

Upon the creation of a strict settlement, the tenant for life has a split role:

- legal title to the estate disposed by the settler will vest in the tenant for life, assuming that he is capable (otherwise, it may vest in 'statutory owners', typically the trustees: see below). He will hold that legal title on trust on behalf of the beneficiaries under the settlement (here, himself and C). As holder of the legal title numerous powers are invested in him by statute relating to the management and administration of the settled land; and

- he is a beneficiary under the settlement holding an equitable life interest in the land. (C is the other beneficiary holding an equitable remainder interest.) He is the one entitled to physically possess the settled land for the duration of his lifetime. Only once he dies, and his interest in the land expires, will C, the remainderman, be entitled to physically possess and enjoy the settled land.

His powers

As well as dealing independently with his own beneficial life interest in the settled land, numerous powers are conferred upon the tenant for life by statute. Whilst such powers can be expanded by express provision in the settlement (s 109 SLA 1925), attempts to restrict or prohibit their exercise are deemed void: s 106(1) SLA 1925. Since the tenant for life is in a position of being a trustee of the settled land, holding it on trust for himself and others beneficially entitled, the exercise of such powers are subject to normal fiduciary obligations imposed upon trustees.

A tenant for life has numerous powers to deal with the settled land, which include:

- selling or exchanging it, when he must achieve the best consideration reasonably obtainable: s 39 SLA 1925;
- granting a lease over it as permitted by s 41 SLA 1925;
- mortgaging it: s 71 SLA 1925; and
- granting an option over it.

When exercising any of the above powers, the tenant for life must first give one month's notice to the trustees of the settlement (who are discussed below) unless the trustees have waived this requirement: s 101 SLA 1925.

The trustees

Trustees appointed under the trust instrument by the settlor may include a beneficiary under the settlement. Their function is not, as is usual with normal trustees, to hold legal title to the land, which is instead held by the tenant for life as discussed above. (Trustees may hold the legal title as 'statutory owners' in circumstances where there is no tenant for life to hold legal title because, for example, the tenant for life is a minor.)

Their role is essentially a supervisory one in overseeing the affairs of the strict settlement conducted by the tenant for life. This includes:

- receiving purchase monies upon a sale of the settled land. By paying purchase monies to the trustees of the settlement (of whom there must be at least two), a purchaser of settled land will overreach the beneficial interests of the settlement and thus take the land free from such interests: s 18 SLA 1925; ss 2 and 27 LPA 1925. The beneficial interests, having been swept off the land by the process of overreaching, now rest in the purchase monies. (Overreaching is discussed in more detail in chapters 3 and 4.);
- giving consent to the tenant for life in respect of certain transactions, for example to effect improvements of the settled land;

- receiving notice upon the exercise of certain powers by the tenant for life, such as sale as discussed above;
- executing vesting documents and documents of discharge;
- exercising the tenant for life's powers where he wishes to purchase the settled land.

Concurrent interests and the role of trusts

Where land is vested in one person, he becomes the sole owner of that land. No distinction is made between legal and equitable ownership.

Where land is conveyed so as to create concurrent interests, where more than one person is entitled to enjoy and possess the land at the same time, such land will be held by way of a trust. A distinction is therefore made between those who hold legal title as trustees on trust for those who hold the equitable title as beneficiaries. Whilst holding the legal title merely confers upon you fiduciary duties and administrative responsibilities in managing the trust property, it is the holding of the equitable title that confers true value and substance of owning a property since it determines beneficial enjoyment of the land.

Prior to TLATA 1996, the trust established in the creation of concurrent interests was a trust for sale.

Trusts for sale

Trusts for sale are defined in s 205(1)(xxix) LPA 1925. A key feature of a trust for sale is that the trustees had a duty to sell the trust property. This duty did not have to be acted upon immediately, since trustees also had a power to postpone sale. Nevertheless, the overriding duty to sell meant:

- Where a dispute arose between concurrent owners as to whether the land should be sold or not, and a subsequent application was made to the court under s 30 LPA 1925 to request a court order to settle the dispute, the court would be pre-disposed towards ordering a sale (see chapter 10).
- The beneficiaries under a trust for sale did not have a right to occupy the trust property since their interests were seen as resting in purchase monies rather than the land itself. Equity views as done that which ought to be done. In respect of a trust for sale, what should be done is that the trustees sell the trust property. Since equity views this as having already happened, the beneficial interests were viewed as resting in the purchase monies, rather than the actual trust property. This was known as the doctrine of conversion and has since been abolished under s 3 TLATA. (Discussed further below.)
- As social attitudes changed and land was beginning to be appreciated more for its use, as a place to live, rather than its economic value, postponement of the duty to sell became commonplace. The idea behind a trust for sale, that trustees had a duty to sell, was becoming inappropriate.

This last point was the principal motivation for wishing to replace trusts for sale with a new type of trust that was not focused upon an underlying duty to sell: the trust of land.

The effect of TLATA on trusts for sale

- All trusts for sale *impliedly created by statute* before TLATA came into force have been automatically converted into trusts of land on 1 January 1997: s 5 and Sch 2 TLATA 1996.

- Trusts for sale *expressly created* before TLATA came into force, can continue to exist as trusts for sale. Indeed, it remains possible even now to create new express trusts for sale. However, the trustees of these trusts for sale have an irreducible power to postpone sale indefinitely, despite any express contrary intention: s 4 TLATA 1996. To some extent, therefore, trusts for sale have lost their key feature and thus their continued creation may be somewhat pointless.

Trusts of land

Trusts of land are defined in s 1 TLATA 1996 as being any trust of property which consists of or includes land whether expressly or impliedly created (the type of trust implied may be a resulting or constructive trust – see below); whether arising before or after 1 January 1997. Unlike a trust for sale, trustees under a trust of land have no duty to sell, but merely a power to do so.

Trusts of land may be:

- express; or
- implied, of which there are two types:
  - resulting; and
  - constructive.

Revision tip

The creation of trusts, and particularly the circumstances in which implied trusts will arise, is dealt with in more detail in the Equity and Trusts book accompanying this series. You must be guided by your individual course as to how much knowledge of this topic you require for your land examination.

Express trusts of land

When do they arise?

These arise in circumstances where:

- the legal owner expressly declares himself a trustee, holding the land on trust for another; or
- land is conveyed to another expressly subject to a trust.

Formalities required for their creation

---

s 53(1)(b) LPA 1925

The express declaration must be 'manifested and proved by some writing signed by the person declaring the trust'.

The effect of an express declaration of trust

Generally, and assuming the express declaration satisfies the formalities above, it will be conclusive as to the nature and extent of the beneficial rights held under the trust of land: *Pettitt v Pettitt* [1970]. The conclusive nature of the express declaration can only be rebutted with evidence of fraud or, in rare circumstances, where evidence is produced showing the express declaration does not accurately reflect the intention of the parties.

Implied trusts of land

These are discussed in greater detail in the Equity and Trusts book accompanying this series. The focus of this chapter is to look at actual trusts of land themselves, however they arise. Nonetheless, some key points are outlined below.

When do they arise?

In some circumstances, a person may not be the legal title holder of a piece of land but may have acted in such a way towards that land that it would be unfair and unjust to fail to recognize him as having some rights in that land. The classic example is where a person has contributed towards the purchase price of a property. Although legal title may not be vested in him, his contributions towards the purchase price should be given some sort of recognition. This is achieved by implying a trust. Although not a legal title holder, he will become a beneficiary under that trust with his beneficial interest in the land reflecting the contributions he made towards the purchase price.

Resulting trusts

These generally arise in situations where a person makes contributions towards the purchase price but legal title is not vested in him. A resulting trust is imposed to give recognition to the fact that he has contributed towards the purchase price. His contributions will be reflected in the beneficial interest he holds under that trust; such beneficial interest generally being proportionate to the contributions he made (*Dyer v Dyer* (1788)).

Of course, it is possible to rebut the presumption of a resulting trust where it is clear that the contributor did not intend to acquire a beneficial interest in the property or where the contribution was intended to be a gift or a loan. The contributor must be making his contributions in the character of a purchaser for a resulting trust to be implied, which is assumed in the examples given overleaf.

Trusts of land

✳✳✳✳✳✳✳✳✳✳

Example 1

Alex provides all the purchase monies for the purchase of a property by Bert. Although legal title to that property will be vested in Bert, a resulting trust will be imposed so that Bert holds legal title on trust for Alex, the sole contributor and thus sole beneficiary under the trust. This type of trust is also known as a *bare trust*. The trustee, Bert, holds no more than the bare legal title. His powers over the property are minimal and he must act in accordance with directions given by his beneficiary, Alex.

Example 2

Alex provides one third of the purchase monies for the purchase of a property by Bert. Whilst legal title is vested in Bert, a resulting trust will be imposed and he will hold the property on trust for himself as to two thirds and Alex as to one third, since beneficial interests under the trust are generally proportionate to contributions made.

Financial contributions made to a property after the purchase, for example by helping to pay mortgage instalments, now tend to be dealt with by way of a constructive trust.

Constructive trusts

These generally arise in situations where it would be unconscionable not to give effect to a common intention or bargain between the parties as to how the property is to be shared beneficially (*Gissing v Gissing* [1971]). Where an agreement or understanding that the property should be shared has been reached and, upon the strength of this common intention, a party acts to his detriment, it would be inequitable for that party not to be recognized as having some interest in the property. The equitable interest that this party has, arises under the construct of a constructive trust (*Bannister v Bannister* [1948]).

In the case of *Lloyds Bank plc v Rosset* [1991], Lord Bridge identified two ways in which such common intention may be found and hence a constructive trust emerge:

- Where there is evidence that the parties expressly reached an agreement, arrangement or understanding that the beneficial ownership of the property was to be shared, and a party relies upon this to his detriment, perhaps by giving up his own home, then that party will have a beneficial interest in the property arising under a constructive trust. This is known as an express bargain constructive trust. Its creation is dependent upon an express communication between the parties regarding a common intention to share the property. Where the agreement goes as far as to identify how shares will be proportioned (for example, 'if you move in with me the house will be half yours'), such proportions should be enforced. Otherwise, shares will be calculated upon the basis of what is fair and just: *Oxley v Hiscock* [2005].

- Where there is no express discussion, the conduct or mutual dealings between the parties may be evidence of a common intention that the property is to be shared beneficially. Where such common intention can be found, an implied bargain constructive trust will arise. Such common intention could be discerned from direct contributions towards the purchase of the property, whether initially or ongoing, such as the payment of mortgage instalments. Indirect financial contributions, such as decorating the house, will not suffice to establish the requisite common intention (*Burns v Burns* [1984]) (although between married couples such indirect contributions may give rise to a beneficial interest in the property under the Matrimonial Proceedings and Property Act 1970). As above, shares in the property will be calculated upon the basis of what is fair and just.

Formalities required for their creation

---

s 53(2) LPA 1925

These trusts are exempt from formalities demanded for the creation of express trusts under s 53(1)(b) LPA 1925.

Trustees of land

Appointment

Who appoints?

Trustees can be appointed by:

- the person specifically named in the trust deed as being able to appoint: s 36(a) Trustee Act 1925;
- current trustees: s 36(b) TA 1925;
- where the last surviving trustee dies, his personal representatives: s 36(1) and (6) TA 1925; or
- the court: s 41 TA 1925.

Beneficiaries acting unanimously and of full age and capacity can, in some circumstances, give written directions as to who should be selected to act as a trustee either as an addition to, or a replacement of, existing trustees. Such circumstances exist where a person has not been specifically named in the trust instrument (if there is one) to appoint trustees and nothing excludes the beneficiaries from so doing: s 19 TLATA 1996.

Who can be appointed?

Anyone who is *sui juris* and willing to act, although only a maximum of four trustees can hold legal title (see chapter 10). Trustees can also be beneficiaries under the trust. However, their role as trustees (the duties and responsibilities that it brings) remains quite distinct from beneficial enjoyment they derive from being equitable title holders.

Trustees of land

✹✹✹✹✹✹✹✹✹✹

Formalities for appointment

A trustee should be appointed by deed. Where this occurs, the trust property is automatically vested in the trustee, with the already existing trustees as joint tenants without the need for a separate transfer: s 40 TA 1925.

Removal

A trustee may retire from being a trustee. However,

- he may not do so, where there is not going to be a simultaneous appointment of a new trustee, without first seeking consent of his co-trustees; and
- he may not retire if, upon his retirement, just one trustee remains.

Beneficiaries, acting unanimously, of full age and capacity and absolutely entitled to the trust property, can in some circumstances give written directions that one or more of their trustees should retire or that an existing trustee(s) should appoint a specific person as a replacement: ss 19 and 21 TLATA 1996. (Circumstances discussed above.)

Formalities

Retirement should be by deed. The remaining trustees will automatically be vested with the legal estate to hold as joint tenants without the need for a separate transfer: s 40 TA 1925.

Where the trustee is also a beneficiary

Retirement as a trustee will not stop that person from being a beneficiary under the trust. If he also wishes to dispose of his beneficial interest in the property, he may do so by disposing of his equitable interest to another in compliance with s 53(1)(c) LPA 1925. Likewise, where a trustee does dispose of his beneficial interest in the property, he will still remain a trustee of that property until such point as he retires, is removed, or dies.

Powers

As a starting point, trustees of land have 'all the powers of an absolute owner': s 6(1) TLATA 1996.

What do these powers entail?

They include:

- the power to sell, lease, mortgage, grant options, easements etc. (Remember that a purchaser will only take free from beneficial interests existing behind the trust where the mechanics of overreaching have been satisfied: discussed in chapters 3 and 4 regarding registered and unregistered land respectively.);

- the power to acquire freehold or leasehold estates, whether for investment or for occupation by a beneficiary under the trust: s 6(3) TLATA 1996;

- the power to exclude or restrict the rights of one or more of the beneficiaries to occupy the trust land: s 13(1) TLATA 1996 (see below);

- the power to delegate their trustee functions to one or more of the beneficiaries of full age: s 9(1) TLATA 1996;

- the power to transfer trust land to the beneficiaries, where they are of full age and capacity, and absolutely entitled to the land, even where the beneficiaries do not require it.

What duties does a trustee owe when exercising these powers?

According to s 1(1) Trustee Act 2000, a trustee is under a duty to exercise 'such care and skill as is reasonable in the circumstances'. Regard shall be had to experience and any special knowledge the trustee may have when assessing whether an appropriate level of care and skill has been exercised.

How are these powers curtailed?

- The powers are only available to the trustees for the purpose of exercising their functions as trustees: s 6(1) TLATA 1996.

- The powers can be excluded or restricted by express provision in the disposition creating the trust of land: s 8(1) TLATA 1996.

- The powers must not be exercised in a way that contravenes any other enactment, rule of law, or equity: s 6(6) TLATA 1996.

- When exercising these powers, trustees must have regard to the rights of the beneficiaries: s 6(5) TLATA 1996. They must, for example, get the best possible return for the trust property.

- So far as practicable, and in the absence of express contrary intention, trustees must consult beneficiaries of full age and beneficially entitled to an interest in possession in the trust land when exercising their powers. Trustees should then give effect to the wishes of the beneficiaries and, where dispute between the beneficiaries exists, give effect to the wishes of the majority in value so far as is consistent with the general interests of the trust: s 11(1) TLATA 1996. It is for the trustees to decide what is in the general interest of the trust.

- The exercise of the powers may be made subject to the consent of the beneficiaries but only where this is expressly provided for in the trust instrument or by a court order.

Delegation of their powers

All trustees may jointly delegate their powers to beneficiaries entitled to an interest in possession in the trust land: s 9 TLATA 1996.

Rights of beneficiaries

These include:

Consultation

As discussed above, in most circumstances beneficiaries have a right to be consulted when trustees exercise their powers: **s 11 TLATA 1996**.

Consent

As discussed above, where required trustees exercise of power may be subject to obtaining the consent of beneficiaries.

Occupation

Revision tip

Examiners often focus on how the law has changed since the introduction of TLATA 1996. The issue of occupation is one such area where comparisons between pre and post TLATA can be made.

Pre TLATA – under trusts for sale

Whilst a beneficiary who was also a legal owner of the property, had a right to occupy the property, the position was less certain for beneficiaries who did not also hold legal title as trustees. Their right to occupy would depend upon:

- Whether they were already in actual occupation of the property. If they were, their right to occupy was safeguarded by virtue of **s 14 LPA 1925**. If they were not, it seemed they had no right to insist upon taking occupation of the property.

- In addition, where the purpose of the trust was not to provide a home for the beneficiaries, such beneficiaries would find it hard to insist upon a right to occupy the trust property: *Barclay v Barclay* [1970].

Remember, that under a trust for sale, where trustees had a duty to sell, beneficial interests were seen as resting in the sale proceeds, rather than the land itself (*the doctrine of conversion*), which seemed to tip the balance against them having rights of occupation (discussed above).

Post TLATA – under trusts of land

When does a beneficiary have a right to occupy trust property?

As before TLATA, a beneficiary who is also a legal owner of the trust property has a right to occupy that property. **Sections 12** and **13 TLATA 1996** govern rights to occupy trust property by beneficiaries who are not also the legal title holders.

According to s 12 TLATA 1996, a beneficiary is entitled to occupy trust property at any time if at that time:

- the purpose of the trust includes providing land for beneficiaries to occupy; and
- such land is both available (so not, for example, already leased to a tenant) and suitable for occupation (so not, for example, an office block unsuitable for residential occupation or a situation where the beneficiary seeking occupation does not get along with the other occupiers).

How are disputes resolved?

Trustees can exercise their powers to restrict or exclude one or more, but not all, of the beneficiaries from occupying the land. In doing so, the trustees:

- must act unanimously; and
- must act reasonably.

In acting reasonably, trustees must have regard to factors specified under s 13(4) TLATA 1996 namely:

- the intentions of the person(s) who created the trust;
- the purpose for which the land is held; and
- the circumstances and wishes of all beneficiaries entitled to occupy under s 12

When exercising their power to restrict or exclude occupation, trustees may impose financial or other conditions on the beneficiary/beneficiaries occupying, for example:

- to pay for any repairs to the property or other expenses the property incurs;
- to pay an occupation rent to those beneficiaries whose rights to occupy have been restricted or excluded, as a way of compensation: *Dennis v McDonald* [1982], where a male partner was allowed to continue to occupy the property but ordered to pay rent to the female partner who had left the property due to his violence.

Trustees even have the power to physically partition the land, where appropriate, to allow different beneficiaries the ability to occupy exclusively different parts of the building: *Rodway v Landy* [2001].

What is clear is that in exercising this discretion, a beneficiary already in occupation should not be removed and prevented from occupying without either his consent or court approval (where the court would consider criteria under s 13(4) listed above): s 13(7) TLATA 1996.

Making an application to court

Beneficiaries have a right to make an application to the court under s 14 TLATA 1996 to request a court order, for example to settle a dispute between beneficiaries as to whether the trust land should be sold or not (see chapter 10) or to resolve disputes over the trustees allocation of rights to occupy (see above).

Revision tip

Make sure you link material covered in chapter 10 on applications to sell co-owned property and the way in which the law has changed since TLATA 1996 came into force.

Capital proceeds

Where trust land is sold, and beneficial interests are successfully overreached (see chapters 3 and 4) beneficiaries have a right to the capital proceeds where their interests now lie, proportionate to the interest they held in the land.

Protection for a purchaser of trust land

Unregistered land

Although trustees of land have a power to sell trust property, the exercise of such powers must not be done in contravention of any rule of law or equity, for example without getting consent of the beneficiaries where such consent is required or without prior consultation of the beneficiaries.

However, by virtue of s 16 TLATA 1996, even where trustees exceed their powers to sell, a purchaser of unregistered land will still take that land free from any beneficial interests existing under the trust provided:

- he satisfied the requirements of overreaching; and

- had no actual notice that the disposition to him was in breach of trust.

Registered land

Section 16 TLATA 1996 does not apply to registered land. It is assumed that any restrictions on the rights of the trustees to deal with the land have been entered as a restriction on the register for the purchaser to see. A valid sale of the property will not occur unless such restrictions as have been entered are complied with. No further protection therefore need be afforded to the purchaser.

However, in the case where such restrictions are not present, s 26 LRA 2002 appears to provide purchasers of registered land with adequate protection. The effect of this provision seems to be that a purchaser takes an unimpeachable title to the registered land even in circumstances where the trustees have acted in breach of the trust.

✅ Looking for extra marks?

Remember that the key focus of this chapter is TLATA 1996. It is therefore important that when citing the legislation you do so accurately, referring to actual sections of the statute rather than just the statute generally. This equally applies when citing appropriate legislation in other topic areas.

✳ Key cases

Case	Facts	Principle
Bannister v Bannister [1948] 2 All ER 133	The freehold interest in two cottages was conveyed by the defendant sister-in-law to her brother-in-law, with an oral promise that he would allow her to remain in one of the cottages rent free for the rest of her life. The purchase price reflected this. When he later sought to evict her from the cottage, on the grounds that their oral agreement was ineffective, the Court of Appeal found that he held legal title on constructive trust to give effect to her life interest. To hold otherwise would allow him to benefit from a fraud.	Where a legal title holder has entered into an agreement to share beneficial ownership of a property in some way, such agreement having been acted upon, a constructive trust is implied so as to prevent that title holder from unconscionably denying that beneficial interest.
Gissing v Gissing [1971] AC 866	Indirect financial contributions made by a wife over a period of 25 years to the family home failed to be sufficient for her to acquire a beneficial interest in the property under a constructive trust.	In the absence of any express agreement, arrangement or understanding between the parties that the property is to be beneficially shared, upon which a party relies to his detriment, for a constructive trust to arise common intention to beneficially share the property may be found in the conduct or mutual dealings between the parties. Such common intention will not be inferred from mere contributions to general household expenditure.
Lloyds Bank plc v Rosset [1991] 1 AC 107	A wife assisted substantially in the renovation of the family home, legal title to which was vested solely in her husband. The House of Lords declined to find that a constructive trust had arisen as a result of her work on the property.	In the absence of any express agreement, arrangement, or understanding between the parties that the property is to be shared beneficially, upon which a party relies to his detriment, a constructive

Exam questions

Case	Facts	Principle
		trust may arise where such common intention can be found from the conduct or mutual dealings between the parties. However, such conduct must amount to a direct contribution to the purchase of the property.
Oxley v Hiscock [2005] QB 211	Legal title of a home was vested solely in the name of Mr Hiscock, although both he and his partner, Mrs Oxley, had contributed financially towards the purchase price (approximately 80% and 20% respectively). Mrs Oxley was held by the Court of Appeal to have a beneficial interest in the property under a constructive trust of around a 40% share.	The quantum of a beneficial interest under a constructive trust should be calculated with regard to the whole course of dealing between the parties in relation to the property and not merely by reference to actual financial contributions.

(?) Exam questions

Problem question

Alan is the sole legal owner of 'Bleak House'. The property was largely purchased with his savings. A quarter of the price was paid by his son Bill and Bill's partner Claire. Bill and Claire live in the property.

Alan has fallen out with Bill and wishes to sell the property. He has found a buyer David.

Alan seeks your advice on the following questions:

1. whether he can sell the property without consulting Bill and Claire;
2. whether he can ask Bill and Claire to leave the house so that it has vacant possession and is therefore more saleable;
3. whether Alan can sell the house without the consent of Bill and Claire;
4. whether David will take free of any interests if he does complete the sale.

An outline answer is available at the end of the book

Essay question

The provisions contained within the Trusts of Land and Appointment of Trustees Act 1996 now make sure that a correct balance is achieved between the rights of trustees and those of beneficiaries under a trust.

Discuss.

An outline answer is available online at www.oxfordtextbooks.co.uk/orc/concentrate/

#10
Co-ownership

This topic area may be examined alone or combined with other aspects of law, notably trusts of land (discussed in chapter 9) and/or principles governing enforcement of beneficial interests behind a trust against purchasers of trust land (discussed in chapters 3 and 4).

Problem questions are common and may require you to:

- assess the fact that the property is co-owned and held on trust and consequently analyse how the property is held both at law and in equity;

- work through a series of events in chronological order assessing how, if at all, the event changes the way property is being held at law and in equity. Such events inevitably involve either a death of a co-owner or an event which could possibly amount to a severance;

- consider how a court would deal with applications to sell trust property either by one of the co-owners themselves or by a trustee in bankruptcy, where one of the co-owners has been declared bankrupt;

- consider the consequences should the co-owned property be sold, both in relation to the co-owners and the purchaser.

An essay question may focus on analysis of severance or require you to assess how the Trusts of Land and Appointment of Trustees Act 1996 has changed the law of co-ownership from that which existed before the Act was passed.

Key facts

- Co-owned property can be held by way of a joint tenancy, requiring all four unities and upon which the right of survivorship operates, or a tenancy in common, requiring only the unity of possession and upon which the right of survivorship does not operate.

- Co-owned property is held on trust and, since TLATA 1996, this is generally a trust of land.

- Legal title can only be held as a joint tenancy, by a maximum of four people. Equitable title can be held as a joint tenancy or a tenancy in common by an unlimited number of people.

- A joint tenancy in equity, but not at law, can be severed to create a tenancy in common.

- Methods of severance are outlined in s 36 Law of Property Act 1925, which itself confirms methods of severance recognized in *Williams v Hensman* (1861).

- Different methods of severance have their own specific requirements but all methods must occur *inter vivos* and demonstrate an irrevocable intention (express or implied) or act to exclude the operation of the right of survivorship.

- Disputes between co-owners as to whether the co-owned property should be sold can be resolved by making an application to the court requesting a court order to settle the dispute under s 14 TLATA. The court shall have regard to factors listed under s 15 TLATA 1996 upon reaching a decision.

- Applications for sale by a trustee in bankruptcy upon a co-owner being declared bankrupt are also made under s 14 TLATA but in reaching a decision the court shall have regard to factors listed under s 335A Insolvency Act 1986.

Chapter overview

Co-owned property: where two or more people are entitled to possess and enjoy the property at the same time. Held by way of a trust:

Legal title: held by a maximum of four trustees (**s 34 TA 1925**) as a joint tenancy (**s 1(6) LPA 1925**)

Four unities must be present for a joint tenancy: *AG Securities v Vaughan* [1990] and benefits from the right of survivorship.
Only unity of possession required for tenancy in common and does not benefit from right of survivorship.

Equitable title: held by any number as a joint tenancy or tenancy in common

Possible to sever joint tenancy in equity (but not at law) to create a tenancy in common. Must occur *inter vivos* and severed share generally quantified upon basis of equality: *Goodman v Gallant* [1986]

Section 36 LPA 1925: modes of severance include:
- written notice
- act operating on your own share
- mutual agreement
- mutual conduct
- homicide

Applications for sale:

By co-owners in dispute. Governed by **ss 14** and **15 TLATA 1996**

By trustee in bankruptcy. Governed by **s 14 TLATA 1996** and **s 335A IA 1986**

Human Rights Issues: *Barca v Mears* [2005] *Donohoe v Ingram* [2006]

Termination

Types of co-ownership

Co-owned property concerns property where two or more people are entitled to possess and enjoy the property at the same time. Today, there are two types of co-ownership: a **joint tenancy** and a **tenancy in common**. You should remember the key differences between the two:

Figure 10.1

Joint tenancy	Tenancy in common
Co-owners are together seen as a single legal entity; holding the whole of the property as one single owner, with no separate shares in the property.	Co-owners hold a distinct, individual, although as yet undivided, share in the property ('undivided'as it is not possible to say which part of the property the share relates to). The share often reflects proportions initially contributed towards the purchase price.
All four unities must be present: • Possession • Interest • Title • Time (*AG Securities v Vaughan* [1990] and discussed further in chapter 6).	Requires only unity of possession, although others may be present.
Since joint tenants are seen as a single owner together, no one joint tenant has a separate share in the land that he may deal with independently of the others. Instead, each has the potential to claim a separate share through a process of **severance** (in equity only and discussed further below).	Since a tenant in common owns a separate, although undivided, share in the property, he can deal with this share in his lifetime, for example, by selling or mortgaging it.
Upon the death of a joint tenant, there is no share for his heirs to inherit. The death extinguishes any entitlement that joint tenant had to the land. Instead, the co-owned estate 'survives to' the remaining joint tenant(s). This is known as the **right of survivorship**. Through this process, the last remaining joint tenant, when all the others have died, will become the sole owner of the land, at which point co-ownership will cease.	The right of survivorship does not operate. Instead, the share will pass in accordance with provisions in a will or, where there is no will, in accordance with the rules governing intestacy. The shares of any remaining tenants in common will remain unaffected by the death, (unless they inherited the share of the dead tenant in common).

The imposition of a trust

Wherever there is co-owned property, that property will be held by way of a trust. This trust may be expressly created or may arise in circumstances where, out of a desire to do justice, a trust is imposed to give recognition to a person's interest in the land where legal title has not been vested in them.

Revision tip

Whilst the creation of implied trusts is explained briefly in chapter 9, a more detailed discussion can be found in the Equity and Trusts book that accompanies this series.

Before 1997, the type of trust imposed upon co-owners was a *trust for sale:* ss 34 and 36 LPA 1925. Today, following TLATA 1996, which came into force on 1 January 1997, such trusts are now generally *trusts of land.*

Revision tip

Some examiners may require you to analyse differences between the two types of trust. An understanding of material covered in the previous chapter will therefore be required.

As trust property, there are two levels of ownership: legal and equitable.

The legal title

Those on the legal title are the trustees of the property, responsible for the overall management and administration of the property, which must be carried out in accordance with their duties and responsibilities as trustees (discussed in chapter 9).

Who?

There can only be a maximum of four legal title holders. Where there are more than four, those who will be deemed to hold the legal title will be the first four who are named on the conveyance and who have capacity to be a trustee: s 34 Trustee Act 1925.

Whilst no statute specifies a minimum number of people who should hold legal title, ideally there should be at least two as this will aid overreaching upon subsequent transactions of the property (see chapters 3 and 4).

Is a co-owner disadvantaged if they are not on the legal title?

Not really, especially when you consider that under s 11(1) TLATA 1996, trustees have a duty to consult all beneficiaries prior to exercising their functions as trustees (discussed in chapter 9). Indeed, since being on the legal title is tantamount to being an administrator of the co-owned property, many would prefer not to be on the legal title.

The imposition of a trust

✷✷✷✷✷✷✷✷✷✷

How?

Legal title will be held by way of a joint tenancy. This is the only way in which legal title can be held: **ss 1(6)** and **34 LPA 1925**.

Example

Property is conveyed to Anna, Bert, Camilla, Duncan, Edward, and Freda. Bert is 14 years old. Legal title will be held by Anna, Camilla, Duncan, and Edward as joint tenants. Bert cannot hold legal title as, at 14 years old, he does not have the capacity to be a trustee. Freda cannot be on the legal title at this stage as there are already four people on the legal title (the first four named with capacity).

(Remember, that when a minor, such as Bert, reaches 18 years he will not automatically become a trustee and hold legal title, even if events have occurred in the interim whereby there no longer exists the maximum four trustees (perhaps following the death/retirement of original trustees.) Where a gap on the legal title exists making it possible for him to become a trustee having reached 18 years, Bert may be appointed as one, following appropriate formalities, as discussed in chapter 9.)

The equitable title

Those on the equitable title hold a beneficial interest in the property. The value and substance of owning a co-owned property comes from holding the equitable title.

Who?

There is no maximum number of people who can be on the equitable title. Those on the equitable title may also differ from those on the legal title.

How?

The equitable title can be held as either a joint tenancy or a tenancy in common. The flow chart in Figure 10.2 provides a guide as to how to determine whether the equitable title is held as a joint tenancy or a tenancy in common:

Revision tip

When assessing the initial equitable position it is vital that you consider the points in the order outlined in Figure 10.2. For example, an express declaration of a joint tenancy could not prevail where the four unities are missing. This is why you must look for the unities first.

✅ *Looking for extra marks?*

Occasionally, express declarations may be contradictory, for example to hold as 'beneficial joint tenants in common in equal shares'. Such words were held to create a tenancy in common in

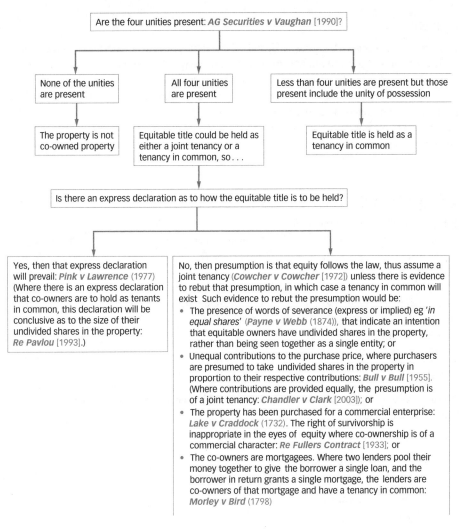

Figure 10.2

Martin v Martin (1987), as the court found that the declaration of a joint tenancy was immediately severed with the words 'in common in equal shares'. However, in the case of *Joyce v Barker Bros* (1980), the same words were held to create a joint tenancy. This shows that ultimately how a court determines what a contradictory express declaration means rests upon the construction of the whole document in which those words are contained. Where contradictions appear throughout, the fairest result is to declare a tenancy in common.

Example

A property is purchased by Mike, Nils, and Olive for the purpose of running a boutique hotel. Mike contributes £100,000 towards the purchase price with Nils and Olive each contributing £50,000. The property is conveyed to them to hold as beneficial joint tenants.

Assuming all four unities are present, the express declaration that they are to hold the property as joint tenants in equity prevails over the fact that they provide unequal contributions to the purchase price, and that the property is to be used for a commercial activity. Only if no express declaration is present, would these facts lead to the conclusion that they hold a tenants in common.

Severance: the principles

It is not possible to sever the joint tenancy at law: s 36(2) LPA 1925.

It is, however, possible to sever a joint tenancy in equity to create a tenancy in common.

Why?

The principal motivation would be a desire to escape the operation of the right of survivorship. Whilst a joint tenant has no separate share in the land that he can pass to a chosen successor, a tenant in common does.

How?

The ability to sever is governed by s 36 LPA 1925. The recognized modes of severance under this provision include:

* written notice; or
* others acts or things which include:
  - an act operating on your own share;
  - mutual agreement;
  - mutual conduct; and
  - homicide.

(All recognized as effective modes in *Williams v Hensman* (1861).)

When?

Whatever method of severance is employed, it is essential that severance takes place during the lifetime of the severing tenant. This is why, generally, it is not possible to sever by will as a will does not take effect until the death of the person to whom it relates: *Re Caines* [1978]. (Severance may be possible by execution of mutual wills: see below.)

Result?

A successful severance will have no effect on how the legal title is held.

 Looking for extra marks?

Where a severing tenant is also a joint tenant at law, he will remain so even after successive severance in equity. If he wished to remove himself from legal title, he would need to:

- release his legal estate to other joint tenant(s): s 36(2) LPA 1925; or
- retire as a trustee: ss 39 and 40 TA 1925; or
- be removed from the trust: s 19 TLATA 1996.

Severance only affects the equitable title. By severing, the co-owner will acquire a separate and distinct, if yet undivided, beneficial share in the land and become a tenant in common in equity.

Generally, severance has a unilateral effect ie only the co-owner who is severing will be affected and become a tenant in common. The other joint tenants from whom he has severed continue to remain joint tenants as between themselves.

Example 1

Claus, Gill, and Victor hold property on trust for themselves as beneficial joint tenants:

| LAW | Claus, Gill, Victor | *Joint tenants* |
| EQUITY | Claus, Gill, and Victor | *Joint tenants* |

Gill successfully severs. The position would then be:

LAW	Claus, Gill, Victor		*Joint tenants* (no change to legal title)
EQUITY	Claus, Victor	+	Gill
	Joint tenants		*Tenant in common*

Where there are only two joint tenants in equity and one decides to sever, this action will have a bilateral effect, with both becoming tenants in common in equity. You cannot be a joint tenant by yourself.

Example 2

Claudine and Gemima hold property on trust for themselves as beneficial joint tenants:

| LAW | Claudine, Gemima | *Joint tenants* |
| EQUITY | Claudine, Gemima | *Joint tenants* |

Claudine successfully severs. The position would then be:

LAW	Claudine, Gemima		*Joint tenants* (no change to legal title)
EQUITY	Claudine	+	Gemima
	Tenant in common		*Tenant in common*

Generally, the severed share is quantified on the basis of equality, irrespective of the initial contributions made to the purchase price of the property: *Goodman v Gallant* [1986]. In other words, where there are *x* number of joint tenants at time of severance, the severing tenant's severed share will equate to 1/*x*th.

So, in example 1 above, Gill's severed share would be one third; in example 2, Claudine and Gemima would each have a half.

This principle of equality is subject to express contrary intention.

Modes of severance

Written notice: s 36(2) LPA 1925

- This can be a unilateral action by the severing joint tenant. There is no need to get the consent of the other joint tenants.

- The written notice need not comply with any particular form. Whilst it must be in writing, it need not state that it is a s 36 notice; nor must it be signed by the severing joint tenant: *Re Draper's Conveyance* [1969].

- The notice must convey an unequivocal and irrevocable intention to sever immediately, whether express or implied: *Harris v Goddard* [1983]. This requires the severing joint tenant to communicate a clear desire to regard himself from this point on as having a distinct and realizable share in the property and therefore no longer wishing to benefit from the right of survivorship.

  For example, if a joint tenant writes the words 'I wish to sever the joint tenancy now' this clearly would satisfy the test. These express words clearly show the joint tenant no longer wishes to be part of a joint tenancy from this point on. Difficulties arise when the words used are not so clear and indeed may not even have been originally directed towards severance.

....

Re Draper's Conveyance [1969] 1 Ch 486

A court summons requesting for the matrimonial home to be sold and the proceeds divided in accordance with the interests of the spouses, was deemed effective written notice to sever. By requesting a sale and receipt of her share of the proceeds, the wife had clearly demonstrated an intention to regard herself as having a distinct and realisable share in the property, separate from that of her husband, and which should be effective immediately.

....

By contrast...

Harris v Goddard [1983] 1 WLR 1203

A divorce petition containing a prayer that the divorce court should make such order in respect of the matrimonial home as may be considered just, did not amount to effective written notice. There was insufficient immediacy, as the request related to future court orders that may be made, and insufficient intention to sever, as any future court order may not have involved any severance.

✅ *Looking for extra marks?*

Whilst in the case of *Nielson-Jones v Fedden* [1975], it was suggested that divorce documentation should never amount to effective written notice as it is not sufficiently irrevocable, this criticism has not held much weight. It is difficult to see what type of document would not be considered revocable.

- The notice must be served on all the other joint tenants in equity. This can be achieved by:
  - handing the notice over to them personally; or
  - leaving it at their last known place of abode or business in person or posting it to that address: **s 196(3) LPA 1925**. The severing joint tenant must be able to establish that the notice arrived at that address. If he uses registered post, he can take advantage of **s 196(4) LPA 1925**, which declares notice to have been sufficiently served where it is addressed to the person(s) on whom it should be served, sent to the appropriate address, and not returned undelivered. Where he uses normal post, he would have to prove that the notice actually arrived: *Kinch v Bullard* [1999].

However, remember that the notice does not need to have been read by the intended recipients for it to be effective:

Re 88 Berkley Road [1971] Ch 648

A joint tenant (G) sent a written notice of severance by recorded delivery to the co-owned property, 88 Berkley Road, which she owned and occupied with the other joint tenant (E), the co-owned property thus being E's place of abode. When the postman delivered the notice and requested a signature, E (the intended recipient) had already gone to work. G therefore signed for the notice herself. G died shortly afterwards and the issue arose as to whether there had been an effective severance by G. It was held that there had been and the fact that E swore that she had never seen the notice was irrelevant. It was proven to have arrived at her place of abode and that was sufficient to establish it had been appropriately served.

✅ *Looking for extra marks?*

There has been some suggestion that written notice is not available as a means of severance where the names on the legal title do not mirror those who hold beneficially in equity; for example, where A and B hold on trust for X, Y, and Z. This has come from a technical interpretation of s 36(2) LPA 1925 and specifically the words 'where a legal estate…is vested in joint tenants beneficially'. Arguably, a more liberal interpretation of the section should be taken allowing all equitable joint tenants the opportunity to sever by this method.

An act operating on your own share

This is where the joint tenant acts unilaterally to sever his beneficial interest in the co-owned property, and sometimes his acts may even be concealed from the other joint tenants. The act must have a final and irrevocable character that precludes the severing joint tenant from claiming, by the right of survivorship, any interest in the joint tenancy.

There are numerous acts that fall into this mode of severance:

- *total alienation* ie where the severing tenant sells or disposes of his beneficial interest in the co-owned property. This includes entering into a specifically enforceable contract to sell: *Brown v Raindle* (1796). To be an effective disposal, and thus an effective severance, there must be compliance with s 53(1)(c) LPA 1925 (see chapter 2).

Example

Vlad, Anish, and Pete are legal joint tenants holding property on trust for themselves as beneficial joint tenants.

| **LAW** | Vlad, Anish, Pete | *Joint tenants* |
| **EQUITY** | Vlad, Anish, Pete | *Joint tenants* |

Anish sells his share to Gabriel. The position would now be:

LAW	Vlad, Anish, Pete		*Joint tenants*
EQUITY	Vlad, Pete	+	Gabriel
	Joint tenants		*Tenant in common*

Remember, severance does not affect the legal title. Should Anish no longer wish to be a trustee of a property he no longer holds a beneficial interest in, he should take action to remove himself from the legal title, for example by retiring as trustee.

Anish could have sold his share to one of the other joint tenants, for example Vlad. The position would then be:

LAW	Vlad, Anish, Pete		*Joint tenants*
EQUITY	Vlad, Pete	+	Vlad
	Joint tenants		*Tenant in common*

It is quite possible for one co-owner to be both a joint tenant and a tenant in common in equity of the same property: *Wright v Gibbons* (1949).

- *Partial alienation* ie where the severing tenant mortgages (*First National Securities Ltd v Hegarty* [1985]) or leases his beneficial interest in the co-owned property.

- *Involuntary alienation* for example bankruptcy of a joint tenant: *Re Pavlou (A Bankrupt)* [1993]. Upon bankruptcy, the severed share will vest in the bankrupt's trustee in bankruptcy (see below).

- *Commencement of litigation* where it concerns the court taking direct action on the joint tenancy itself. This is despite the fact that court proceedings could be discontinued and therefore arguably are neither final nor irrevocable. Provided the intention to sever can be seen as final at the time of commencing proceedings, this will be sufficient: *Re Drapers Conveyance* [1969].

A mere unilateral oral declaration of an intention to sever is insufficient to amount to severance. To be effective, it would have to be incorporated into a written document. This is to avoid any issues that might arise from uncertainty.

Mutual agreement

Form

The agreement:

- must be between *all* beneficial joint tenants: *Wright v Gibbons* (1949);
- can be oral or in writing;
- need not be contained within a specifically enforceable contract (*Burgess v Rawnsley* [1975]). The fact that the agreement may be legally unenforceable was further illustrated in *Hunter v Babbage* [1994]. A divorcing couple's agreement to sell the matrimonial home and split the proceeds was held effective severance, despite being contained in a *draft* consent order which had yet to receive court approval;
- must be fixed and unchanging so it probably needs to go beyond an 'agreement in principle', which suggests that the parties have reserved the right to change their positions: *Gore and Snell v Carpenter* (1990).

Content

The agreement must convey an unequivocal common intention to sever, whether express or implied. (An example of implied common intention could be where joint tenants agree that upon death their interests should pass to their child: *McDonald v Morley* (1940)).

A mere agreement just to sell the co-owned property is not sufficient, as it does not eliminate the possibility of holding the sale proceeds as a joint tenancy to which the right of survivorship applies: *Nielson-Jones v Fedden* [1975]. If the agreement was to sell the co-owned property *and* split the sale proceeds, this would be sufficient as it shows a clear intention on the part of the joint tenants to see themselves as having distinct shares in the co-owned property.

Burgess v Rawnsley [1975] Ch 429

A couple (H and R) purchased a property, each contributing half towards the purchase price, which they held as legal and equitable joint tenants. Upon their relationship breaking down, negotiations began for H to buy R out. Initially, R orally agreed to sell her interest in the property to H for £750. She then revoked that agreement and demanded a higher price. H then died before negotiations were concluded. The Court of Appeal held that there had been effective severance prior to H's death. By both parties reaching the initial agreement, although later revoked, it indicated a common intention that they have separate shares in the property and that the right of survivorship should no longer operate between them.

Mutual conduct

- Where there is no express or implied *agreement* to sever, it may be possible to infer from the conduct of the joint tenants that the interests of them *all* are to be treated as tenancies in common.

- There must be a clear intention from the joint tenants' course of dealings with the property that the right of survivorship should no longer operate between them. In *Greenfield v Greenfield* (1970), the co-owned property was physically partitioned. Severance had not resulted from this conduct as it seemed apparent that the co-owners were still happy for the right of survivorship to operate.

- The execution of mutual wills, directing where each joint tenant's 'share' should go upon death, indicates a common intention that their interests in the co-owned property be severed and that the right of survivorship should no longer operate: *Re Wilford's Estate* (1879).

- In the case of *Burgess v Rawnsley* [1975], Sir John Pennycuick noted that negotiations between joint tenants in relation to each other's share in the property, could serve to indicate a common intention to sever, even where such negotiations fail to result in a final agreement. However, it was his opinion that a mere offer from one joint tenant to buy the other out for £X, and that other makes a counter offer of £Y, would be insufficient to indicate a common intention to sever.

Homicide

A person cannot benefit from the right of survivorship where he unlawfully kills another joint tenant: *Cleaver v Mutual Reserve Fund* (1892). His action of unlawful killing, therefore, generally severs his interest.

Applications for sale by co-owners in dispute

Where a dispute arises between co-owners as to whether a co-owned property should be sold, it is possible for an application to be made to the court requesting a court order to resolve that dispute.

Pre TLATA – under trusts for sale

Under a trust for sale, trustees had a *duty* to sell, with a statutory power to postpone. When a court received an application requesting a court order to settle a dispute between co-owners as to whether to sell the trust property or not under s 30 LPA 1925, it was predisposed towards ordering a sale. This assumption to sell would be lost in cases where the co-owners had agreed, prior to the acquisition of the trust property, only to sell if all co-owners agreed. In such cases, a court would only order a sale where such agreement was forthcoming.

A further consideration that might persuade a court to postpone an order to sell would be if the purpose for which the trust property had been purchased, for example to provide a home, was continuing and thus could still be fulfilled.

Post TLATA – under trusts of land

When an interested party, which includes a beneficiary, makes an application to the court by virtue of s 14 TLATA 1996, requesting an order to settle a dispute regarding whether to sell a co-owned property, the court should have regard to factors listed in s 15 TLATA 1996, namely:

* the intention of the person(s) who created the trust;
* the purpose for which the property subject to the trust is held;
* the welfare of any minor who occupies or might reasonably be expected to occupy any land subject to the trust as his home;
* the interest of any secured creditor of any beneficiary.

According to s 15(3), the court should also have regard to the circumstances and wishes of the beneficiaries or the majority of them, having regard to the size of their interests.

Remember, however, that the criteria listed under s 15 are not exhaustive, and a court may regard other factors which it considers significant, for example the interest of a disabled adult as in *First National Bank v Achampang* [2003].

Applications for sale by co-owners in dispute

✳✳✳✳✳✳✳✳✳✳

Case law influence

The consideration of purpose under s 15 TLATA largely reflects what the court used to consider when receiving applications to resolve disputes prior to TLATA coming into force (when applications were made under s 30 LPA 1925). It would therefore appear that pre TLATA case law may provide a useful guide as to how purpose influences a court when deciding whether to order a sale or not.

In circumstances where the purpose for which the property was purchased can still be fulfilled, a court may be inclined not to order a sale:

Re Buchanan-Wollaston's Conveyance [1939] Ch 738

Four separate home owners clubbed together to buy a piece of land adjacent to their own properties in order to prevent the land from being built upon, thus preserving a sea view for their properties. They covenanted not to sell the land except with unanimous or majority vote. One of the home owners, upon selling his home, applied to the court for an order that the adjacent land be sold. The court declined to order a sale. The purpose for which the land had been purchased (to preserve a sea view) could still be fulfilled. In addition, it would be improper for the court to go against the contractual arrangement regarding the conditions agreed between the co-owners for any sale of that land.

The purpose of providing a home for a couple may be declared dead upon the relationship breaking down, in which case a court may order a sale: *Jones v Challenger* [1961]. However, the presence of any minors may sustain the purpose for a longer period:

Re Evers Trust [1980] 1 WLR 1327

A co-habiting couple purchased a property as joint tenants to provide a home for themselves and their three children. Upon the relationship ending, the male partner applied for a sale of the property to release his capital investment. The court declined to order a sale holding that the greater part of the purpose for acquiring the property, as a family home, could still be fulfilled. (The court also took into account the fact that the male partner did not need to realize his capital as he had a secure home with his mother.)

✅ Looking for extra marks?

Remember that pre TLATA, a court was predisposed towards ordering a sale since under a trust for sale, trustees had a duty to sell. Under a trust of land, trustees have a power to sell, rather than a duty. Since the emphasis under the 1996 Act has moved away from a duty to sell to a mere power, there is less of presumption towards ordering a sale. As such, whilst pre TLATA case law may provide a court some guidance when reaching decisions under s 14 TLATA applications, it should be treated with caution: *Mortgage Corporation v Shaire* [2001].

Possible outcomes

Remember, that when a court receives an application to resolve a dispute over whether to sell co-owned property, it can make whatever order it sees fit. It could:

- order a sale of the property, for example where the house is excessively large and unsuitable for sole occupation by the co-owner resisting the sale: *Jackson v Jackson* [1971];

- order a sale but postpone it for a short period, for example to enable the co-owners wanting to stay in the property the opportunity to buy out the co-owner wishing to sell: *Ali v Hussein* (1974); or because one of the co-owners occupying the property is ill: *Bank of Ireland Home Mortgages Ltd v Bell* [2001]; or until minors living in the property reach school leaving age;

- refuse to order a sale of the property, for example where one co-owner uses the property as a place to work: *Mayes v Mayes* (1969);

- refuse a sale but require the occupying co-owner to pay rent to a co-owner no longer occupying: *Dennis v McDonald* [1981].

Applications for sale by a trustee in bankruptcy

Where a co-owner is declared bankrupt, his beneficial interest in the co-owned property will vest in his trustee in bankruptcy. If he is a joint tenant at the time of becoming bankrupt, the declaration of bankruptcy has the effect of severing his beneficial interest (under an act operating on your own share: *Re Pavlou (A Bankrupt)* [1993], discussed above) so that his now separate beneficial interest in the property can vest in his trustee in bankruptcy.

Remember that only the beneficial interest vests in the trustee in bankruptcy. Where the bankrupt is also a legal title holder, he will continue to remain so upon declaration of bankruptcy.

Example

Gordon, Simone and Mario hold a property on trust for themselves as beneficial joint tenants.

| LAW | Gordon, Simone, Mario | *Joint tenants* |
| EQUITY | Gordon, Simone, Mario | *Joint tenants* |

Mario is declared bankrupt. As a joint tenant in equity, bankruptcy will have the effect of severing his interest in equity. His severed share will then vest in his trustee in

Applications for sale by a trustee in bankruptcy

bankruptcy. There will be no change to the legal title. The position following bankruptcy will thus be:

LAW	Gordon, Simone, Mario	Joint tenants
EQUITY	Gordon, Simone	+ Trustee in Bankruptcy
	Joint tenants	*Tenant in common*
	two thirds	*a third (Goodman v Gallant rule)*

What happens next?

The trustee in bankruptcy has a statutory duty to 'get in, realize and distribute' the bankrupt's interest to pay off the creditors: s 305(2) Insolvency Act 1986.

Where the interest is in the principal residence of the bankrupt, steps to realize the interest must be taken within 3 years from the date of bankruptcy: Enterprise Act 2002. Failure results in the interest reverting back to the bankrupt (s 283A IA 1986).

To realize the interest, the trustee in bankruptcy will make an application to the court requesting a sale of the property under s 14 TLATA 1996 (as an interested party).

When considering whether to grant an order to sell, the s 15 TLATA criteria (discussed above) are irrelevant: s 15(4) TLATA.

Instead, the court should have regard to s 335A IA 1986 and 'make such order as it thinks just and reasonable having regard to the interests of the bankrupt's creditors' and 'all the circumstances of the case other than the needs of the bankrupt'.

In addition, where the application is in respect of a family home, the court should also have regard to:
- the conduct of the (former) spouse/civil partner in contributing towards the bankruptcy;
- the needs and financial resources of the (former) spouse/civil partner; and
- the needs of any children.

Where application for sale is made within the first year of bankruptcy: court may grant the bankrupt a breathing space (moratorium) up to the first year anniversary of the bankruptcy, in order that he may sort out his financial affairs or make alternative living arrangements.

Where the application for sale is made after the first year of bankruptcy: court assumes interests of creditors outweigh all other considerations, save where exceptional circumstances may exist: s 335A(3) IA 1986.

Figure 10.3

What amounts to exceptional circumstances under s 335A(3) IA 1986?

- These must be truly extreme and typically involve issues of severe illness or disability.
  - *Re Raval* [1998]: the fact that the bankrupt's spouse suffered from paranoid schizophrenia which would have been adversely affected if an immediate sale took place, led the court to agree to postponing the sale for one year.
  - *Claughton v Charalambous* [1999]: the court agreed to an indefinite postponement of sale where the bankrupt's wife suffered from severe ill health and restricted mobility.
  - *Re Bremner* [1999]: the bankrupt had terminal cancer with a life expectancy of six months. Sale was postponed to three months after his death to allow for his elderly wife to care for him in his own home in the final stages of his life.
- Generally, any adverse effect a sale might have on the children of the bankrupt would not be considered exceptional enough to warrant a sale being postponed.
  - *Re Citro* [1991]: disruption of the children's education and eviction from their home, in circumstances where the wife of the bankrupt was unable to buy a comparable property in the neighbourhood or elsewhere, did not amount to exceptional circumstances.

✅ *Looking for extra marks?*

Whilst pre TLATA the courts adopted a similar approach to applications made by secured creditors for sale as those made by a trustee in bankruptcy, resulting almost inevitably in an order to sell, post TLATA the creditors needs are not paramount under s 15 TLATA and are just one factor to be considered with others listed under that section: *Mortgage Corporation v Shaire* [2001]. However, post-TLATA case law suggests that the courts still have a tendency to order a sale, not wishing to keep creditors waiting for repayment of debts owed. Issues of ill health or disability are unlikely to do more than postpone a sale, if that: *Bank of Ireland Home Mortgages Ltd v Bell* [2001].

Human rights issues

In *Barca v Mears* [2005] and *Donohoe v Ingram* [2006], consideration was given to the courts strict approach to finding exceptional circumstances and whether such an approach was compatible with ECHR Art 8 (right to family life and home) and ECHR Art 1 (right to peaceful enjoyment of possessions).

In both cases, arguments raised to establish exceptional circumstances justifying postponement of a sale, were not successful. Although the courts recognized that a broader interpretation of what is exceptional may be required, so as not to offend Art 8, in both cases, even taking such a broader interpretation, circumstances were not of an exceptional nature. The *usual* stress and upheaval caused by the sale of a family home (which both cases involved) cannot be relied upon as an *exceptional* circumstance.

Termination of co-ownership of land

Partition

This is where the land is physically divided up between the co-owners so that each becomes absolute owner of his own portion. Powers to partition are given to trustees under s 7 TLATA 1996 (see chapter 9).

Union in sole ownership

This is where the co-owned property falls into the absolute ownership of one of the tenants, for example through the operation of the right of survivorship where the land finally vests in the sole surviving joint tenant.

Conveyance to a single purchaser

Where trust property is sold to a single purchaser, and the mechanics of overreaching are complied with (discussed in chapters 3 and 4), that purchaser will take the property free from the trust.

 Key cases

Case	Facts	Principle
Burgess v Rawnsley [1975] Ch 429	Oral negotiations between co-owners for one to buy the other out, where an agreement had been reached as to the price to be paid, although later revoked with a higher price being demanded, was held effective severance. In reaching the initial agreement, although later revoked, both parties had indicated a common intention to have separate shares in the property and that the right of survivorship should no longer operate between them.	When severing by mutual agreement, the agreement need not be in a specifically enforceable contract. Any agreement must convey an intention to preclude the future operation of the right of survivorship.

Case	Facts	Principle
Harris v Goddard [1983] 1 WLR 1203	A divorce petition merely requesting for such orders to be made in respect of the matrimonial home as may be considered just, did not amount to effective written notice. There was insufficient immediacy, as the request related to future court orders that may be made, and insufficient intention to sever, as any future court order may not have involved any severance.	Written notice must convey and irrevocable and unequivocal intention to sever immediately, whether express or implied.
Re 88 Berkley Road [1971] Ch 648	A joint tenant's written notice was deemed effectively served when it was sent by registered post to the co-owned home, even though it was signed for by the severing joint tenant and had never been read by the intended recipient. The fact remained that it could be proved written notice had arrived at the last known place of abode of the other, non-severing joint tenant and that was sufficient.	Provided written notice has been effectively served, it need not be read by the intended recipient(s) to be effective.
Re Buchanan-Wollaston's Conveyance [1939] Ch 738	The purpose behind a joint purchase of land, to provide four home owners with sea views, was considered to still be continuing when one of the home owners applied to the court under s 14 TLATA 1996 requesting a sale of that land. This, together with the fact that the home owners had covenanted not to sell the land without unanimous or majority vote, led a court to decline ordering a sale of the land.	Upon receiving an application by an interested party under s 14 TLATA 1996 requesting an order to settle a dispute as to whether to sell trust property, a court may decline ordering a sale where the purpose for which trust property was purchased can still be fulfilled (a consideration under s 15 TLATA 1996).
Re Draper's Conveyance [1969] 1 Ch 486	An affidavit in support of a divorce petition, requesting a sale of the matrimonial home and the division of proceeds between spouses amounted to effective severance by written notice. It indicated sufficient immediacy, in wanting a sale to occur as soon as possible, and by requesting her share of sale proceeds, the wife showed that she considered herself to have a distinct and realizable share in the property, separate from that of her husband.	Written notice must convey and irrevocable and unequivocal intention to sever immediately, whether express or implied.

Exam questions

✱✱✱✱✱✱✱✱✱✱

Case	Facts	Principle
Re Evers Trust [1980] 1 WLR 1327	A request for the sale of a co-owned family home under s 14 TLATA 1996, was declined by the court since the presence of three children meant that the purpose for which the property had been purchased (to provide a family home) could still be fulfilled (a consideration under s 15 TLATA 1996).	As for *Re Buchanan-Wollaston's Conveyance* [1939] above.

(?) Exam questions

Problem question

Alex, Bobby, Carl, and David are keen surfers and run a surf school business in Cornwall. In 2004, they decided to purchase a large house located near to the surf school, with the intention of living there and using it to offer bed and breakfast to the surfers. At this time, Bobby was only 17 years old and could only afford to contribute £5,000 towards the £250,000 purchase price. The remainder was provided by Alex, Carl, and David in equal shares. The house was conveyed to them as beneficial joint tenants.

In 2006, Carl needed to raise some capital to buy himself a car, so he mortgaged his share in the house to Surfs Up Bank plc.

Last year, after a series of heated arguments with Alex, Bobby moved out of the house. He spoke to Alex, Carl and David and told them that he could no longer live with them. He offered to sell his interest in the house to them. They all agreed that this would be for the best and that steps should be taken as soon as possible to achieve this, although no final agreement was reached as to the price.

Two days later, Bobby was involved in a surfing accident and was killed. His will left all his property to David.

Two weeks ago, having had very few surfers come to their school since it opened in 2004, Alex wrote a letter to Carl and David informing them that he wanted the house sold so that he could get his money out as soon as possible. Carl opened the letter when it arrived at the house, but he became so angry upon reading its contents that he tore the letter up and threw it away. He mentioned nothing about the letter to David.

Alex now wishes to take action to get the house sold.

Advise Alex, Carl and David as to their interests in the house and how, if at all, Alex could achieve his desire of getting the house sold and his share out.

An outline answer is available at the end of the book

Essay question

To what extent is it true to say that severance should be final and irrevocable to be effective? Discuss in relation to all modes of severance.

An outline answer is available online at www.oxfordtextbooks.co.uk/orc/concentrate/

#11

Licences

This is a topic that can be tested both in the format of a problem question or an essay question. It can be examined as a self-contained question or be combined with another topic area, typically leases where the focus is often upon how you can distinguish a lease from a licence. Examiners often look to use the topic of licences as a way of testing whether you understand the nature of the distinction between personal and proprietary rights and in what circumstances the distinction is blurred.

Key facts

- A licence is permission given by the licensor to the licensee to allow the latter to enter the land of the former, which, without such permission would otherwise amount to a trespass: *Thomas v Sorrell* (1673).

- A licence should be distinguished from a lease (see also chapter 6).

- There are different types of licences. Each type has different rules when it comes to the effect that it has on the original parties and on a third party who purchases the land over which the licence exists.

- Probably the most common type of licence, a bare licence, can arise expressly or impliedly. It does not afford much protection to a licensee. The licensor can revoke it provided that he gives reasonable notice and allows a packing up period. It does not bind a third party.

- A licence coupled with an interest is based upon the idea that a licence is necessary in order for the licensee to enjoy some other proprietary interest over the licensor's land, for example a *profit à prendre*. The licence is irrevocable for as long as the proprietary interest remains. It has the ability to bind a third party only by virtue of being a shadow of another proprietary interest.

- Contractual licences are licences that arise under the terms of a contract. Where a licensor attempts to revoke such a licence he is in breach of contract. In some cases equity will intervene by granting an injunction to restrain the breach or an order of specific performance to enforce the licence. Consequently, a licensee can enjoy better protection than mere damages. Whether or not a contractual licence can bind third parties has proved controversial. Modern orthodoxy suggests that it cannot unless protected by an estoppel or constructive trust.

- An estoppel licence arises as a result of a representation by the licensor and a detrimental reliance by the licensee. It is binding between these two parties but is also capable of binding a third party.

Chapter overview

Introduction

A **licence** can be described as permission given by one person (the licensor) to another (the licensee) allowing that other to enter the licensor's land which, without such permission, would amount to a trespass: *Thomas v Sorrell* (1673). It may extend beyond permitting mere entry and give the licensee occupational rights over the land in question.

Revision tip

Remember that a licence is distinguishable from a lease. Any occupational rights granted under a licence will fall short of exclusive possession and/or fail to meet the formalities for the creation of a lease. Examiners often test the distinction between the two so make sure you review material covered in chapter 6.

A licence does not convey a proprietary interest over the land where it is exercised: *Ashburn Anstalt v Arnold* [1989]. Rather it creates a mere personal right between the person giving the permission, the licensor, and the person receiving that permission, the licensee. As a personal right, it is not capable of:

- being transferred to another; or
- being binding upon a third party.

(*Clore v Theatrical Properties* (1936))

However, the law has developed so that, in some circumstances, a licence can be enforced against both the licensor and a third party purchaser. This, therefore, provides some licences with characteristics of a proprietary nature, considered further below.

✅ *Looking for extra marks?*

A licence can sometimes appear very similar to an easement giving someone a right of way through the land of another. However, to be an easement, the requirements under *Re Ellenborough Park* [1956] must be met and the right must have been acquired as an easement (discussed in detail in chapter 12). Such requirements do not apply for a licence to exist. The finding of an easement to enter on to the land of another is arguably preferable to the finding of a licence since an easement, as a proprietary interest, is capable of binding third parties. However, do remember that a licence to be, or do something, on the land of another can convert into an easement where (i) it meets the requirements under *Re Ellenborough Park* and (ii) s 62 LPA 1925 has operated (again discussed in more detail in chapter 12).

Categories of licences

Bare licences

When do they arise?

These arise where the licensee is given permission to be, or enter, on the land of the licensor without the need to provide the licensor with any consideration. They may be created:

- expressly, for example by giving an invitation to another to attend your house for dinner; or
- impliedly, for example, it is generally accepted that people have an implied licence to walk through your garden gate and along your garden path up to your front door.

By acquiring a bare licence, the licensee is prevented from being a trespasser on the land, so long as he does not exceed the scope of the licence.

Termination

A bare licence may be revoked by simply telling the licensee to leave and then giving him a reasonable time to do so (*Greater London Council v Jenkins* [1975]). What amounts to a reasonable time will vary according to the circumstances but in all cases only if that reasonable time expires and the licensee remains on the land, does he then become a trespasser.

Enforcement against third parties

A successor in title to the licensor is just as capable of revoking a bare licence as the original licensor. Thus, such licences have never been held as binding upon third parties.

✅ Looking for extra marks?

The extent to which an estate owner can give and, more particularly, revoke licences preventing people from being on his land may well be subject to future challenges under the Human Rights Act 1998. This may especially be the case where the land in question is privately owned but open to public use. To ensure liberties of citizens are protected, landowners in some circumstances in the future may be allowed to prevent persons from being on their land only where reasonable grounds can be established: *Appleby v UK* (2003).

Licences coupled with an interest

When do they arise?

These arise in circumstances where a proprietary interest has been granted and, in order for that interest to be exercised and enjoyed, access on to land of another must also be given. The licence giving such access arises as a consequence of the proprietary interest that has been granted and thus can be seen as ancillary to that interest. For example, such licences arise with the granting of *profits à prendre* (discussed in more detail in chapter 12). A right to take something from the land of another can only be exercised where it is accompanied by a licence to enter that land.

Some older case law decisions expanded upon the concept of 'interest', to which the licence is coupled, beyond those of a proprietary status. For example, in *Hurst v Picture Theatres Ltd* [1915] the Court of Appeal held that the interest to which the licence was coupled was a contractual right to watch a film at a cinema. However, more recent cases with similar contractual rights under consideration as that in *Hurst*, have declined to apply a similarly wide view as to what is meant by an 'interest', rather limiting it to one that is in property: *Hounslow LBC v Twickenham Garden Developments Ltd* [1971].

Termination

As long as the proprietary interest remains, the licence that accompanies it is irrevocable.

Enforcement against third parties

As this licence effectively shadows a proprietary interest, it is regarded as having the same enforceability as the proprietary interest to which it is attached. Thus, it could be binding upon not only the original licensor but also his successors in title: *Webb v Paternoster* [1619]. The enforceability of such licences beyond the original licensor has allowed this type of licence to been seen as creating a proprietary interest, albeit indirectly.

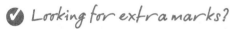 **Looking for extra marks?**

The fact that this licence may bind a third party has led some to suggest that, albeit indirectly, this type of licence creates a proprietary interest. However, when you consider that its enforceability against a third party is merely a consequence of the fact that it shadows an existing proprietary interest, such as a *profit*, this view may be defeated. Indeed, some have suggested that this category of licence should not exist as a separate category at all. The licence to enter the land of another, in order for an existing proprietary interest to be exercised and enjoyed, is perhaps merely just a component of that proprietary interest and not a separate licence.

Contractual licences

When do they arise?

This is a licence that is given upon the licensee providing some form of consideration. Such licences may arise, for example, when you pay for admission to a cinema or pay for a ticket to a race course.

Whilst past case law appeared to ignore the need for all the usual requirements of a contract to exist, such as offer, acceptance, consideration, intention etc, today such prerequisites seem necessary before a contractual licence can arise.

Categories of licences

✳✳✳✳✳✳✳✳✳✳

Termination

Historically, the licensor could revoke a contractual licence at any time, upon providing reasonable notice, even if it amounted to a breach of the contract upon which the licence was based. Where this was the case, the premature termination of the contract might allow the licensee to seek contractual damages, but no further remedy was available: *Wood v Leadbitter* (1845).

However, today, with the intervention of equity in some cases, this approach is changing. Where a contractual licence is given to occupy land for a specific period of time or specific purpose, the courts may be willing to imply that it is a term of the contract that the licence should not be revoked before this period has been completed or the purpose fulfilled. A threat of bringing the licence to an end before this can be achieved may be resolved by the intervention of equity in granting an injunction to restrain a breach of the licence.

....

Winter Garden Theatre (London) Ltd v Millennium Productions Ltd [1948] AC 173

A licence was granted to present plays in the licensor's theatre. The licensor purported to revoke the licence. It was found on the facts of the case that this particular licence was intended to be revocable and thus could be revoked upon giving reasonable notice. However, importantly, the House of Lords recognized that an injunction could be awarded to prevent a premature termination of a contractual licence in circumstances where it was intended to be irrevocable until a purpose had been fulfilled or a period of time completed.

....

In some circumstances, where the licensee has not yet taken possession of the land, an order for specific performance may be awarded where the licensor is refusing entry to a licensee who has a contractual right to enter.

....

Verrall v Great Yarmouth BC [1981] QB 202

The National Front had contracted to hire a hall for its annual conference. When the Labour council sought to revoke the licence, an order for specific performance was granted. Damages were deemed inadequate as the National Front had not been able to find an alternative venue. With the intervention of equity, the contractual licence was enforced and thus could not be revoked at will.

....

Despite the intervention of equity, as illustrated in the cases above, you must appreciate that this does not mean that all contractual licences will now be prevented from being revoked by the licensor when he wishes, with the implementation of equitable remedies. Remember that the provision of equitable remedies is subject to discretion and will only be provided in circumstances where damages for breach of contract appear inadequate. The question will be one of construction of the contract and whether, upon true construction of the contract, it was intended to be irrevocable (Megarry J in *Hounslow LBC v Twickenham Garden Developments Ltd* [1971]).

Where equitable remedies are not available, an action for assault may be brought in the event of being forcibly ejected from the land or refused entry on to it.

Enforcement against third parties

Traditionally, it was considered that contractual licences are not enforceable against third parties.

King v David Allen & Sons [1916] 2 AC 54

A contractual licence was granted to allow the licensee to affix posters to the wall of the licensor's cinema. When the licensor leased the cinema to a third party, it was held that the third party was not bound by this contractual licence and could refuse to allow the licensee to continue fixing posters to the cinema wall.

However, with the intervention of equitable relief making some contractual licences irrevocable in certain circumstances, this view has been subject to challenge. Indeed, some challengers have gone as far as to suggest that the use of equitable remedies, both to prevent premature revocation of contractual licences and to ensure their performance in accordance with the terms of the contract, not only makes contractual licences enforceable against third parties but also confers a proprietary status upon them. This was certainly the view of Lord Justice Denning in the case of *Errington v Errington & Woods* [1952].

✅ *Looking for extra marks?*

In *Errington v Errington & Woods* (1952) Denning LJ deemed that the availability of equitable remedies, enforceable against the licensor in order to prevent him from revoking the licence, gave rise to an 'equity' in favour of the licensee. This equity would then be enforceable against a third party according to the doctrine of notice and thus have the effect of conferring proprietary status upon a contractual licence. A comparison was drawn with the development of restrictive covenants. The willingness of equity to intervene and provide remedies in certain circumstances where restrictive covenants have been breached led to such rights gaining equitable proprietary status and thus the ability to bind third parties (see chapter 13). However, this approach was rejected by the House of Lords in *National Provincial Bank Ltd v Ainsworth* [1965]. The availability of an equitable remedy to enforce a right does not, by itself, make that right proprietary in nature. Other factors must be present, clearly demonstrated in the law of restrictive covenants where several conditions must be met before restrictive covenants can be enforced in equity against third parties.

Final clarification on the issue of enforceability against third parties was found in the case of *Ashburn Anstalt v Arnold* [1989].

Ashburn Anstalt v Arnold [1989] Ch 1

A shop was purchased for the purpose of development. It was sold to the purchaser expressly subject to a licence whereby the licensee would retain the shop rent free until the re-development took place. The court clearly found that contractual licences cannot bind successors in title. (On the facts of this case, the purported licence was in fact held to be a lease and was deemed binding upon the purchaser.)

By finding that contractual licences are not capable of binding third parties, which is an essential characteristic of a proprietary interest, the case of *Ashburn Anstalt v Arnold* [1989] has also determined that contractual licences do not have proprietary status. This is perhaps a sensible decision, as to rule otherwise might:

- blur the boundaries between licences and proprietary interests such as leases and easements; and
- lead to some land becoming inalienable by a subsequent increase in the number of proprietary interests existing over it.

However, it is true to say that if the facts of the case give rise to an estoppel or constructive trust, both of which are equitable proprietary interests capable of binding third parties, the licence may be protected and thus enforceable against a third party. This was held in *Ashburn Anstalt v Arnold* [1989] as being the true explanation for holding the licence to be binding against a third party in the case of *Errington v Errington & Woods* [1952].

 Looking for extra marks?

It is worth noting that the decision in the case of *Bruton v London & Quadrant Housing Trust* [2000], as discussed in chapter 6, has led to the existence of a contractual or non-proprietary lease. This lease, whilst having some of the characteristics of a proprietary term of years, such as the granting of exclusive possession, and the protection of Landlord and Tenant legislation, was found, unlike a proprietary term of years, not to be capable of binding a third party. This decision has clearly blurred the distinction between a contractual lease and a contractual licence.

Licences protected by constructive trusts

When do they arise?

Whilst it is true that any type of licence may be protected by the imposition of a constructive trust, a constructive trust most notably arise in respect of contractual licences.

In the case of *Ashburn Anstalt v Arnold* [1989] (discussed above), clarification was given as to the circumstances in which a constructive trust may arise to protect a licence. Fox LJ deemed that it would not be enough simply for a purchaser to agree to buy the land subject to the licence. Rather, that purchaser must have acted in such a way that it would be unconscionable for the licence to be denied. For example, that purchaser may have agreed to buy the land subject to the licence and consequently paid a lower price for that land. Any later attempt to deny the licence would thus be deemed inequitable.

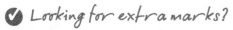 Looking for extra marks?

The imposition of a constructive trust upon a licence arrangement is a difficult one to reconcile, when you consider that the very nature of a trust creates a separation between legal and equitable title to the land. Where the trust is being imposed upon a licence to enter the land of another that falls short of actual occupation, there is no such separation of legal and equitable title. In these circumstances, how can a trust exist?

Enforcement against third parties

As an equitable proprietary interest, a constructive trust is capable of being enforced against third parties. In cases where it is protecting a licence, that licence is consequently also found capable of being enforced against third parties.

Binions v Evans [1972] Ch 359

Following her husband's death, a widow was given a licence to remain living rent free in a cottage she had shared with her husband. The property was then sold to a purchaser expressly subject to her rights and indeed this was reflected in the purchase price paid. The purchaser was found to take the property subject to a constructive trust in favour of the widow.

However, in *Ashburn Anstalt v Arnold* [1989], Fox LJ made it clear that the constructive trust which arises as a result of the particular conduct of the purchaser, will only be binding on that particular purchaser. It is not, strictly speaking, binding upon the actual land. Should this purchaser, who is bound to give effect to the licence by means of a constructive trust that has arisen as a result of his conduct, sell to another, this other will not be bound by the licence unless he too acts in such a way that it would be unconscionable to deny the licence.

Licences protected by an estoppel

When do they arise?

- One person, A, makes an assurance to another, B, that B can go on A's land and occupy it for a specific purpose or period of time. This assurance may come from conduct or words.

- B relies upon this assurance to his detriment. The detriment might be:
    - spending money (for example *Inwards v Baker* [1965]: a son was encouraged by his father to build a bungalow on his father's land. The encouragement given, together with the fact that it was acted upon by the son to his financial detriment, led the court to find the son had acquired a licence to occupy the bungalow for his lifetime.);
    - Making improvements to a property (for example *Dodsworth v Dodsworth* [1973]: having been assured that they could live in a bungalow for as long as they wanted

to, a couple spent money making improvements to the bungalow. Having acted upon this assurance to their detriment, they had acquired an estoppel allowing them to stay in the bungalow until such time as their expenditure had been reimbursed.);

– Changing your circumstances (for example *Crabb v Arun DC* [1976]: in relying upon an assurance that the claimant would be allowed a right of access across the defendant's land, the claimant sold land that provided him with an alternative route of access. The defendant was then estopped from denying the claimant the right of access he had assured him.).

The reliance must be reasonable and must have been known (or should have been known) by the person who gave the assurance.

• Where it would be unconscionable for A to go back on his assurance, taking into account the reliance placed upon it, and detriment consequently incurred, an estoppel will arise.

Termination

The existence of the estoppel allows equity to intervene and do justice in circumstances where it would be unjust for a person, such as a licensor, to deny rights of another, such as the licensee, even if those rights are not themselves proprietary in nature. The existence of the estoppel means that equity does not allow the licensor to revoke the licence at will so that the purpose or period for which the licence was given cannot be fulfilled.

Instead, discretion is exercised by the court in granting an equitable remedy in favour of the person whose rights are sought to be denied ie the licensee. What will be considered as an appropriate remedy depends upon the individual facts of the case and what is considered as necessary to do justice to the wronged party. Often, the remedy given entails making sure that the assurance that was given, is met.

Pascoe v Turner [1979] 1 WLR 431

A man encouraged his mistress to make improvements to a house on the assurance that it would be hers. When the man tried to evict her, the court found that an estoppel had arisen and ordered that the freehold in the property be transferred to her. The assurance that she had acted upon to her detriment was met.

Sometimes, the remedy may just require a repayment of the detriment suffered (see, for example *Dodsworth v Dodsworth* [1973], as discussed above).

What is clear is that where a licence is protected by an estoppel, the remedies available to protect that licence are more flexible and far reaching than the equitable remedies available to enforce contractual licences (limited to injunctions and orders of specific performance, as discussed above).

Enforcement against third parties

An estoppel is an equitable proprietary interest and is therefore deemed capable of binding third parties. Where an estoppel has arisen to protect a licence, the licence's association with that estoppel will make that licence capable of being enforced against third parties: *Ives v High* [1967].

Where title to land is registered, a licence protected by an estoppel may be enforceable against a third party by virtue of s 116 LRA 2002. Where the licensee, benefitting from the estoppel protection, is also in actual occupation of the land, his right may bind as an overriding interest under Sch 3 para 2 LRA 2002 (see chapter 3).

Where title to land is unregistered, a licence protected by an estoppel may be enforceable against a third party where that third party is not a *bona fide* purchaser of a legal estate for value without notice: (see the doctrine of notice as discussed in chapter 2 and 4).

What type of licence will arise?

The type of licence that is found to exist, be it a contractual one, one protected by an estoppel, or the imposition of a constructive trust, may ultimately depend upon the remedy that is being sought. Clearly, if an estoppel or constructive trust is to be relied upon to protect a licence, the characteristics upon which they are based must be present. Constructive trusts are largely a construct of intention. Where no such intention is found, then an estoppel will have to be relied upon for the licence to be protected. Ultimately, there appears to be a flexible approach adopted by the courts as to the construct it finds in existence to achieve the result it desires.

What is important to remember is that for a licence to be capable of being enforced against a third party, either an estoppel must have arisen or a constructive trust must be found to have been imposed. A licence, existing by itself, has no such capability.

 Key cases

Case	Facts	Principle
Ashburn Anstalt v Arnold [1989] Ch 1	A shop was purchased for the purpose of development. It was sold to the purchaser expressly subject to a licence whereby the licensee would retain the shop rent free until the redevelopment took place. It was held that the purported licence was in fact a lease and this was deemed binding upon the purchaser.	Contractual licences are not proprietary interests and cannot bind third parties. However, where the facts are such that a constructive trust or estoppel arises, protecting the licence, the licence may be enforceable against a third party.

Key cases

✳✳✳✳✳✳✳✳✳✳✳

Case	Facts	Principle
Binions v Evans [1972] Ch 359	A widow was given a licence to remain living rent free in a cottage she had shared with her husband following her husband's death. The property was then sold to a purchaser expressly subject to her rights and indeed this was reflected in the purchase price paid. The purchaser was found to take the property subject to a constructive trust in favour of the widow.	Where a licence is protected by a constructive trust, that licence may be enforceable against a third party.
King v David Allen & Sons [1916] 2 AC 54	A contractual licence was granted to allow the licensee to affix posters to the wall of the licensor's cinema. The right to do so was found not to be binding against a third party.	Contractual licences are not capable of binding a third party.
Pascoe v Turner [1979] 1 WLR 431	A man encouraged his mistress to make improvements to a house on the assurance that it would be hers. When the man tried to evict her, the court found that an estoppel had arisen and ordered that the freehold in the property be transferred to her. The assurance that she had acted upon to her detriment was met.	Where a licence protected by an estoppel has been infringed, the appropriate equitable remedy will be determined in accordance with making sure that justice is achieved for the wronged party.
Verrall v Great Yarmouth BC [1981] QB 202	An attempt to revoke a contractual licence granted to the National Front in respect of hiring a hall for its annual conference, was met with an order of specific performance against the licensor to enforce the licence.	An order for specific performance may be awarded where a licensor is refusing entry to a licensee who has a contractual right to enter.
Winter Garden Theatre (London) Ltd v Millennium Productions Ltd [1948] AC 173	A contractual licence to present plays in the licensor's theatre was deemed to be revocable upon giving reasonable notice.	An injunction could be awarded to prevent a premature termination of a contractual licence in circumstances where it was intended to be irrevocable until a purpose had been fulfilled or a period of time completed.

Exam questions

Problem question

Albert is the registered freehold proprietor of a large estate which includes a wooded area.

In 2000 Albert entered into an oral agreement with Brian. Brian is a sculptor of wood. Albert agreed that Brian could take any fallen wood to use in his sculptures for as long as he wanted. In return Brian gives Albert an occasional sculpture.

Albert's friend Colin is a poet. He finds sitting in the wood inspires some of his best poems. In 2003 Albert tells Colin that he can sit in the wood as much as he likes.

In 2006 Albert enters into an agreement with one of his neighbours, David. The agreement is in writing. Albert agrees that David can store some farm machinery on Albert's land for five years. In return David agrees to pay five hundred pounds a year.

In 2008 Albert decides to sell the whole of the estate including the wooded area to Eric. He conveys the land to Eric who becomes registered freehold proprietor. Before the conveyance he tells Eric about David but does not mention Brian and Colin.

Eric is now refusing access to Brian, Colin and David.

Advise the parties.

An outline answer is available at the end of the book

Essay question

Whilst licences are rights connected to the use of land they are unusual since, in theory at least, they do not confer any proprietary interest upon the licensee and thus the protection they afford a licensee is limited.

Discuss.

An outline answer is available online at www.oxfordtextbooks.co.uk/orc/concentrate/

#12

Easements and profits

The examination

This is a largely self-contained topic area and the principle focus of a question is usually on easements, but bear in mind that *profits à prendre* may pop up as a minor element of a question. In addition, aspects of enforcement of easements against third parties may be examined within a question, which is discussed in this chapter but also link to chapters 3 and 4.

A typical problem question will require you to:

1. identify the rights being claimed as easements;

2. assess whether such rights have the capacity to be easements by considering the requirements from *Re Ellenborough Park* [1956]. (Where they do not, you may be required to assess what type of right they could be, whether personal, such as a licence (see chapter 11) or proprietary, such as a lease (see chapter 6));

3. where capacity is established, assess whether they have been acquired as easements;

4. where acquired appropriately, assess whether they are legal or equitable; check they have not been extinguished and consider remedies where there is actual or threatened infringement.

Any issues that may arise regarding enforcement of the easements against third parties can be dealt with by applying the appropriate rules, dependent firstly upon whether they exist over registered or unregistered land, and secondly whether they are legal or equitable.

Essay questions may focus upon whether the boundaries have been set appropriately as to what can and cannot amount to an easement. This might involve discussion of those rights that fall outside the boundaries, such as licences. Alternatively, questions may focus on a particular aspect of the law, for example acquisition, and require you to analyse how the law works and whether reform is required.

Key facts

- An easement gives either a positive or, less often, a negative right of use over land of another (the servient land), which must be seen to benefit a dominant piece of land.

- For a right to be capable of being an easement, it must satisfy the four requirements under *Re Ellenborough Park* [1956].

- Even where such requirements are satisfied, a right may not be an easement if the exercise of that right requires expenditure by the servient owner, amounts to exclusive possession of the servient land, or is not exercisable as of right.

- A right that is capable of being an easement will only become an easement where it has been acquired by one of the recognized methods of acquisition.

- Where a person claims to have been granted an easement by another over land of that other, this may be substantiated by evidence of an express grant. Alternatively, where there is no such evidence, a court may imply the easement was granted out of necessity, common intention, the operation of s 62 LPA 1925 or the rule in *Wheeldon v Burrows* (1879).

- Where a person claims to have reserved an easement in his favour over land he has transferred to another, this may be substantiated by evidence of an express reservation. Where there is no such evidence, a court may imply the easement was reserved out of necessity or common intention. Acquisition by the operation of s 62 LPA 1925 or the rule in *Wheeldon v Burrows* (1879) is not available.

- Alternatively, an easement may have been acquired out of long use, known as prescription, of which there are three modes: common law, lost modern grant and the Prescription Act 1832.

- An easement can be either legal or equitable in status, depending upon which formalities have been satisfied. The status of an easement will determine the relevant rules governing the enforcement of that interest against a third party. These rules differ depending upon whether the easement exists over registered or unregistered land.

Chapter overview

Chapter overview

An easement gives either a positive or, less often, a negative right of use over land of another (the servient land), which must be seen to benefit a dominant piece of land.

To be capable of being an easement, the right must satisfy the four requirements under *Re Ellenbrough Park* [1956]:

1. there must be a dominant land and a servient land;
2. the right must accommodate the dominant land;
3. there must be diversity of ownership and/or occupation of the dominant and servient lands; and
4. the right must lie in grant.

Even where these requirements are met, the right cannot be an easement if its exercise:

1. requires the servient owner to spend money; or
2. amounts to exclusive possession of the servient land; or
3. is not as exercisable of right.

Once deemed capable of being an easement, it must be established that the right has been acquired as an easement by one of the recognized methods of acquisition:

- Express grant or reservation
- Implied...
- Prescription

Grant by virtue of either:
- necessity
- common intention
- s 62 LPA 1925; or
- *Wheeldon v Burrows* (1879)

Reservation by virtue of either:
- necessity; or
- common intention

Either:
- common law
- lost modern grant
- **Prescription Act 1832**

The easement acquired may be legal or equitable depending upon the formalities that have been satisfied.

Whether the burden of an established easement binds a successor in title to the servient land will depend upon:

1. whether the easement is legal or equitable in status; and
2. whether it exists over registered or unregistered land.

The benefit of an established easement will pass to a successor in title to the dominant land by virtue of **s 62 LPA 1925**

Remedies where an easement has been infringed include:
- abatement
- damages

where infringement is threatened, an injunction may be sought.

Termination of easements is possible by:
- merger
- release

Introduction

An **easement** is a right over the land of another, either positive in nature, allowing you to use the land of another in a particular way (for example, a right to store), or, less frequently, negative in nature, requiring another to refrain from certain action over his own land (for example, a right to light). It gives no right of possession or occupation over the land, save to the extent that is required to enjoy that right.

It is one of the proprietary interests that is capable of being legal (s 1(2) Law of Property Act 1925), if created in the appropriate way (see below).

Capability

To be an easement, a right must satisfy the four requirements laid down in *Re Ellenborough Park* [1956]:

1. There must be a **dominant** and **servient tenement**.
2. The right must accommodate the dominant tenement.
3. There must be diversity of ownership and/or occupation of the dominant and servient tenements.
4. The right must lie in grant.

There must be a dominant and servient tenement

There must be two separate and identifiable pieces of land: one that enjoys the benefit of the easement (the dominant tenement), and one that is burdened by the exercise of the easement (the servient tenement): *London & Blenheim Estates v Ladbroke Retail Parks Ltd* [1994]. An easement cannot exist **'in gross'** ie unattached to a dominant piece of land.

Revision Tip

Remember that if a person is given a right to use land of another independently of any land that he may own (ie where there is no dominant tenement), that right is likely to be a mere licence (discussed in chapter 11). Some examiners may link the two topics.

The right must accommodate the dominant tenement

To meet this requirement you are looking for evidence that the right makes the dominant tenement a better and more convenient property. This improvement to the utility of the dominant tenement should be something connected to its normal enjoyment and apply indifferently to any owner of that land. In other words, rather than conferring a mere personal benefit on the current owner, incidental to his ownership of the land, it must be shown to confer an advantage on the actual dominant tenement itself.

Capability

✱✱✱✱✱✱✱✱✱✱✱

Hill v Tupper (1863) 2 H&C 121

A claim to an exclusive right to put boats on a canal was rejected as an easement. The business monopoly that the right created did not make occupation of the land on the bank of the canal (the dominant tenement) better or more convenient. Rather it created a mere commercial advantage for the particular tenant of that land.

That is not to say that rights connected to commercial activity can never be easements.

Moody v Steggles (1879) 12 Ch D 261

The right to put an advertisement on a neighbour's property advertising a pub was held to be an easement. The trade of running a pub on the dominant tenement was a necessary incident to the normal enjoyment of that land. The business had been present on the land for hundreds of years. Therefore, the business and the land had become intertwined, to such an extent that something benefiting the business would also benefit the land itself. Future owners of that land would see it as a benefit to have this right and thus it was clearly not merely personal to the current owner.

Ultimately, whether a right accommodates the dominant tenement is a question of fact. An enhancement to the value of that land may be evidence of accommodation but is not, by itself, conclusive of that fact: *Re Ellenborough Park* [1956].

What is certain, is that if a right is going to be deemed to accommodate the dominant tenement, the dominant and servient tenements must be sufficiently proximate to one another: *Bailey v Stephens* (1862); although the two pieces of land need not be next to each other: *Pugh v Savage* [1970].

There must be diversity of ownership and/or occupation of the dominant and servient tenements

You cannot enjoy an easement against your own land: *Roe v Siddons* (1888). Such enjoyment amounts to a **quasi easement**; something that has the potential to become an easement should diversity of ownership/occupation of the land subsequently arise. This may occur, for example, when you sell part of your land to another (see later under the *Wheeldon v Burrows* (1879) rule).

The right must lie in grant

Since an easement is a right capable of existing at law, it must be capable of being granted by deed. This essentially involves looking for three separate requirements:

A capable grantor and grantee

There must be two separate legal personalities, each having legal capacity ie be of sound mind, over 18 years old etc.

A right that is capable of reasonably exact definition

This is so the servient owner knows the full extent of his obligation. A right to a scenic view, for example, could never be an easement since defining what is scenic rests too heavily upon subjective views: *William Aldred's Case* (1610).

In other cases, a right, normally capable of being an easement, may fail to meet this requirement simply because of ambiguities within the documentation: *Chaffe v Kingsley* (2000).

A right that is within the nature of rights traditionally recognised as easements

Where the right in question has not been given judicial recognition in the past, this does not mean that the right could not be an easement. You need to consider two further authorities:

In *Dyce v Lady James Hay* (1852), it was held that the list of recognized easements is not closed. The categories of easements may expand to take into account social changes that take place. So, just because a right has not been given judicial recognition as an easement in the past, does not mean that it will not be given such recognition in the future.

However, this has to be qualified with the acknowledgement that the courts will not recognise new negative easements: *Phipps v Pears* [1965].

✅ Looking for extra marks?

Arguably, today with the development of the law of restrictive covenants, any attempts to restrict what a landowner can do over his own land are now better served by establishing restrictive covenants. This may be the motivation for declining to recognise new negative covenants. In some cases, decisions have also been influenced by public policy. In *Hunter v Canary Wharf Ltd* [1997], the House of Lords rejected the claim of an easement to receive a television signal. To allow such an easement would have prevented the defendant from being able to build on its land, itself not desirable considering the positive economic impact such building works would have.

Additional factors

Where you have succeeded in satisfying the four *Re Ellenborough Park* [1956] criteria outlined above, the right in question may be capable of being an easement. However, there are three additional factors that could defeat such a claim and you must give them consideration where appropriate, before drawing your conclusions regarding capability.

The right must not require any expenditure on the part of the servient owner

Whilst the servient landowner is under an obligation to refrain from taking any action that would impede the enjoyment of an easement, he should be under no obligation to spend money so as to enable the dominant landowner to enjoy the right: *Regis Property Co Ltd v Redman* [1956]. This is subject to one exception being the spurious easement of a right to fence, where the servient owner is required to fence his land for the purpose of enclosing livestock: *Crow v Wood* [1971].

Capability

✳✳✳✳✳✳✳✳✳✳

Revision tip

Remember, expenditure does not include costing the servient owner by him losing money. The question is rather whether the servient owner has to spend money for the right to be exercised.

You should also remember that the servient owner is under no obligation to maintain and repair so as to enable the right to be enjoyed: *Jones v Pritchard* [1908]. A servient owner's only obligation in this respect is to allow the dominant owner access onto the servient land, so that the dominant owner may carry out the repair and maintenance for himself. Such rights of access have now been incorporated into the **Access of Neighbouring Land Act 1992**. The right to enter another's land for the purpose of repair and maintenance under this Act is not, itself, an easement, but rather a licence.

Of course, there may be cases where the parties agree, either expressly or impliedly, that the servient owner will bear the cost of repair and maintenance as in *Liverpool City Council v Irwin* [1977].

The right must not amount to exclusive possession of the servient land

Revision tip

This requirement is often used to assess your ability to apply the law to a novel set of facts. To do well, make sure you know the case law, both facts and legal reasoning behind the decisions, so that you can draw good comparisons and distinctions between the cases and the facts in your question and thus strengthen your overall conclusions.

Where the exercise of the right precludes the servient landowner from having reasonable use of the servient land for himself, it will be rejected as an easement: *Copeland v Greenhalf* [1952].

This may be determined by looking at the extent to which the physical space of the servient land is being used by the dominant landowner. This is especially the case when trying to establish whether a right to store is an easement. Where storage takes up most of the space, leaving little or none for the servient owner to use for himself, the right may be rejected as an easement: *Grigsby v Melville* [1974].

This approach has also been adopted when looking at whether a right to park can exist as an easement.

Hair v Gillman (2000) 80 P&CR 108

The right to park on a forecourt that could accommodate four cars was held to be an easement. Even when the right was being exercised by the dominant owner, there remained three other parking spaces available for the servient owner's use. The servient owner thus retained reasonable use of the forecourt for himself.

In contrast:

....

Batchelor v Marlow [2003] 1 WLR 764

The right to park a car in a parking space between 8.30am and 6.00pm Monday to Friday was rejected as an easement. Although the exercise of the right did not amount to exclusive use of the physical space by the dominant owner, since the servient owner could have used the space at night and on weekends, it would have precluded the servient owner from using the space during working hours. Considering the parking space related to business premises, the court concluded that if the right existed it would preclude the servient owner from reasonable use of the space for himself.

....

✅ *Looking for extra marks?*

When assessing whether there is exclusive possession, the case law above shows that the court may consider not only the extent to which the physical space is being used, but also the nature of the land itself. In addition, it might also consider the nature of the right actually being claimed. A right to use a neighbour's toilet, for example, was accepted as an easement in *Miller v Emcer Products* [1956]. This was despite the fact that when it was exercised the whole of the physical space of the toilet was being used by the dominant owner to the exclusion of the servient owner. The nature of the right made this inevitable and yet it did not ouster the servient owner's rights over the space completely. The physical occupation of the toilet by the dominant owner was not constant and thus the servient owner retained reasonable user of the toilet for himself.

The right must be one exercised as of right

Whilst there will initially be an element of permission given by the servient owner when the easement is being created initially, the dominant owner must not have to seek constant permission every time he wishes to exercise that right thereafter. It must not be precarious upon the constant approval of the servient owner.

Where a right has passed all of the above hurdles, it is merely one *capable* of being an easement. To actually become an easement, it must have been acquired in one of the recognized ways.

Acquisition of easements

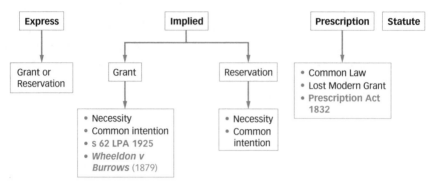

Figure 12.1

Express

An easement may arise by incorporating express words of creation into a deed. For example, X, the vendor, decides to sell part of his land to Y, the purchaser. In the deed transferring the legal estate to Y, an easement may be expressly *granted* in favour of Y for the benefit of the land that he is purchasing. Alternatively, an easement may be expressly *reserved* in favour of X for the benefit of the land he is retaining.

Implied

Where express words creating an easement do not appear in the actual documentation, a court may be willing to imply such words are present. It will, however, be less willing to do so in favour of a transferor claiming to have reserved an easement for himself over land that he is transferring to another. The general expectation, in these circumstances, is that the transferor should expressly reserve for himself any rights that he wishes to exercise over the land that he is transferring. So, whilst a court may be willing to imply that an easement has been granted in four different circumstances, only two (necessity and common intention) can be used to imply that an easement has been reserved: *Re Webbs Lease* [1951].

Necessity

A court may be willing to imply an easement has been acquired in circumstances where the land in question cannot, in fact, be used without having the benefit of that easement. The easement in question has to be essential to the use of the land, rather than merely desirable: *Pryce v McGuiness* [1966]. Fundamentally, this has limited acquisition of easements by this means to rights of way and only in circumstances where the land would be landlocked without the right of way being implied. It would not be possible to acquire a right of way out of necessity where alternative, even if less convenient, access routes to the land are available: *Manjang v Drammah* [1990].

✅ *Looking for extra marks?*

It is clear that this method of acquisition is dependent upon the parties' intention. In *Nickerson v Barraclough* [1981], a piece of land was purchased and the document transferring the legal estate of that land to the purchaser, expressly stated that the vendor was not also granting the purchaser a right of way over land that the vendor retained. The court was unwilling to see that the right of way had been impliedly granted to the purchaser out of necessity, despite the fact that the land sold to the purchaser was landlocked without such a right. There was no public policy to grant the right. The purchaser had simply entered into a bad deal and should sue his conveyancer for the misfortune of ending up with an unusable piece of land.

Common intention

A court may be willing to imply the acquisition of an easement in circumstances where the parties' mutual intention is for the land to be used in a particular way and the easement in question is absolutely essential to fulfilling that intention.

....

Wong v Beaumont Property Trust Ltd [1965] 1 QB 173

A lease was granted over a cellar specifically for use as a restaurant. In order to comply with health and safety regulations, a ventilation system was required to be fixed to the landlord's property. An implied easement to fix such a system was found to exist as, without such a right, the tenant could not use the cellar for the purpose intended by the lease.

....

In determining whether an easement would be implied out of common intention, you should therefore ask yourself two questions:

- What use of the dominant land have the parties mutually intended?
- Is the right being claimed essential for that use to be fulfilled?

Where the answer to the second question is yes, an easement may be implied. Where the answer is no, a court may not be willing to imply acquisition by way of common intention.

How does this mode of acquisition differ from necessity?

An easement will be implied by way of necessity where it is essential for *any* use of the land to be enjoyed. An easement will be implied out of common intention where it is essential for the land to be enjoyed for the specific *purpose* which the parties have mutually intended.

Section 62 LPA 1925

Revision tip

Remember, this mode of acquisition cannot be relied upon in a reservation scenario. It can only operate in favour of a grantee (eg a purchaser), not a grantor (eg a vendor).

Acquisition of easements

✴✴✴✴✴✴✴✴✴✴

This section is essentially a word-saving provision. It has the effect of automatically passing to a successor in title all existing rights, privileges, easements etc attached to the land without the need for express mention in the conveyance. Judicial interpretation of the operation of this section has given it an even wider effect so that, in some circumstances, it will convert a mere licence upon conveyance into a legal easement.

> ### Wright v Macadam [1949] 2 KB 744
>
> A tenant's revocable licence to store coal in a coal shed converted, upon the granting of a new lease, into a legal easement to store.

However, to establish acquisition of a legal easement by virtue of s 62 LPA 1925, you must satisfy all of the following:

- **There must be a conveyance**
  Defined in s 205 LPA 1925, it includes:
  - a legal sale of a freehold;
  - a grant of a legal lease over three years in duration;
  - a grant of a legal lease less than three years in duration in writing;
  - an assent by personal representatives.

  It will not include:
  - a contract to purchase/lease land;
  - an oral grant of a legal lease less than three years in duration orally (*Rye v Rye* [1962]);
  - a will.

- **The right must exist at the date of the conveyance**
  Section 62 cannot be used to revive rights that were used in the far past: *Penn v Wilkins* (1974).

- **There must be prior diversity of occupation between the dominant and servient lands immediately before the conveyance:** *Sovmots Investments v Secretary of State for the Environment* [1979].
  Without such diversity, it would be difficult to identify any 'rights', 'privileges' etc that come under the operation of s 62 LPA 1925.

 ✓ Looking for extra marks?

There has since been some debate as to whether this condition needs to be met in all cases. In the Court of Appeal decision of *P&S Platt v Crouch* [2004], Peter Gibson LJ observed that it would not be necessary to establish prior diversity where the right in question was continuous and apparent (requirements identified under the rule in *Wheeldon v Burrows* (1879) as discussed below). Arguably, however, the *obiter* statement regarding the need for prior diversity made in the House of Lords decision of *Sovmots* still stands as a requirement for s 62 LPA 1925 to operate. *P&S Platt v Crouch* failed to consider the *Sovmots* decision when passing judgment and, if correct, would limit any role the rule in *Wheeldon v Burrows* (1879) might have in the implied acquisition of easements. (Note, it is accepted that no requirement of prior diversity is required where the right in question is a right to light: *Payne v Inwood* (1996).)

- **There must be no contrary intention**
  It is possible for the parties to exclude the operation of s 62 LPA 1925: s 62(4) LPA 1925.

Wheeldon v Burrows *(1879)*

Revision Tip

Remember, this mode of acquisition cannot be relied upon in a reservation scenario. It can only operate in favour of a grantee (eg a purchaser), not a grantor (eg a vendor).

This rule has the effect of elevating quasi easements ie those rights exercised over, and for the benefit of, your own land, into full easements, whether legal or equitable.

For example, X owns and occupies a large plot of land, which has a house on the western boundary of the plot. Out of convenience, he uses a short cut across his land to get from his house to the main road on the eastern boundary of the property. Whilst X owns and occupies the whole plot, this right has the status of a quasi easement. Should X decide to transfer part of his land, including the house, to another, Y, the benefit of the short cut which X had previously enjoyed and exercised may also transfer to Y and in so doing, elevate into a full easement. Likewise, should X decide to split the plot into two and have a contemporaneous sale of both parts, each transferee will acquire as an easement any quasi easements that were exercised prior to the transfer for the benefit of the land they now own: *Swansborough v Coventry* (1832).

Once again, you need to establish a number of conditions if an easement is to be acquired by this mode:

- **There must be common ownership and occupation of the potential dominant and servient lands prior to the transfer**

- **The right must be continuous and apparent**
  A right will be continuous where there is evidence that it has been used regularly. It need not be incessant use, but it must be regular enough to convey a degree of permanence.
  A right will be apparent where it is discoverable upon careful physical inspection of the property. For example, a worn tarmac road across a field would make a right of way across the field apparent: *Hansford v Jago* [1921].

An example of a right that was not found to be continuous and apparent was a right to take water from a neighbours pump from time to time: *Polden v Bastard* (1865).

- **The right must be necessary for the reasonable enjoyment of the dominant land**
  The right must facilitate reasonable enjoyment of the property. It need not be something that it absolutely essential for the land to be enjoyed but has to be more than a mere

convenience: *Wheeler v JJ Saunders Ltd* [1996]. So in *Goldberg v Edwards* (1950), a right to access an annexe to a house via an indoor passageway, was not acquired under the rule in *Wheeldon v Burrows* (1879), since the annexe could be accessed by an outdoor passage. However, in *Borman v Griffith* [1930], a secondary access route to the dominant land was acquired under the rule in *Wheeldon v Burrows* (1879) since it was the only means by which to access the front door to the house and was the only practical access route for heavy vehicles involved in the claimant's business.

 Looking for extra marks?

There has been some debate as to whether the two tests above both have to be met or whether they are alternatives. Indeed, the case of *Wheeldon v Burrows* (1879) is ambiguous on the issue. In the case of *Ward v Kirkland* [1967] a suggestion arose that the requirement the right be necessary for reasonable enjoyment related to the acquisition of negative easements. Acquisition of positive easements need only be continuous and apparent. However, the dominant view is that both requirements must be met. Perhaps, as was suggested in the case of *Wheeler v JJ Saunders* [1996], this is inevitable since the two requirements tend to interact with one another; if something is found to be necessary for reasonable enjoyment, it is also likely that it will be found to be continuous and apparent.

- **The right must be used, for the benefit of the piece of land that it to become dominant, immediately before the grant**
  This does not mean that the right was actually being used at that exact time. Rather it requires that the right was exercised in the recent past and it was expected that it would be exercised again sometime in the near future.

- **There must be no contrary intention**
  The parties can exclude acquisition of easements by this method: *Borman v Griffith* [1930].

Key similarities between s 62 LPA **and** *Wheeldon v Burrows* (1879)

- Both modes require the right to be capable of being an easement; and
- both modes can be excluded by the parties from operating.

Key distinctions between s 62 LPA 1925 **and** *Wheeldon v Burrows* (1879)

Figure 12.2

	Section 62 LPA 1925	***Wheeldon v Burrows* (1879)**
Situation	Can only apply where, prior to the transfer of the dominant land, there is diversity of occupation between the dominant and servient lands	Can only apply where, prior to the transfer of the dominant land, both the servient and dominant lands are under common ownership and occupation

Figure 12.2 *(continued)*

	Section 62 LPA 1925	***Wheeldon v Burrows* (1879)**
Transaction	Can only operate where there is a conveyance of land (see above)	Can operate upon a conveyance or a valid contract of land
Type of right	The right must be one that exists at the date of the conveyance	The right must be one that is continuous and apparent, and reasonably necessary for the enjoyment of the land. It must also be in use at the date of the grant

Prescription

This mode of acquisition allows for the creation of easements which have been exercised over the land of another for a long period of time, but where no actual grant of the right can be traced.

There are three modes of **prescription**:

* Common Law

* Lost Modern Grant

* Prescription Act 1832

Regardless of the mode under consideration, you must first satisfy three conditions if you are to be successful in establishing an easement has been acquired.

Figure 12.3

The user must be 'as of right'	It must have been exercised: • *nec vi* – without force. The user must not have been contentious in any way. • *nec clam* – without secrecy. The user must be open, such that a reasonable person would have the opportunity to discover its exercise. • *nec precario* – without permission, whether written or oral. Mere tolerance or acquiescence (knowledge of the user but abstaining to stop it where it is within your power to do so) of the exercise of the right, without any express permission, will not defeat a possible claim to an easement being acquired by prescription: *Mills v Silver* [1991].
The user must be 'continuous'	This may be intermittent provided there is a reasonably uniform quality to the frequency of user and intervals between use are not excessive. Use of a right 3 times in 20 years was deemed insufficiently continuous in *Hollins v Verney* (1884).

Figure 12.3 *(continued)*

The user must be by/on behalf of one fee simple owner against another fee simple owner	The claimant must show that either he is the fee simple owner of the dominant tenement or, if he is the tenant of that land, show that he is claiming the right on behalf of the fee simple owner. An easement cannot be acquired by prescription where a tenant occupies the servient tenement, unless it can be established that the use of the right began before the tenant took occupation, against the fee simple owner: *Pugh v Savage* [1970].

Where the three conditions above have been satisfied, you then have to ask yourself whether the right has been used for the requisite period of time. This will differ depending upon the particular mode of prescription you are seeking to rely upon.

Common law

The user must be shown to have been exercised since time immemorial ie 1189. This will be presumed where the claimant can show that the right has been enjoyed for 20 years (which need not be the 20 years immediately prior to the action). This presumption will be rebutted where there is evidence that the right could not have been enjoyed since 1189, for example a claim to a right of light through a window of a house that had only been built in the 1800's, or evidence that the dominant and servient tenements had been in common ownership some-time after 1189.

Lost modern grant

Where 20 years or more user can be established, the court is willing to presume a valid grant of that right was given some time in the past ie that a deed was executed granting that right in 'modern times' (post 1189), but that that document has since been lost.

It is not possible to rebut this presumption with evidence that in fact no grant was ever made: *Tehidy Minerals v Norman* [1971]. The presumption can only be rebutted if it can be shown that such a grant was legally impossible, perhaps, for example, because there was no legally competent grantor throughout the period of use: *Oakley v Boston* [1976].

Prescription Act 1832

All easements other than right to light

An easement may be acquired where you can establish either 20 or 40 years uninterrupted use as of right. Unlike under common law, acquisition will not be defeated by showing that the use began some time after 1189.

What is the difference between the two time periods?

When relying upon 20 years uninterrupted use, a claim will be defeated where it is shown to be based upon either oral or written consent. However, where the use continues for 40 years, the existence of oral permission will not defeat a claim. Only if the use as of right is exercised with written consent will a claim be defeated.

When must the 20 or 40 years period of user occur?
It must be the period immediately before the claim is litigated. The period of user must continue up to the date of the action. Where there is a gap between the period of user and the issuing of the writ, acquisition under the Prescription Act will be of no use, irrespective of the length of user.

What will amount to an 'interruption'?
An interruption in use, that has been submitted to or acquiesced in by the dominant owner for at least a year, will defeat a claim. So interruptions for less than a year will be disregarded. This effectively means that a claim could be established where interruption occurs within the twentieth year ie before 20 years full user can be established. In *Flight v Thomas* (1841), the dominant owner enjoyed the use of an easement as of right for 19 years and 11 months, when the use was then interrupted. A few months passed before the writ was issued. Since, at the date of the issue of the writ, there had been at least 20 years user as of right and the interruption was for less then one year, the right was deemed acquired under the Prescription Act.

Right to light

Twenty years' uninterrupted use of the right immediately prior to an action being taken will result in an 'absolute and indefeasible' easement being acquired, unless it is being enjoyed with written consent (s 3). What amounts to an interruption is the same as above. In addition, under the Rights to Light Act 1959, the servient owner can register a 'light obstruction notice' as a local land charge, thus interrupting user as of right.

Statute

This would cover, for example, the right for an electricity company to put pylons up over land belonging to another.

Status of the easement acquired

Once you have established that a right is capable of being, and has been acquired as, an easement, whether expressly or by a process of implication, you should then consider whether it is legal or equitable. Essentially, an easement will be:

Legal when:	Equitable when:
• created by a competent grantor; and • created by deed: s 52 LPA 1925 (deed requirements in s1 Law of Property (Miscellaneous Provisions) Act 1989); and • equivalent in duration to one of the legal estates in land: s 1(2)(a) LPA 1925; and	• created merely in compliance with s 53(1)(a) LPA 1925; or • created merely by an equitable estate owner; or • an attempt to create a legal easement fails to meet all legal formalities, provided this failed attempt amounts

- where expressly acquired (by grant or reservation) in respect of registered land, registered in accordance with **s 27(2)(d) Land Registration Act 2002**.

to a valid contract (**s 2 LP(MP)A 1989**) that is specifically enforceable: *Walsh v Lonsdale* (1882).

Remember, that these formalities must be met irrespective of whether the easement has arisen expressly or through implication. The status of an implied easement will largely depend upon the nature of the document into which the courts are implying it has been acquired. Where this document is a deed then, subject to satisfying all other requirements above, the easement has the potential to be legal. But where the courts are implying an easement has been acquired in a contract, for example, at best, it could only have equitable status.

Enforcement of the easement against third parties

Whether an easement that has been acquired is legal or equitable holds particular importance when determining whether a successor in title to the servient land is bound by any easements burdening that land.

Essentially:

Registered land

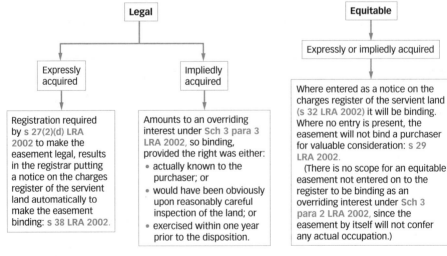

Figure 12.4

Unregistered land

Legal	Equitable
Bind the whole world	Where registered as a Class D(iii) land charge it will be binding: s 198 LPA 1925. Where not registered, it will not bind a purchaser of a legal estate for money/'s worth: s 4(6) Land Charges Act 1972.

Figure 12.5

Revision tip

Link your revision here to relevant material discussed in both chapters 3 and 4 on the issue of enforcement of interests against third parties.

Remember that the benefit of an easement appertaining to the dominant land will automatically pass to the successor in title of that land by virtue of s 62 LPA 1925.

Termination of easements

Merger

Where there is union of ownership of the fee simple of both the dominant and servient tenements, easements existing for the benefit of what was the dominant land, will cease. They will not be later revived if the lands come into separate ownership again in the future.

Where there is union of occupation, any existing easements will cease to exist, although these could be later revived should occupation of the lands separate again some time in the future.

Release

Express

This should be done by deed although if done in a valid contract, the release from the burden will be effective in equity. Where the servient owner acts on a promise that he has been released from the burden of an easement to his detriment, the dominant owner may be estopped from denying the easement has been extinguished.

Implied

Mere non-user of the easement is not sufficient, although if the easement has not been used for a long period, it could lead to a presumption of abandonment, provided there is some evidence of intention to that effect.

Statute

For example, where a compulsory purchase order is made by a local authority.

Remedies

Abatement

A self-help remedy allowing the dominant owner to remove any obstruction that prevents him from enjoying the exercise of the easement. He must do so without using any unreasonable force or injuring any person. Its use should be limited to cases of urgency. Preference should be to seek remedy through the courts.

Damages

To be awarded, there must be some substantial interference with the enjoyment of the easement, rather than a mere trivial incident: *Weston v Lawrence Weaver Ltd* [1961].

Injunction

To restrain the interference of the right that the dominant owner complains of, although it will not be justified where the infringement is trivial or temporary.

Profits à prendre

These allow a person to go onto the land of another, the servient land, and take either part of the natural produce of the land, itself capable of ownership (for example crops but not water), or animals. The exercise of the right may or may not be for the benefit of a dominant tenement. Where it is not, the profit exists '*in gross*'. It can be unrestricted as to the amount that can be taken from the land and amounts to a personal right.

Where it is for the benefit of a dominant piece of land, it is known as a profit appurtenant and the conditions necessary for a right to exist as an easement would equally apply. The profit is restricted as to the amount that can be taken from the land and amounts to a proprietary interest.

Key cases

Case	Facts	Principle
Batchelor v Marlow [2003] 1 WLR 764	The right to park a car in a commercial parking space between 8.30am and 6.00pm Monday to Friday was held not to be an easement as it amounted to exclusive possession. The servient owner would only want to use the parking space during business hours and to recognize the right as an easement would have prevented him from doing so.	The exercise of an easement must not exclude the servient owner from having reasonable use of the servient land for himself. The nature of the land in question shall be taken into account when making this assessment.
Copeland v Greenhalf [1952] Ch 488	A right to store vehicles on a narrow strip of land was held not to be an easement. The exercise of that right would have amounted to effectively claiming the whole of the beneficial use of that strip, to the exclusion of the servient owner.	The exercise of an easement must not exclude the servient owner from having reasonable use of the servient land for himself. The extent to which the physical space is being used is taken into account when making this assessment.
Hair v Gillman (2000) 80 P&CR 108	The right to park on a forecourt that could accommodate four cars was held to be an easement. There was no exclusive possession as there would always be three other parking spaces for the servient owner to use.	The exercise of an easement must not exclude the servient owner from having reasonable use of the servient land for himself. The extent to which the physical space is being used shall be taken into account when making this assessment.
Hill v Tupper (1863) 2 H&C 121	A claim to an exclusive right to put boats on a canal was rejected as an easement. The exercise of the right was deemed to confer a mere commercial advantage on the claimant, rather than an advantage on the dominant land.	For a right to be capable of being an easement it must accommodate a dominant tenement, rather than confer a mere personal advantage on the current owner.
Moody v Steggles (1879) 12 Ch D 261	The right to put an advertisement on a neighbour's property advertising a pub was held to be an easement. The right would accommodate the land in connection with its normal use as a pub and thus benefit any future occupier of that land, irrespective of who they are.	A right which confers a commercial benefit may not be precluded from being an easement where the commercial activity and the land upon which it is carried out have become interlinked, so that any benefit to the business also benefits the land.

Key cases

✳✳✳✳✳✳✳✳✳

Case	Facts	Principle
Phipps v Pears [1965] 1 QB 76	A claim of an easement to have a house protected from the weather by another house was rejected as an easement. To allow otherwise would have precluded the owner of the other house from demolishing it.	Negative easements, restricting what a servient owner can do over his own land, can no longer be created.
Re Ellenborough Park [1956] Ch 131	A right for residential property owners to use a park adjacent to their houses for recreational use was deemed to be an easement. The right accommodated the land since use of the park was akin to use of a garden; such use being connected to normal enjoyment of a house.	Four requirements must be met for a right to be capable of being an easement. On the issue of accommodating the dominant land, the right should be connected to normal use of the dominant land and thus benefit any occupier of that land.
Regis Property Co Ltd v Redman [1956] 2 QB 612	The claim of a right to hot water as an easement was rejected.	The exercise of an easement should not involve the servient owner spending any money.
Wheeldon v Burrows (1879) 12 Ch D 31	Two plots of land, in common ownership, with one enjoying a quasi easement of light over another. The quasi servient plot was sold to B and a year later the quasi dominant plot was sold to W. When B erected hoardings blocking light to W's land, W was held not to have an easement of light.	Quasi easements may elevate to full easements when the quasi dominant land is transferred to another and three conditions are met.
Wong v Beaumont Property Trust Ltd [1965] 1 QB 173	An easement to fix a ventilation system to the landlord's property was impliedly acquired by the tenant when granted a lease over the landlord's cellar, specifically for use as a restaurant. Without such an easement, the tenant could not comply with health and safety regulations and thus could not use the cellar in the way the lease intended.	Where an easement is essential for the dominant land to be used in accordance with the purpose mutually intended by the parties, that easement may be impliedly acquired by common intention.
Wright v Macadam [1949] 2 KB 744	A tenant's revocable licence to store coal in a coal shed converted, upon the granting of a new lease, into a legal easement to store.	A conveyance in respect of the dominant land may elevate in favour of the transferee any pre-existing licences into easements.

Exam questions

Problem question

In May 2006, Danielle, the registered freehold owner of a large Victorian house, decided to con-vert the top floor of the building into a flat. She then granted a two-year lease of the top floor flat to Shirley. The lease provided for access to the flat via an outside set of stairs, together with residential parking at the front of the building.

When Shirley moved in, Danielle orally agreed for her to access the flat via the internal stairs. Although she gave no express agreement, Danielle also raised no objection when Shirley set up a flower stall in the residential parking area at the front of the building, which she advertised by fixing a sign to the side of the house.

When Shirley's lease expired, she was granted a new lease by Danielle, containing similar provi-sions to the original lease. Shirley continued to use the internal stairs and sell flowers from the flower stall advertised by the sign.

At the end of 2008, Danielle sold the freehold to the property to Roger. Roger has since told Shirley that she can no longer use the internal stairs to access the flat and that her flower stall must be removed from the parking area at the front of the house. He has already removed the sign from the house.

Advise Shirley.

An outline answer is available at the end of the book

Essay question

Whilst the list of rights recognized as easements is not a closed one, are the boundaries which the courts have imposed to limit the expansion of this list appropriate and consistent?

An outline answer is available online at www.oxfordtextbooks.co.uk/orc/concentrate/

#13
Freehold covenants

The examination

This is typically examined as a self-contained problem question. Such a question frequently involves:

- The sale of part of a freehold estate to another. Covenants are extracted at the time of sale, from the purchaser for the benefit of the vendor. This is so the vendor can retain some control over the land that he is selling, for the benefit of the land that he is retaining for himself.

- The purchaser's land then passes to a successor in title who breaches the original covenants and the question then is who can be held liable for that breach: the successor in title who committed the breach or the original purchaser who gave the covenant, or both.

- In addition, the vendor's land may also have passed to a successor in title, so you will need to assess who can enforce that breach: the original vendor, who extracted the promise or his successor in title?

Once you have a formula for how to deal with these issues, the good news is that this formula can generally be applied to any problem question set in this topic area.

Essay questions may focus upon a general analysis of the circumstances in which covenants run with the land. Questions may also focus upon areas of controversy such as the decision in *Federated Homes Ltd v Mill Lodge Properties Ltd* [1980]. Alternatively, although perhaps less frequently, you may be required to assess the differences between this type of proprietary interest with another, such as an easement for example.

Key facts

- All freehold covenants are enforceable between the original covenanting parties based upon principles of contract law.

- Where successors in title to the original covenanting parties wish to enforce covenants, they must establish the burden and benefit of the covenants passed to them.

- Whilst common law may pass the benefit of a covenant to a successor of the dominant land (express or implied), it will not pass the burden of any covenant to a successor of the servient land.

- Equity will pass the burden of a covenant to a successor of the servient land but only where the four requirements developed from *Tulk v Moxhay* (1848) are met. This is limited to restrictive covenants.

- Where the burden of a covenant has passed to a successor in equity, the benefit must also pass to a successor of the dominant land in equity.

- A benefit of a covenant may pass in equity in one of three ways: annexation, express assignment, or under a scheme of development.

- Following the decision in *Federated Homes Ltd v Mill Lodge Properties Ltd* [1980], the benefit of a covenant will typically pass by statutory annexation, unless expressly excluded by the parties.

- The burden of positive covenants will not pass to a successor of the servient land whether at common law or in equity. Whilst common law has developed ways to circumvent this problem and make positive covenants enforceable against successors, whether directly or indirectly, such methods are of limited application.

Chapter overview

Freehold covenant: a promise extracted by the covenantee from the covenantor, the latter undertaking to do/not to do something over his servient land for the benefit of the covenantee and/or his dominant land

Enforcement between the original covenanting parties: based upon contractual principles

A third party, not named in the document creating the covenant, may enforce a covenant if he satisfies rules under either:
- s 56 LPA 1925; or
- Contracts (Rights of Third Parties) Act 1999

Enforcement between successors in title: must demonstrate the burden and benefit of the covenants have passed

At Common Law

Benefit will pass if either:
- express assignment under s 136 LPA 1925; or
- implied assignment under *P&A Swift Investments v Combined English Stores Group plc* [1989]

Burden will not pass: *Rhone v Stephens* [1994]

The burden of a covenant may be enforceable against a successor in title to the original covenantor:
- indirectly via a chain of indemnity covenants; or
- using the rule in *Halsall v Brizell* [1957]

In Equity

Burden will pass if satisfy requirements from *Tulk v Moxhay* (1848)

Limited to restrictive covenants. Enforcement of positive covenants between successors in title relies upon common law

Where burden has passed in equity, benefit must pass in equity. Benefit will pass either by:
- annexation (express/statutory/implied); or
- express assignment; or
- scheme of development

Equitable remedies available

Covenants no longer enforceable where:
- extinguished; or
- discharged

Introduction

Freehold **covenants** are promises extracted by one freehold owner (the **covenantee**) from another freehold owner (the **covenantor**), whereby the latter undertakes either to do (positive covenant) or not to do (negative covenant) something over his land. The land burdened by the promise becomes the servient tenement. The land benefiting from the promise becomes the dominant tenement.

Covenants commonly arise when a freehold owner is selling off part of his freehold to another and wishes to maintain some degree of control over the land being sold in order to preserve the value and enjoyment of the land he is retaining. Such covenants could include, for example, restrictions on the ability to build on the land or restrictions as to how the land can be used. Such covenants effectively amount to a form of private planning control. However, despite the development of this area of law, they have not eradicated the need for public planning controls.

Revision tip

Remember not to confuse a question on freehold covenants with one on leasehold covenants, where the promises are extracted between a landlord and his tenant.

Enforcement

This is the key area of focus in an exam problem question and it is very important you understand how freehold covenants are enforced not only between the original contracting parties but, more importantly, between their successors in title.

Between the original parties to the covenant

Enforcement between the original covenantor and covenantee is based upon their contractual relationship. Privity of contract exists between them. Should the covenantor breach his covenant, the covenantee could enforce the breach using normal contractual principles.

Generally, only the parties to a deed/contract can enforce the terms of that deed/contract. This rule is subject to two exceptions:

* **Section 56 Law of Property Act 1925**
  This allows a person who is not a party to a covenant to sue upon it provided the covenant was purported to be made with him, rather than simply confer a benefit upon an unidentifiable third party: *Re Ecclesiastical Commissioners for England's Conveyance* [1936]. It is therefore essential that the third party is identifiable at the time of the creation of the covenant. Consequently, a covenant made with *successors in title* would not benefit those future owners of the land since, at the time the covenant was made, they are not identifiable: *Kelsey v Dodd* (1881).

Enforcement

✳✳✳✳✳✳✳✳✳

Once a benefit of a covenant has been acquired this way by a third party not named in the deed of creation, he is treated in the same way as an original covenantee and may pass the benefit of the covenant to his successor.

- **Contracts (Rights of Third Parties) Act 1999**
This applies to contracts entered into on/after 11 May 2000. Under s 1(1), a third party may enforce terms of a contract to which he was not a party where:

  - the contract expressly provides that he can; or

  - a term of the contract purports to confer a benefit upon him.

Thus a party, other than the original covenantee, may be able to enforce the terms of a covenant. To do so, the covenant must have named this person or identified them as a member of a class (here 'successors in title' would suffice). This person need not have been in existence when the covenant was created.

Between successors in title

The benefit of a covenant

In theory, even after the dominant and servient lands have passed to successors in title, the covenants are still enforceable between the original parties due to their contractual relationship. The reality, however, is that the original covenantee is unlikely to take action to stop any subsequent breaches of covenant since:

- he may not be aware of the breach, having disposed of the dominant land and moved away;

- even if aware, he may not wish to spend time and money enforcing it since, as he no longer owns the dominant land, he's not incurring any loss as a result of the breach being committed;

- consequently, if he were to take any action to enforce the breach, his remedy would be limited to nominal damages only.

It is rather his successor in title, the current owner of the dominant land and the person actually being affected by the breach, who will wish to take action. However, he will only be in a position to do so if he can establish that he has the benefit of the covenant that is being breached. The question of whether that benefit passed to him when he took over the dominant tenement is a key one for you to answer.

The burden of a covenant

Although the original covenantor remains liable for subsequent breaches committed after he has transferred the servient tenement to a successor, he may not be the best person to pursue for the breach since:

- he may be difficult to trace and, if he can be found, any remedy obtained against him would be limited to damages as he no longer owns the servient tenement; and

- pursuing him would provide little motivation for the successor actually committing the breach to stop (unless there exists an indemnity covenant between himself and the original covenantor – discussed below).

It is rather his successor in title, the current owner of the servient tenement and the person actually committing the breach, who should be pursued. However, it will only be possible to do so if it can be established that the burden of the covenant passed to him upon the transfer of the servient tenement. This again is a key issue for you to understand.

Revision tip

An exam problem question is unlikely to have the original parties staying as owners of the dominant and servient tenements, since there would be insufficient law for you to discuss. You must be prepared to be able to identify the original parties, their respective successors in title and how, if at all, the benefit and/or burden (as appropriate) of the covenant has passed to those successors.

At common law

Passing the benefit of a covenant

Express assignment

As a chose in action, the benefit of a covenant, provided it is not purely personal, can be expressly assigned by the holder of the benefit, to any third party in accordance with ordinary rules of law.

For the benefit to have passed successfully under this mode, you need to establish that the requirements under **s 136 LPA 1925** have been met, namely:

- the assignment is in writing; and
- express notice of the assignment has been given to the covenantor.

Once the benefit has been shown to have passed to a successor in this way, it is no longer open to the assignor to enforce the covenant. That ability has passed to their assignee.

Implied assignment

Where there is no evidence of an express assignment, you may be able to show the benefit has been impliedly assigned instead. To do so, you need to establish that the requirements from *P&A Swift Investments v Combined English Stores Group plc* [1989] have been met:

The covenant must touch and concern the dominant land

The covenant must be for the benefit of the land itself, rather than merely a personal benefit for just the original covenantee. A covenant that affects the land as regards mode of occupation or value, in the sense that the owner of that land gets more from his land by reason of the covenant being attached to it, may be deemed to touch and concern that land: *Smith &*

At common law

Snipes Hall Farm Ltd v River Douglas Catchment Board [1949]. In addition, if the covenant only benefits a party whilst they are the owner of the dominant land, and will be of no benefit to them when they part with that land, it is likely to be seen as a covenant that touches and concerns: *P&A Swift Investments v Combined English Stores Group plc* [1989].

A covenant will not be deemed to touch and concern the land where it has been expressed as personal to the covenantee, even where the tests above are met: *P&A Swift Investments v Combined English Stores Group plc* [1989].

The original parties must have intended for the benefit to pass

The covenant must not have been expressed to be personal to the covenantee. The intention that the benefit should pass to a successor can be found either:

- in the express wording of the covenant; or
- for all covenants created after 1925, it is implied by virtue of s 78 LPA 1925.

At the time the covenant was created, the covenantee must have held a legal estate in the land to be benefited

Since 1925, there now only exists two legal estates in the land – the freehold and the leasehold: s 1(1) LPA 1925. The covenantee must have held one of these estates in the dominant land.

The successor in title to the covenantee, who seeks to enforce the covenant, must also hold a legal estate in the dominant land

Although originally, it was thought that the original covenantee and their successor in title must have held the same legal estate in the dominant land, this is no longer the case: *Smith & Snipes Hall Farm Ltd v River Douglas Catchment Board* [1949]. The only requirement is that the person seeking to enforce the breach has a legal estate in the land, regardless of whether it is the same as the original covenantee.

Passing the burden of a covenant

At common law, the burden of a covenant will never pass to a successor of the servient land. This was established in the Court of Appeal case of *Austerberry v Corporation of Oldham* (1885), and was later confirmed in the House of Lords' decision of *Rhone v Stephens* [1994]. Consequently, at common law any attempt to privately control the use of land and preserve the character of neighbouring land, will come to an end once there has been a change of ownership to the servient property. Whilst the covenant may remain enforceable against the original covenantor, this will have little practical benefit for the person seeking to enforce the covenant, as discussed above.

 Looking for extra marks?

Why does the common law adopt this position that the burden of a covenant will not pass to a successor in title to the servient land? Arguably, it reflects the common law reluctance to allow restraints to be placed on a piece of land that could affect future generations. To allow this might result in the land becoming so bogged down with obligations that eventually the land becomes inalienable. This could have far-reaching negative economic consequences.

There have been attempts to undermine this common law position. For example, it has been suggested that s 79 LPA 1925 allows the burden to pass at common law since it implies into every covenant created after 1925, subject to contrary intention, that the covenant is *'deemed to be made by the covenantor on behalf of himself his successors in title and the persons deriving title under him or them'*. This argument has been rejected in *Tophams Ltd v Earl of Sefton* [1967], where it was declared that s 79 is no more than a word-saving provision and does not have the effect of passing the burden of a covenant to successors of the servient land.

The Contracts (Rights of Third Parties) Act 1999 will also provide no assistance in passing the burden of a covenant to a successor. Whilst it allows, in some circumstances, the benefit of a covenant to be enjoyed by persons not a party to its creation, the statute is unwilling to extend this rule to the burden.

In equity

Passing the burden of a covenant

Equity, recognizing the inadequacy of the common law position discussed above, has been willing to allow the burden of a covenant to pass from an owner of the servient tenement to his successor in title, where certain conditions are satisfied.

These conditions have been developed from the case of *Tulk v Moxhay* (1848), and you must establish all four are met for the burden of a covenant to pass in equity:

1. The covenant must be negative in nature; and

2. The covenant must accommodate the dominant land; and

3. The original parties must have intended for the burden to pass with the servient land; and

4. The purchaser of the servient land must have had notice of the covenant.

The covenant must be negative in nature

A covenant will be deemed negative when it does not require action/expenditure of money in order to be complied with: *Haywood v Brunswick Permanent Benefit Building Society* (1881).

This must be ascertained by looking at the substance, and not just the wording, of the covenant. For example, a covenant *'not to allow a brick wall to fall into disrepair'*, whilst worded negatively, will require action, ie maintenance work, if it is to be complied with. It is therefore a positive covenant.

In equity

✱✱✱✱✱✱✱✱✱✱

How should you treat a mixed covenant, for example a covenant not to build (the negative component) without first submitting building plans for approval (the positive component)?

There are two possible approaches:

Shepherd Homes v Sandham (No 2) [1971]: where a covenant has both positive and negative components, it may be possible to sever the positive component away from the negative, thus allowing the latter to pass. This will only be possible if the positive component is not dependent upon the negative ie it must be able to exist by itself. Essentially, this approach may be appropriate where one covenant can actually be interpreted as imposing two separate obligations.

Alternatively, *Powell v Hemsley* [1909]: where the positive component is no more than a mere condition to the performance of the negative component (as may be the case in the example given above), the covenant as a whole will be viewed as negative and will pass this requirement. In effect, the court will look to see which component of the covenant is dominant and this will provide the status of the covenant as a whole, the other component being considered as a mere condition to the performance of the former.

Revision tip

Unless obvious in an exam question which of the two above approaches should be adopted, you should discuss each approach and then adopt the most appropriate, justifying your reasons for doing so.

Equity will not pass the burden of positive covenants: *Rhone v Stephens* [1994]. It does not wish to contradict the common law rule of enforcement being dependent upon privity of contract.

The covenant must accommodate the dominant land

This has three components which must all be met:

- There must be identifiable land that can enjoy the benefit of the covenant, both at the time of creation and the date of enforcement of the covenant: *LCC v Allen* [1914].
- The covenant must touch and concern the dominant land. It must provide an actual benefit to the land itself rather than merely a personal benefit to the original covenantee. According to *Re Gadd's Land Transfer* [1966], a covenant may do this where it:
  - affects the value of the dominant land, though this need not be monetary; or
  - affects the mode of occupation or enjoyment of the dominant land.

Revision tip

Remember that you must establish the covenant benefits the *dominant* land. Where possible, use the facts given in the question to enhance your arguments here.

- There must be sufficient proximity between the dominant and servient lands: *Rogers v Hosegood* [1900]. Whilst the two pieces of land need not be adjacent to each other, clearly the further apart they are from each other, the harder it will be to satisfy this point.

✅ *Looking for extra marks?*

Is it possible for a covenant to touch and concern the land when the dominant land is a very large estate? In *Re Ballards Conveyance* [1937], where the estate was 1,700 acres, it was held that the covenant in question was not effective as it could not be seen to benefit the entire estate. The current view on this point is probably that adopted in *Wrotham Park Estate Co v Parkside Homes Ltd* [1974]: covenants should be seen to touch and concern the whole of the dominant land unless it can be shown that that opinion could not reasonably be held. Here the covenant in question was held to benefit the whole of a plot just less than 4,000 acres in size.

The original parties must have intended for the burden to pass with the servient land

This may be:

- in the express wording of the covenant; for example, '*the covenantor covenants on behalf of himself and his successors in title*'; or
- such words will be implied by virtue of s 79 LPA 1925, subject to contrary intention.

✅ *Looking for extra marks?*

Any suggestion that s 79 LPA 1925 by itself will make the burden of a covenant run with the servient land, thus rendering the other three requirements for passing the burden in equity redundant, has been rejected. In *Morrells of Oxford Ltd v Oxford United Football Club* [2001], Robert Walker LJ confirmed that the role of s 79 is merely to simplify the conveyancing process by creating the rebuttable presumption that covenants are made not just with the original covenantor, but also with his successors in title. It will not, by itself, pass the burden of a covenant.

The purchaser of the servient land must have had notice of the covenant

Today, this is essentially a question of registration and the conditions for meeting this requirement therefore differ depending upon whether the covenant affects registered or unregistered land.

In equity

✳✳✳✳✳✳✳✳✳✳

Registered land

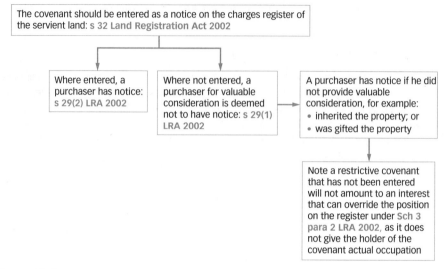

Figure 13.1

Unregistered land

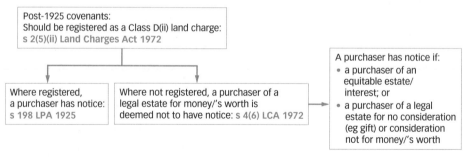

Figure 13.2

Covenants created over unregistered land before 1926, are governed by the doctrine of notice in determining whether a purchaser buys the servient land with notice of the covenant (see chapters 2 and 4).

Passing the benefit of a covenant

Where the burden of a covenant has passed in equity, a successor in title to the dominant land must prove that the benefit of that covenant passed to him in equity too, if he is to be in a position to enforce the breach: *Miles v Easter* [1933]. Establishing that the benefit passed under common law would not suffice.

Equity will pass the benefit of a covenant to a successor of the dominant land provided:

- the covenant is one which touches and concerns the land; and
- the covenant is shown to have passed by one of three recognised methods:
    - annexation;
    - express assignment; or
    - scheme of development.

(*Renals v Cowlishaw* (1878))

Annexation

This takes place at the time that the covenant is created and results in the benefit of the covenant becoming permanently attached to the dominant land. Consequently, once annexed the benefit has effectively become part of that land and will automatically pass to all successive owners of that land without specific mention, and irrespective of whether they know about its existence at the time of transfer.

You can establish annexation has occurred in one of three ways:

Express

This is where the wording of the covenant shows that the benefit is being attached to the dominant land. The express words must show the benefit is being attached to the actual land itself, rather than being entered into merely for the benefit of the covenantee. This can be achieved either by:

- ensuring that the covenant is expressly made '*for the benefit of*' the dominant land: *Rogers v Hosegood* [1900]; or
- ensuring that any reference made to the covenantee is done so *in their capacity as owner of the dominant land*. In *Renals v Cowlishaw* (1878), a covenant entered into expressly for the benefit of the vendor and his assigns was insufficient to result in annexation, since the parties referred to had not been explicitly linked to the dominant land.

Once deemed expressly annexed to the dominant land, the benefit is regarded as annexed to the *whole* of that land. This result has caused problems in the past:

- To be seen as annexed to the whole of the dominant land, you would need to show that the covenant touches and concerns the whole of that land. This may prove problematic where the dominant land is a very large estate.

. . . .

Re Ballards Conveyance [1937] Ch 473

A 16 acres plot was sold off from a 1,700 acres estate. A covenant extracted by the vendor, for the benefit of the land retained, was held not to have been annexed to that land. Whilst the covenant not to build private dwelling houses on the 16 acres plot, had been expressed to benefit the whole of the retained estate, it was deemed that such a covenant would only benefit that part of the estate which was in the immediate vicinity of the 16 acres plot. Since express annexation had proved ineffective, the benefit of the covenant could not pass to successive owners of the dominant land.

- Where the benefited estate is broken up and sold off in parts, it ceases to exist as a whole and any annexation that had existed would cease to be effective, both in respect of the land retained and the land sold off: *Russell v Archdale* [1964].

Today, these problems appear to be surmountable:

- A covenant should be seen to touch and concern the whole of the dominant land unless it can be shown that that opinion could not reasonably be held. Consequently, annexation may be effective irrespective of the size of the dominant land.

Wrotham Park Estate Co Ltd v Parkside Homes Ltd [1974] 1 WLR 798

Forty-seven acres of a 4,000 acres estate was sold off subject to a covenant not to build without the prior approval of the dominant owner to the development plans. The covenant was expressed to be for the benefit of the remaining estate. When building works commenced in breach of the restriction, it was held that the covenant benefited the whole of the dominant land, despite it being almost 4,000 acres in size.

- *Marquess of Zetland v Driver* (1939): where a covenant is expressly annexed to *each and every part of the land*, upon sale of part, the benefit will pass. The benefit will also continue for that land retained, thus overcoming the problem with annexation identified in *Russell v Archdale* [1964].

Statutory

In *Federated Homes Ltd v Mill Lodge Properties Ltd* [1980], the issue arose as to whether the benefit of a covenant, restricting the number of buildings that could be built on a neighbouring plot, had been annexed to the dominant land and subsequently passed to a successive owner of that land. Whilst there had been insufficient words to satisfy express annexation, the Court of Appeal held annexation had been successful. It reached this conclusion by interpreting s 78 LPA 1925 as causing automatic annexation, an interpretation of the provision which, up until that date, had not been recognized. Prior to this decision, s 78 had been interpreted as a mere word saving provision. It would operate to pass the benefit of a covenant to successors in title of the dominant land, without the need to expressly mention them in the wording of the covenant, but only once a valid express annexation had already been established. Brightman LJ rejected this narrow interpretation of the provision. Instead, he favoured the view that s 78 LPA 1925 operates to annex the benefit of a covenant to a covenantee's land automatically, without the need for express words. Indeed, he went further and held that this automatic annexation would attach the benefit of the covenant to *each and every part* of the dominant land, thus eliminating the need to do so expressly (as discussed in *Marquess of Zetland v Driver* (1939) and consequently overcoming the problem highlighted above in *Russell v Archdale* [1964]).

 Looking for extra marks?

Whilst this fully distributive effect of annexation has been accepted, the decision that annexation can occur automatically without the need for any express words has been criticized:

- Arguably, Parliament only ever intended s 78 LPA 1925 to operate as a word-saving provision. There is no indication that it was ever intended, by itself, to effect automatic annexation of the benefit of covenant to a dominant land. Indeed, the provision itself makes no mention of the word 'annexation'. If this is the case, the decision in *Federated Homes Ltd* goes too far in producing a result that is contrary to Parliament's intention.

- If the interpretation of s 78 LPA 1925 is truly correct, it renders express assignment, as an alternative method of passing the benefit, defunct. If this is true, you have to question why so much case law has arisen surrounding the issue of express assignment if, as is declared to be the case in *Federated Homes Ltd*, the benefit would have automatically passed anyway by virtue of s 78 LPA 1925.

- Section 78 LPA 1925 provides no provision for contrary intention. Arguably, it makes annexation a compulsory consequence of entering into a covenant, irrespective of the parties intention. This particular criticism has been addressed (see below).

Is it possible to avoid automatic statutory annexation from occurring?

The answer to this is yes.

. . . .

Roake v Chadha [1984] Ch 40

A conveyance stipulated that the benefit of a covenant would not pass to any owner or subsequent purchaser of the dominant land unless it had been expressly assigned to them. This was held to be a valid clause which effectively excluded the operation of automatic statutory annexation.

. . . .

The ability, by way of careful wording, to exclude automatic annexation by virtue of s 78 LPA 1925 has since been confirmed in *Crest Nicholson Residential (South) Ltd v McAllister* [2004].

 Looking for extra marks?

This case indicated that *Federated Homes Ltd v Mill Lodge Properties Ltd* [1980] represents the current law. However, it added that in order for statutory annexation under s 78 LPA 1925 to operate, it would be necessary for the wording of the covenant to actually identify the dominant land. If this is the case, such wording may alone be sufficient to find that the benefit has passed by way of express annexation. This being so, perhaps the decision in *Federated Homes Ltd* is less radical than at first thought.

In equity

✳✳✳✳✳✳✳✳✳✳

Revision tip

The decision of *Federated Homes Ltd* and its overall effect, is often the issue for debate in an essay question. Be sure to be aware of criticisms and views surrounding the decision. Those outlined above can be explored further.

Implied

Where the court may not find sufficient words of express annexation, it may look at the surrounding circumstances and imply annexation: *Marten v Flight Refuelling Ltd* [1962]. It is a very rare method of annexation and, arguably, has been made largely redundant following the decision in *Federated Homes Ltd v Mill Lodge Properties Ltd* [1980].

Express assignment

The benefit of a covenant will pass to a successor to the dominant land where it is expressly assigned to him. The assignment of the benefit of a covenant must occur contemporaneously with the transfer of the dominant land: *Miles v Easter* [1933]. An assignment of the benefit that occurs after the dominant land has been transferred will not be effective: *Re Union of London & Smith's Bank Ltd's Conveyance* [1933].

How does an express assignment of the benefit of a covenant differ from annexation of the benefit?

Figure 13.3

	Annexation	Assignment
Timing	This takes place at the time of the creation of the covenant. When looking for evidence of express annexation, one must look at the conveyance between the original covenanting parties.	This occurs on the transfer of the dominant land from the covenantee to his successor in title. The words of assignment will be found in the conveyance that transfers the dominant land from one owner to the next, and not in the conveyance between the original covenanting parties.
Effect	Annexation permanently attaches the benefit of the covenant to each and every part of the dominant land. From that date onwards, the benefit will automatically pass to successive owners of the whole, or part, of the dominant land, without the need for further words/action.	Since assignment transfers the benefit of the covenant to a successor in title of the dominant land personally, it must be expressly assigned upon every subsequent transfer of that dominant land.

In what circumstances might this method be relied upon to pass the benefit of a covenant?

Essentially, if the covenant was not annexed to the land at the time of its creation, and thus will not automatically pass on any transfer of that land, it may instead be expressly assigned upon a subsequent transfer of the land in question.

There has been some attempt to suggest that assignment of the benefit of a covenant will be implied automatically by virtue of s 62 LPA 1925. This provision provides that *'a conveyance of land shall be deemed to include…rights, and advantages whatsoever, appertaining or reputed to appertain to the land…'*. This suggestion was rejected in *Roake v Chadha* [1984], declaring that a covenant that has not been annexed to the land does not appertain to the land. A similar view was held in *Kumar v Dunning* [1989].

Scheme of development

This arises in situations where you have a large estate, owned by a single owner, who subsequently decides to sell the estate off in lots. Upon the sale of each lot, the vendor seeks covenants from the purchasers, with the aim of preserving the overall value and residential amenity of the whole estate. At the time of obtaining these covenants, the dominant land will comprise those unsold lots owned by the vendor. So long as the vendor retains some of these unsold plots, for the benefit of which the covenants were given, he is in a position, as the original covenantee, to enforce any breaches. The difficulty arises when the final lots are sold and the vendor no longer owns any of the estate and indeed, probably no longer cares about whether the covenants are being observed. Those who do care will be the current owners of the lots. Some such owners may be able to claim the benefit of the covenant has passed to them using the rules outlined above. However, those who own lots that were sold before the covenant being breached had been obtained, will not be able to do so. This is because their lots did not form part of the dominant land at the time the covenant was given. To overcome this problem, a scheme was established which essentially allowed for covenants in such a situation to be mutually enforceable between the various owners of the lots.

Following the decision in *Re Dolphin's Conveyance* [1970], there are two key requirements that must be met for such a scheme to operate:

- there must be an identifiable scheme; it must be possible to identify the perimeters of the land to which the scheme relates; and

- of paramount importance, there must be a mutually perceived common intention; that a scheme was clearly intended to be established for the reciprocal enforcement of obligations.

Remedies

Since equity is being used to enforce restrictive covenants, the remedies sought are equitable and are subject to discretion, exercised in accordance with settled principles.

Injunction

The specific type sought depends upon whether the breach has actually been committed and discontinuance is sought, or merely threatened.

Damages in lieu of an injunction: s 50 Supreme Court Act 1981

The principles in *Shelfer v City of London Electric Lighting Co* [1895] will be followed by a court in deciding whether to award damages.

Positive covenants

Despite equity intervening to allow for the enforcement of restrictive covenants between successors to the dominant and servient land, positive covenants, in principle, remain enforceable only against the original covenantor. Neither common law nor equity will pass the burden of a positive covenant to a successor to the servient land. This could lead to problems, so ways have been developed to circumvent these problems and make positive obligations enforceable against successive owners to the servient land.

Indemnity covenants

The original covenantor remains liable on the covenants, after having disposed of the servient land to a successor in title, due to his original contractual position. It is possible, therefore, that upon disposing of the servient land, he extracts an indemnity covenant from his successor, obliging the successor to indemnify him in respect of any damages he pays out as a result of his successor breaching the covenants. It is possible, in situations where the servient land has changed hands many times, that a chain of indemnity covenants will be created. Where a complete chain of indemnities exists (ie upon every disposal of the servient land, the outgoing owner has extracted an indemnity covenant from his successor), ultimately, the party left out of pocket as a result of the breach of covenant, will be the party at the end of the chain ie the person committing the breach in the first place. This, therefore, achieves indirect enforcement of positive obligations against successive owners to the servient land.

There are, however, problems with the efficiency of this system as a means of enforcement of positive obligations:

- Successors in title to the servient land may refuse to give an indemnity covenant to the outgoing owner. Where this is the case, it may create a break in the chain of indemnities. Where such a break exists, the party at the end of the chain committing the breach (ie the current owner of the servient land) will know that he cannot be pursued for the breach either directly or indirectly. He is therefore unlikely to have any motivation to stop committing the breach. The same will also be true where there is a break in the chain through disappearance/insolvency.

- Any remedy obtained using this method of enforcement will be limited to damages against the original covenantor. Since the latter no longer owns the servient land, it would be impossible to obtain an order of specific performance against him, despite this being, in most circumstances, the most appropriate remedy for the breach of a positive covenant.

- After some years, it may not be possible to locate the original covenantor. Thus, even the receipt of damages may not be achievable.

The rule in *Halsall v Brizell* [1957]

A person who wishes to claim the benefit of a deed must also submit to any corresponding burden which is imposed by that deed. This benefit and burden doctrine does not imply that any condition can be rendered enforceable by attaching it to a right. There are two conditions which have to be met for the doctrine to work, as clarified in *Thamesmead Town Ltd v Allotey* [1998]:

- there must be a correlation between the burden and the benefit; the burden must be 'relevant' to the enjoyment of the benefit; and

- the successor in title to the covenantor must have had the opportunity to elect whether to take the benefit or, having taken it, elect to renounce it, even if only in theory, and thereby escape the burden.

Revision tip

Remember that where a successor to the original covenantee wishes to enforce positive covenants indirectly using indemnity covenants or by using the rule from *Halsall v Brizell* [1957], you must show that he received the benefit of such covenants using common law methods of passing the benefit.

Enlargement of a long lease into a freehold

Where this is achieved, the freehold estate that results is subject to the same covenants as the lease from which it has been created: s 153 LPA 1925. In theory, therefore, any positive covenants that had been contained in the lease would be binding upon the freehold owner.

Rentcharges

A rentcharge is an annual sum of money charged on the land, non-payment of which could ultimately lead to termination of the estate. The rentcharge could be made subject to the performance of positive obligations. Where such obligations are not performed, the holder of the charge has a right to enter the estate, perform the positive obligations and charge the freehold owner. Enforcement of positive obligations over freehold land by attachment to a rentcharge has survived the prohibition of new rentcharges under the Rentcharges Act 1977.

Creation of a commonhold scheme

This is possible under the Commonhold and Leasehold Reform Act 2002 and creates a system of landholding which effectively allows for enforcement of positive obligations between freehold owners (discussed further in chapter 5).

Extinguishment and discharge

Extinguishment

A covenant will no longer be enforceable where the dominant and servient lands cease to be in separate ownership/occupation.

Discharge

By the parties affected

This can be done by deed.

By the court – applicable to restrictive covenants only

In accordance with s 84(1) LPA 1925, as amended by s 28 LPA 1969, any person with an interest in the freehold that is affected by a restriction as to its use, may apply to the Land Tribunal for an order to wholly or partially discharge or modify the restriction. This may be granted in the following situations:

- where the restriction has become obsolete, due to *'changes in the character of the property or the neighbourhood or other circumstances'*; or
- the continued existence of the restriction impedes a reasonable user of the land and either
  - the restriction does not provide any practical benefit to any person; or
  - it is contrary to public interest; or
- those entitled to the benefit have agreed, expressly or impliedly to its discharge/ modification; or
- the proposed discharge/modification will not injure persons entitled to the benefit of the restriction.

The power is mainly exercised where the restriction has become obsolete. Where the Land Tribunal agree to discharge/modify the restriction, it has the discretion to require a compensation payment to the owner of the dominant land.

Key cases

Case	Facts	Principle
Federated Homes Ltd v Mill Lodge Properties Ltd [1980] 1 WLR 594	A restrictive covenant limiting building works referred to 'any adjoining or adjacent property retained by' the covenantee. Upon transfer of part of the covenantee's adjoining land, the benefit of this covenant was deemed annexed to the land and thus passed to the transferee.	Provided the conditions under s 78 LPA 1925 are satisfied, annexation of the benefit of a covenant to the dominant land is automatic.
Halsall v Brizell [1957] 1 All ER 371	Purchasers of building plots covenanted to contribute towards maintenance costs of roads and sewers in common use of the owners of all the building plots.	Where you wish to take the benefit of a deed, you must also submit to any corresponding burden that deed imposes.
LCC v Allen [1914] 3 KB 642	A successor in title to the servient land started to build on that land in breach of a covenant. The council was refused an injunction to stop the building work.	To enforce a covenant, you must have a dominant land capable of benefiting from that covenant.
P&A Swift Investments v Combined English Stores Group plc [1989] AC 632	Rent obligation between landlord and tenant. Landlord assigned the reversion to the plaintiff. The tenant failed to pay rent and the plaintiff pursued the defendant, who stood as surety for the rent. The benefit of the rent obligation was deemed to have passed at common law to the plaintiff.	Benefit of a covenant may pass at common law where four requirements are met. A covenant is deemed to touch and concern the dominant land where any holder of that land would benefit, not just the original covenantee personally.
Re Ballards Conveyance [1937] Ch 473	A covenant not to build and extracted for the benefit of a dominant land just less than 1,700 acres, was deemed not to be annexed to that land. Although expressed to benefit the whole of the dominant land, it was deemed to only benefit that part of the dominant land within the immediate vicinity of the servient land, a 16 acres plot. Express annexation had thus been unsuccessful.	For the benefit of a covenant to be annexed to the whole of the dominant land, it must be proven to touch and concern the whole of that land. (But see now *Wrotham Park Estate Co v Parkside Homes Ltd* [1974]
Rhone v Stephens [1994] 2 AC 310	A covenant to keep a roof in repair was deemed unenforceable against a successor to the original covenantor.	The burden of a positive covenant will not pass at common law to a successor in title to the original covenantor.

Case	Facts	Principle
Roake v Chadha [1984] Ch 40	A conveyance stipulating that the benefit of a covenant would not pass to any successor of the dominant land unless it had been expressly assigned to him, was deemed to exclude the operation of automatic statutory annexation.	Automatic statutory annexation by virtue of s 78 LPA 1925 and the decision in *Federated Homes Ltd v Mill Lodge Properties Ltd* [1980] may be expressly excluded from operating.
Smith & Snipes Hall Farm Ltd v River Douglas Catchment Board [1949] 2 KB 500	Defendants entered into a covenant with the freehold owners of land subject to flooding, that they would maintain the banks of a river. An original covenantee conveyed her land to the 1st plaintiff together with the benefit of the covenant. The 2nd plaintiff occupied the dominant land under a tenancy. Both plaintiffs were entitled to enforce a breach of the covenant.	For the benefit of a covenant to pass at common law, the original covenantee and his successor must have held/holds now a legal estate in the dominant land. That legal estate need not be the same.
Tulk v Moxhay (1848) 2 Ph 774	A covenant not to build was deemed enforceable against a successor in title to the original covenantor, since he was aware of the existence of the covenant when purchasing the land affected.	A successor to the original covenantor who has notice of the covenant, takes subject to that covenant. Since extended to incorporate a further three requirements for the burden of a covenant to pass in equity.
Wrotham Park Estate Co v Parkside Homes Ltd [1974] 1 WLR 798	A covenant not to build without prior approval of plans, was extracted for the benefit of a dominant land just less than 4,000 acres. When the successor in title to the covenantor breached the covenant, the plaintiff was entitled to enforce the breach. (Note a mandatory injunction was refused. To demolish the 13 houses already built would be 'an unpardonable waste'. Instead, damages in lieu of an injunction were awarded.)	A covenant will be deemed to touch and concern the whole of the dominant land, however large, unless it can be shown that that opinion cannot reasonably be held.

(?) Exam questions

Problem question

David is the registered owner of a 200 acres farm, which includes a house, separate cottage, and a number of outbuildings. The farm benefits from a natural spring which provides the farm with all the water it needs through a system of pipes that David has installed on the property.

In 2005, David sold 15 acres of his farm, which included the cottage and an outbuilding, to John. The purchase was subject to the following covenants:

1. to use the property for residential purposes only;
2. to contribute towards the upkeep of the water pipes;
3. to plant and maintain conifer trees on the boundary between David and John's property.

Two years later, John became seriously ill and was given just a short time to live. He decided that he should travel the world whilst he still could and so gifted his property to his son, Eric.

Eric is an artist and decided that the property was perfect for establishing an art school. So, in 2008, he converted the outbuilding into a large studio for the art students to work in. To ensure that the outbuilding benefits from as much light as possible, he chopped down the conifer trees and replaced them with a picket fence.

David has recently sold his farm to Gillian who is unhappy that Eric is using his property as an art school as it increases the amount of traffic in the local area. She is also annoyed that the conifer trees have been replaced with a picket fence, providing her property with less privacy. In addition, since a recent argument with Eric about these issues, he has refused to make any contributions towards the upkeep of the water pipes.

Advise Gillian.

An outline answer is available at the end of the book

Essay question

What are the circumstances in which the benefit of a freehold covenant will run with the land? Did the decision in the case of *Federated Homes Ltd v Mill Lodge Properties Ltd* [1980] fundamentally alter the law in this area?

An outline answer is available online at www.oxfordtextbooks.co.uk/orc/concentrate/

#14
Mortgages

This is examined largely as a self-contained topic area. To some extent, there are reasonably distinct issues within the topic that can be the focus of an exam question, notably:

- the rights of the mortgagor and, in particular, the role equity plays in intervening to strike out clauses within a mortgage agreement. Such intervention can be seen as restricting freedom of contract and essay questions may require you to consider the extent to which this is true and how the law balances the contractual nature of a mortgage with its proprietary status;

- the concept of undue influence, in particular how it is established and the consequences of finding the borrower has been subjected to it, especially for the lender who often is not the culprit. Essay questions may focus on the relatively recent re-working of the law following the case of *Royal Bank of Scotland plc v Etridge (No 2)* [2002] requiring you to consider whether the law in this area has been clarified/improved;

- the rights of the mortgagee, in particular the remedies available should a mortgagor default on the mortgage payments. As the availability and operation of remedies differ slightly depending upon whether the mortgage is legal or equitable in status, an understanding of how legal and equitable mortgages are created could be required (although it is true to say that most examiners focus upon legal mortgages).

Key facts

- A mortgage is a proprietary interest that can be legal or equitable in status.

- The equity of redemption encapsulates the rights of a mortgagor and includes the equitable right to redeem and the ability to have certain clauses struck out from a mortgage agreement, perhaps because they prevent the ability to redeem or because they are oppressive.

- The Administration of Justice Act 1970, amended by the AJA 1973, provides the mortgagor with some protection where possession of a dwelling house is being sought by the mortgagee.

- Where a mortgage is obtained under undue influence, be it actual or presumed, it may be possible for the wronged party to have the transaction set aside.

- Where a lender, who is not the wrongdoer, wishes to enforce a mortgage transaction obtained under undue influence, it would have to prove that it took certain steps as identified in *Royal Bank of Scotland plc v Etridge (No 2)* [2002], prior to the mortgage transaction being completed.

- The mortgagee has various remedies available to it should the mortgagor fail to meet the mortgage payments including suing for the debt, taking possession, and selling the mortgaged property or appointing a receiver.

- The remedies available are less where the mortgage is equitable.

- A property may be subject to more than one mortgage and where this is the case and the property is sold, proceeds from the sale will be applied in order of priority.

Chapter overview

Mortgage: a proprietary interest that has capacity to be legal: **s 1(2)(c) LPA 1925**

Formalities for creation: →
Legal:
Unregistered land – **ss 85 and 86 LPA 1925**
Registered land – **s 23(1)(a) LRA 2002**
→ Equitable

Mortgagor's rights: the equity of redemption

A right to redeem the mortgage. Any postponement must not render right illusory: *Fairclough v Swan Brewery Co Ltd* [1912]

A right to have collateral advantages in favour of the mortgagee struck out, whilst respecting freedom to contract: *Jones v Morgan* [2001]

A right to have oppressive/ unconscionable terms struck out: *Cityland & Property (Holdings) Ltd v Dabrah* [1968]. Support provided by statute

Ability to have mortgage set aside where evidence of undue influence: *Royal Bank of Scotland plc v Etridge (No 2)* [2002]

Mortgagee's rights

Sue

Possession: (**AJA 1970/ 1973** where a dwelling house)

Sale:
Arises: **s 101 LPA 1925**
Exercisable: **s 103 LPA 1925**
Proceeds distribution: **s 105 LPA 1925**

Appoint receiver:
Arises: **s 101 LPA 1925**
Exercisable: **s 103 LPA 1925**
Income distribution: **s 109 LPA 1925**

Foreclosure

Priorities

Introduction

A **mortgage** is:

- a contractual arrangement between a lender (the **mortgagee**) and a borrower (the **mortgagor**) creating personal rights between them;

- a proprietary interest over the land of the mortgagor, granted to the mortgagee as security for the money lent by the latter to the former.

A mortgage can:

- be granted over any interest in land, not just the freehold estate;

- exist alongside other mortgages over the same piece of land;

- be either legal or equitable. The significance of the distinction is of particular importance when looking at remedies available to a mortgagee (discussed below).

Formalities for creation

Legal mortgages

Over Registered Land

Under s 85 Law of Property Act 1925, mortgages created over a freehold estate are either a:

- *mortgage by demise*: the mortgagor grants the mortgagee a long lease (usually 3,000 years) over his estate subject to a provision that once the debt is paid, the lease will terminate; or

- *charge by way of a legal mortgage*: by deed, identifying the land in question and expressly declaring it to be charged by way of a legal mortgage. Rather than obtain a legal estate in the land, the mortgagee acquires a legal interest in the land: s 1(2)(c) LPA 1925. In all other respects, his rights and powers are the same as if granted a mortgage by demise.

Under s 86 LPA 1925, mortgages created over a leasehold estate will be the same as above save the mortgage by demise will amount to a sublease of the leasehold estate out of which is has been granted.

Over Unregistered Land

Under s 23(1)(a) Land Registration Act 2002, only

- *charge by way of a legal mortgage*. Not only must it be created by deed, but it must also be registered as a charge at the Land Registry: s 27(2)(f) LRA 2002.

(Pre LRA 2002, mortgages could be created as per unregistered land.)

✳✳✳✳✳✳✳✳✳✳

Equitable mortgages

Created where:

- the mortgage is being granted over a mere equitable interest, eg a beneficial interest under a trust of land. The whole of the equitable interest is conveyed to the mortgagee who promises to reconvey it when the debt is paid. The transfer of the equitable interest must satisfy s 53(1)(c) LPA 1925 (see chapter 2); or

- the parties expressly create an equitable mortgage. There must be compliance with s 53(1)(a) LPA 1925 (see chapter 2); or

- the formalities for creating a legal mortgage have not been satisfied ie there is no deed, but the failed attempt amounts to a valid contract (ie complies with s 2 LP(MP)A 1989) that is capable of specific performance; or

- where the land is registered and the mortgage created has not been registered as a charge at the Land Registry: s 27(2)(f) LRA 2002.

Mortgagor's rights

The principle

A mortgage is mere security for a loan. When a mortgagor wishes to redeem the loan, he should be able to do so, recovering his property in an unencumbered state. The mortgagee is only entitled to have the loan monies repaid, together with any interest that might have accrued.

To uphold this principle, equity has created a bundle of rights in favour of the mortgagor: the **equity of redemption**. Such rights are outlined below.

✅ *Looking for extra marks?*

The issue of whether equity will intervene or not to uphold the basic principle behind a mortgage is one which requires you to understand that a balance must be met between competing interests. On the one hand, there is clearly a desire to ensure borrowers are protected, some of whom may be vulnerable to the sharp practices of lenders. On the other hand, some recognition must be given to the concept of freedom of contract and lending must be encouraged so as to secure property transactions, itself vital to a healthy economy.

The equitable right to redeem

A mortgage agreement specifies a legal date for redemption, before which a mortgagor cannot repay the loan, without consent from the mortgagee. At common law, if the debt was not paid on this exact date, the property vested in the mortgagee, preventing the mortgagor from ever recovering his property. Since this conflicts with the basic principle of a mortgage (discussed above), equity intervened, giving the mortgagor an equitable right to redeem that commences upon the expiry of the legal date for redemption. Any intervention by the mortgagee which either removes this possibility to redeem or renders the right illusory, will be struck out.

Clauses attempting to remove the right to redeem completely

Equity will not tolerate such clauses in a mortgage agreement. In *Toomes v Consent* (1745), a mortgage term specifying that the property was to become the mortgagee's upon a specified event occurring, was struck out. If the event occurred, the mortgagor would be prevented from ever getting his property back, which clearly goes against the basic principle of what a mortgage is.

Options to purchase the mortgaged property

Figure 14.1

Obtained as part of the mortgage transaction	Obtained in a transaction independent of the mortgage
Option is void, irrespective of whether there was oppression or not: *Samuel v Jarrah Timber and Wood Paving Corporation Ltd* [1904]. Why? If the option was allowed and later exercised, the mortgagor would lose his property. Consequently, he would lose the ability to redeem the loan and recover his property, thus contravening the basic principle.	Option might be upheld: *Reeve v Lisle* [1902]. Depends upon the reality of the situation and whether the granting of the option and the mortgage are truly independent transactions: *Jones v Morgan* [2001]. (Remember, a mere delay between completing the mortgage and creating the option will not necessarily mean that the two are independent of one another. Neither will putting the option into a separate agreement from the mortgage.)

✅ Looking for extra marks?

In the case of *Warnborough Ltd v Garmite Ltd* [2004], the vendor was granted a mortgage over property being sold as security for unpaid purchase monies. An option was granted to the vendor to repurchase the property in specified circumstances. The option was upheld. The Court of Appeal declared that it was not part of the mortgage transaction but part of the sale transaction, thus independent of the mortgage. Mortgage rules should not apply when the reality is the transaction in question is of a different commercial character.

Clauses attempting to postpone the right to redeem

A mortgagee may wish to postpone the ability to redeem in order to guarantee for himself a return on his money in the guise of interest payments. Whilst acceptable in principle, equity will not allow postponement to be such that it renders the right to redeem illusory.

Mortgagor's rights

Fairclough v Swan Brewery Co Ltd [1912] AC 565

The mortgage was created over leasehold property and contained a clause postponing redemption until the final six weeks of the lease. The clause was held void. Had the clause been upheld, the mortgagor, upon redemption, would recover an estate that was virtually worthless and substantially different in character from the one he had mortgaged, which had been a 20 year lease.

In contrast:

Knightsbridge Estates Trust Ltd v Byrne [1939] Ch 441

The mortgage was created over freehold property and contained a clause postponing redemption for 40 years. The clause was upheld. Upon redeeming in 40 years, the mortgagor would still recover his property in virtually the same state as when it was mortgaged.

✅ *Looking for extra marks?*

What facts within *Knightsbridge* allowed the court to reach a different view about the postponement clause?

- The property was freehold so the right to redeem had not been made illusory. Upon redemption, even after 40 years, the mortgagor would recover a property of value.

- The clause had not been obtained through oppression. Both parties were experienced and the bargaining had been an arm's length commercial transaction.

- The terms were the most advantageous available at the time.

The right to have collateral advantages for the mortgagee struck out

Equity has been wary of collateral advantages sought by the mortgagee over and above the repayment of the loan with interest, as these go against the basic principle that a mortgage is mere security for a loan.

Traditionally, the view of equity has been:

- Where the advantage is set to continue after the mortgage is redeemed, it will be deemed void: *Noakes & Co Ltd v Rice* [1902]. The continued existence of the advantage would hinder the mortgagor from recovering his property in an unencumbered state upon redemption.

- Where the collateral advantage is to end upon redemption, provided it is not imposed in an oppressive or unconscionable way, it will be upheld: *Biggs v Hoddinott* [1898].

Today, greater acknowledgement is given to freedom to contract. Unless you can establish that the term was imposed in an oppressive way, the collateral advantage may be upheld as a valid term of a mortgage agreement, whether it is to last beyond the mortgage term or not: *Kreglinger v New Patagonia Meat & Cold Storage Co Ltd* (1914).

This greater respect towards freedom to contract was confirmed in *Jones v Morgan* [2001], which confirmed that no rule in equity precluded collateral advantages being obtained by a mortgagee, provided such terms are not:

- unfair/unconscionable;
- a clog on the equity of redemption;
- inconsistent with the right to redeem.

However, the court added that such advantages should be reached in a transaction truly independent of the mortgage.

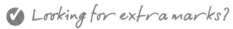 ## Looking for extra marks?

Some collateral advantages may be struck out as void based upon the contractual principle that agreements must not impose unreasonable restrictions on trade. This can be seen with clauses that tie the borrower to buying the lender's products only: *Esso Petroleum Co Ltd v Harper's Garage (Stourport) Ltd* [1968]. Such clauses may also be in breach of EC competition law and especially Art 81: *Courage Ltd v Crehan* [2002].

The right to have oppressive or unconscionable terms struck out

To be struck out, the term must be more than merely unreasonable. It must have been imposed in a morally reprehensible way. In making this assessment, have regard to:

- the equality of bargaining power between the parties;
- the experience of the mortgagor;
- whether the mortgagor received independent legal advice. If yes, it might be hard to show that the term had been imposed oppressively: *Jones v Morgan* [2001].

....

Multiservice Bookbinding Co Ltd v Marden [1979] Ch 84

Linking the interest rate to the Swiss franc, leading to large interest payments when currency values fluctuated, was upheld. Equality of bargaining power existed and, since the lender was a private individual anxious to preserve the capital value of his investment, the court was inclined to see the hard bargain as a fair one.

....

In contrast:

Cityland & Property (Holdings) Ltd v Dabrah [1968] Ch 166

A penal rate of interest was struck out as there had been no equality of bargaining power and the facts suggested the possibility of oppression.

Consumer Credit Act 1974

This may provide the mortgagor with an alternative way of dealing with 'extortionate' agreements. Under this Act, the court has the power to reopen such agreements so as to do justice to the parties. It is used sparingly and in deciding whether an agreement is extortionate, the court will consider:

- rates of interest;
- age and experience of the borrower;
- the financial pressure the borrower was under; and
- the degree of risk taken by the lender

at the time that the loan was given.

Consumer Credit Act 2006

This amends the CCA 1974 and provides the courts with powers to consider 'unfair relationships' by amending the terms of the agreement. The Act itself provides no definition as to what is an 'unfair relationship'.

Unfair Terms in Consumer Contracts Regulations 1999

High rates of interest may be open to challenge as an unfair term under these regulations. If found to be unfair ie one causing a significant imbalance in the parties rights to the detriment of the borrower contrary to the requirements of good faith, it would be unenforceable, with the rest of the mortgage agreement being upheld.

Financial Services and Markets Act 2000

This Act may be useful to a mortgagor claiming excessive charges have been imposed upon him, but only if his mortgage was created after 31 October 2004. To determine whether a charge is excessive, regard must be had to charges for similar products or services on the market at the time the mortgage was created.

Undue influence

Evidence that the mortgage transaction was obtained under undue influence (or by any other equitable wrongdoing), may allow for the wronged party to have the transaction set aside.

Typical exam scenarios which might require you to consider the possibility of undue influence may include:

- where the property is co-owned and the loan appears to benefit just one of the legal co-owners; or
- where the property is co-owned but not all co-owners are on the legal title; or
- where the mortgage is taken to secure the debt of another.

Is there evidence of undue influence between the parties?

Class 1: actual undue influence

You are looking for actual evidence that a person entered into the mortgage, not out of his own free will, but rather through overt acts of improper pressure exerted upon him by another. Where present, the complainant can have the transaction set aside without having to establish anything further.

Class 2: presumed undue influence

Although traditionally divided into two categories, since the decision of *Royal Bank of Scotland v Etridge (No 2)* [2002], this essentially requires you to establish two things:

- that the relationship between the complainant and the alleged wrongdoer is one of trust and confidence, making it more likely that undue influence has been exerted; and
- that the transaction appears to be one that is disadvantageous to the complainant, to the extent that it requires explanation.

Where these two conditions are met, the presumption is not that undue influence exists, but that it will exist if the alleged wrongdoer cannot explain the nature of the transaction. It is for the alleged wrongdoer to prove that the complainant freely entered into the transaction and that no undue influence was applied.

The effect of finding undue influence

Where undue influence of either class is established, the complainant is entitled to have the transaction set aside against the wrongdoer. Usually, however, the wrongdoer is not the lender. The lender will still want to be able to enforce the mortgage. Has the existence of undue influence affected its right to do so?

The position of the lender

The current law regarding the lender's position came from a reworking of the law established in the case of *Barclays Bank plc v O'Brien* [1994]. An essay question might require you to consider the changes made to the position given in *O'Brien*. It might therefore be useful for you to read the decision of Lord Browne-Wilkinson in that case.

Undue influence

✳✳✳✳✳✳✳✳✳✳

In the key case of *Royal Bank of Scotland v Etridge (No 2)* [2002] it was recognized that a balance must be sought between maintaining the confidence of lenders that mortgages created over family homes will be enforceable and protecting potentially vulnerable parties from agreeing to mortgages out of pressure exerted upon them by another.

To assert the continuing validity of a mortgage between itself and the complainant, despite the existence of undue influence, the lender must establish that it took certain steps in making sure that the complainant received independent legal advice, regarding the practical implications of the mortgage transaction, prior to agreeing to the mortgage.

When must the lender take such steps?

- Whenever a wife is standing surety for her husband's debts ie the family home is being mortgaged to provide security for the husband's debts or interests;
- whenever a family home is being mortgaged to support a business activity;
- in any non-commercial transaction where the purpose of the loan does not appear to be for the mutual benefit of the parties involved.

What are the steps the lender should take?

Before the mortgage transaction goes ahead, the lender should:

- obtain from the potential complainant the name of the solicitor acting for him and seek written confirmation from that solicitor that the potential complainant has been advised as to the practical implications of the proposed transaction;
- provide the advising solicitor with all information he requires to be able to give appropriate advice to the potential complainant;
- inform the solicitor of any concerns he may have about the potential complainant's understanding of the transaction/vulnerability.

A lender may assume that the solicitor has advised the potential complainant on his own behalf and that the advice given was sufficient and correct: *Bank of Baroda v Rayerel* [1995]. This is so even if the solicitor was also acting for the alleged wrongdoer (*Banco Exterior International v Mann* [1995]) or the lender itself (*Barclays Bank plc v Thomson* [1997]).

What is the effect of having taken these steps?

Once these steps have been taken and the lender has received written confirmation that the potential complainant has been advised appropriately, the mortgage transaction cannot be set aside against the lender.

Revision tip

Much of the case law in this area concerns husbands and wives and whether the former exerted undue influence over the latter. Remember, however, that the issue of undue influence may arise in any situation where trust between parties may have been abused.

Mortgagee's remedies

What can a mortgagee do if the mortgagor defaults on a legal mortgage?

Revision tip

Be sure you understand what makes a mortgage legal or equitable (explained above). The availability and operation of remedies may differ depending upon the status of the mortgage.

Sue on the personal covenant

The mortgagee sues the mortgagor for any sums outstanding. Perhaps preferable in cases of **negative equity** where recovery of the property alone would not satisfy the debt.

Where the mortgage is equitable

As above.

Possession

Why?

Commonly sought prior to selling since a vacant property is easier to sell. It may also be sought in cases of negative equity. The repossessed property can be let until such time as the market recovers, making a sale more attractive.

When?

Technically, this can be sought by the mortgagee any time after the mortgage has been created, even before any default by the mortgagor: *Four Maids Ltd v Dudley Marshall (Properties) Ltd* [1957]. In practice, a mortgagee is unlikely to seek possession where the mortgagor is not in breach of the mortgage agreement.

How?

A mortgagee can seek possession of a mortgaged property without a court order (*Ropaigealach v Barclays Bank plc* [1999]), although one may be advisable to avoid any criminal liability under Criminal Law Act 1977 (discussed under forfeiture in chapter 6).

Where the mortgaged property consists of, or includes, a dwelling house, s 36 Administration of Justice Act 1970, amended by the AJA 1973, gives the court, upon receipt of a possession application, a discretionary power to:

*   adjourn the proceedings; or
*   grant a stay of execution of an order ie grant the possession order but suspend its operation.

This power may be exercised where it appears likely that within a 'reasonable period' the mortgagor will be able to pay 'any sums due under the mortgage' or remedy any other breach.

Mortgagee's remedies
✳✳✳✳✳✳✳✳✳✳

1. **What is a 'reasonable period'?**

   The starting point should be the remaining years of the mortgage: *Cheltenham & Gloucester BS v Norgan* [1996].

2. **What are 'any sums due under the mortgage'?**

   The mortgagor must convince the court that not only can he make a reasonable attempt to pay off the arrears accumulating within a reasonable period, but that he can also meet future payments. Where this is unlikely, a court will not exercise discretion in his favour: *First National Bank v Syed* [1991].

   In cases where the mortgage contains a default clause ie a clause stipulating that should the mortgagor default on his repayments, the whole sum borrowed becomes due, s 8 AJA 1973 makes it clear that 'any sums due' would simply be those the mortgagor would be required to pay had no such default clause existed.

3. **What will influence a court in deciding whether to exercise its discretion?**

   • The mortgagor's current financial position (not speculative windfalls);

   • Proposed sale of the property by the mortgagor which may mean that the mortgagor is likely to pay sums due within a reasonable time. This may justify a suspension of a possession order provided the prospect of sale is not fanciful: *National & Provincial Building Society v Lloyd* [1996].

✅ Looking for extra marks?

In the case of *Cheltenham & Gloucester plc v Krauz* [1997], the mortgagor sought an order for sale. The mortgagee had already obtained a possession order but had not executed it. In finding that the proposed sale would not have produced sufficient funds to satisfy sums due, the Court of Appeal allowed the possession order to be enforced. It was held that a mortgagor is not entitled to remain in possession in order to sell at a price that would not clear the debt, even in circumstances where that price would be better than one achieved by the mortgagee selling with vacant possession.

Consequences

Having taken possession, the mortgagee can use any income arising from the property in lieu of interest payments due to him under the mortgage. Any surplus may be used to pay off the capital or passed to the next person entitled.

Duty of the mortgagee when possessing

• Where the mortgagee possesses the property himself, he must pay a fair rent and do reasonable repairs.

• Where receiving an income for the property, the mortgagee must account for that income on the footing of *wilful default* ie he must account for not only what he receives but also for what he could have received by acting reasonably: *White v City of London Brewery Co* (1889).

Where the mortgage is equitable

The mortgagee may have the right to take possession where he has obtained a court order: *Barclays Bank Ltd v Bird* [1954]. Otherwise, his right is debateable, although few mortgagees risk taking possession without a court order nowadays.

Sale

Why?

To release capital that can be used to pay off the outstanding debt.

When?

Sell before power of sale arises:
- sale is invalid
- mortgagor simply transfers his own interest in the property ie the mortgage to the purchaser

Power of sale arises when:
- the mortgage is by deed; and
- there is no express contrary intention; and
- the legal date for redemption has passed
  s 101 LPA 1925

Sell now ie after power has arisen but before it has become exercisable:
- good title will normally pass to the purchaser
- mortgagee may have to pay damages to anyone suffering a loss from the improper sale (s 104 LPA 1925)
- where the purchaser knows the power had not become exercisable, he will not get good title and the mortgagor could seek to have the sale set aside

Power of sale becomes exercisable if:
- notice has been served on the mortgagor requiring repayment and three months have lapsed without the mortgagor repaying the whole debt; or
- interest is at least two months in arrears; or
- a term other than one relating to payment has been breached. s 103 LPA 1925

Sell now ie after power of sale becomes exercisable:
- sale is valid (see consequences below)

Figure 14.2

Mortgagee's remedies

✳✳✳✳✳✳✳✳✳✳

How?

The property can be sold without first obtaining a court order and by any method.

Who can buy?

- The mortgagee cannot buy the property himself or through an agent: *Martinson v Clowes* (1882), unless it is under a direction from the court: *Palk v Mortgage Services Funding* [1993]. Any attempt to do so will result in the sale being set aside.

- The mortgagee can sell to:
  - an associated person; or
  - a company in which he holds a substantial shareholding

  but the burden of proving the transaction was in good faith and without fraud would fall on him: *Tse Kwok Lam v Kwong Chit Sen* [1983].

Consequences

The sale transfers the mortgagor's estate to the purchaser free from the mortgagor's equity of redemption and any subsequent mortgages, although it may be subject to any prior mortgages that exist.

The mortgagee is trustee of the proceeds of sale and must distribute them in the order laid down in **s 105 LPA 1925**:

- to discharge total debt owed to any prior mortgagee;
- to discharge any costs of sale;
- to discharge total debt owed to the mortgagee selling;
- any balance remaining, to be paid to any mortgagee next in priority and, if none, the mortgagor.

Where the sale produces insufficient funds to pay off the debt, the mortgagee could then sue on the personal covenant for the remainder.

Duty of the mortgagee when selling

No statutory duties are imposed upon the mortgagee when exercising power of sale.

Duties have arisen through case law and those that exist are owed solely to the mortgagor and not, for example, to a beneficiary where the mortgaged property is held under a trust: *Parker-Tweedale v Dunbar Bank plc* [1991].

- The mortgagee can sell the property whenever he wishes, subject to meeting the statutory requirements discussed above. However, when he decides to sell, he must obtain a fair and true market value for the property: *Cuckmere Brick Co Ltd v Mutual Finance Ltd* [1971]. Failure to do so may lead to the mortgagee having to pay the difference or, worst still, the sale being set aside.

- In seeking to obtain a fair and true market value for the property, the mortgagee is not required to incur expense in securing a better price, for example by pursuing planning applications: *Silven Properties Ltd v Royal Bank of Scotland plc* [2004].

- The mortgagee can seek the mortgagor's consent to sell at less than current market value. Where given, the mortgagor would then be estopped from claiming the mortgagee failed to meet his duty, assuming the mortgagor had not been subjected to any undue influence: *Mercantile Credit Co v Clarke* [1996].

Section 91(2) LPA 1925

This gives a court a wide power to order a sale at the instance of any 'person interested'. It is sometimes requested by the mortgagor where the mortgagee refuses to sell.

....

Palk v Mortgage Services Funding plc [1993] Ch 330

The mortgagee wished to lease the mortgaged property, despite the fact that rent acquired would cover no more than a third of the mortgage interest payments. Realizing that the effect of this would be to increase their debt, the mortgagors requested a sale which was granted by the Court of Appeal.

....

Where the mortgage is equitable

Without any deed, power of sale is not possible under s 101 LPA 1925. However, the mortgagee could apply to the court for an order for sale under s 91 LPA 1925.

Appointing a receiver

Why?

Typically, appointed where the mortgaged property is generating an income which the mortgagee wishes to intercept to help pay off the debt. It is preferable to the mortgagee taking possession himself, since the duties imposed upon the mortgagee in appointing a receiver, are less onerous.

When?

Figure 14.3

Mortgagee's remedies

✳✳✳✳✳✳✳✳✳✳

How?

The appointment must be in writing.

Who?

The mortgagee may choose whosoever he wishes. The receiver need not be a professional.

Consequences

The primary function of the receiver is to collect income from the mortgaged property (eg rents) and apply that money in accordance with s 109 LPA 1925:

- to pay rents, taxes rates, and other outgoings affecting the mortgaged property;
- to pay interest payments on any mortgages having priority;
- to pay the receiver's commission, property insurance, and repairs;
- to pay mortgage interest;
- to reduce the principal sum outstanding where directed to do so by mortgagee in writing;
- to pay any surplus to the next in line eg mortgagor where no inferior mortgages.

Duty of the receiver

The receiver is deemed to be the agent of the mortgagor (although not in the true sense) and, in managing the property, the duty he owes the mortgagor goes beyond acting in good faith. Rather he must manage the property with due diligence subject to trying to achieve a position where the interest payments on the mortgage can be met and the principal sum repaid: *Medforth v Blake* [2000].

Where the mortgage is equitable

Without a deed, the power to appoint does not arise under s 101 LPA 1925. However, the mortgagee could apply to the court under s 37 Supreme Court Act 1981 to request an appointment.

Foreclosure

Why?

The mortgagee seeks to become the outright owner of the property.

When?

Not until the legal date for redemption has expired.

How?

The mortgagee must seek a court order. He commences an action in court by requesting foreclosure unless the mortgagor pays the debt within a specified time. Where no payment is forthcoming:

- the court issues a foreclosure order *nisi*. An account setting out monies owed is prepared. The court declares that if the monies owed are not paid within a specified time after the account has been drawn up (usually six months) then...
- the foreclosure order becomes *absolute*, vesting the property in the mortgagee free from the rights of the mortgagor.

Consequences

- In seeking foreclosure, other remedies are no longer available to the mortgagee.
- If successful, the mortgagee becomes outright owner of the mortgaged property.
- The mortgagor loses all rights over the property. His equity of redemption is extinguished.

However, remember that even once a foreclosure order has been made *absolute*, it can be reopened in exceptional circumstances that may justify the failure to repay monies owed within the specified time limit: *Campbell v Holyland* (1877).

Where the mortgage is equitable

As above.

Priorities

When a property subject to several mortgages is sold, the proceeds of sale will not be shared amongst the mortgagees equally. Rather, the mortgagees will be paid on the basis of who has priority. The rules to determine this will differ depending upon whether the land is registered or not.

Unregistered land

- Where the mortgagee has the title deeds, he will take priority over all other lenders.
- Where the mortgagee does not have the title deeds, and the mortgage is legal, it should be registered as a *puisne* mortgage; a Class C(i) land charge. Where it is equitable, it should be registered as a general equitable charge; a Class C(iii) land charge. Where no such registration has occurred by the time a subsequent mortgage is created, the subsequent mortgage will take priority over the former. Failure to register the mortgage makes it void against subsequent mortgagees: s 4 Land Charges Act 1972.

Registered land

- To create a legal mortgage over registered land, it must be registered: s 27 LRA 2002. It will be entered on the charges register of the land over which it exists, with the date of entry being noted on the register. Priority will then be governed by the order in which the mortgages were entered on the register: **s 48 LRA 2002**.

- Where the mortgage is not registered, it will be equitable only. Priority will then be governed by the chronological date of creation, with those created earlier taking priority over those created later. However, once registered, the mortgage will take priority over those still to be registered, but will rank below any charge already entered on the register.

Revision tip

Remind yourself of some of the rules above by linking to material covered in chapters 3 and 4.

Key cases

Case	Facts	Principle
Cheltenham & Gloucester BS v Norgan [1996] 1 WLR 343	Mrs Norgan had a history of difficulty in paying her mortgage repayments and orders for possession had been made, although postponed. A possession order was finally granted without postponement and Mrs Norgan appealed. Her case was remitted back to the first instance court to determine whether she had the means to pay off the debt and arrears within 13 years, the remaining term of the mortgage.	In assessing what would be a reasonable period to postpone a possession order to allow arrears to be paid, the starting point should be the agreed duration of the mortgage term.
Cityland & Property (Holdings) Ltd v Dabrah [1968] Ch 166	Concerned the sale of a freehold by a landlord to his tenant, with a loan for the purchase being provided by the landlord. The loan repayments amounted to a 57% premium on top of the actual sum advanced for the loan. This was held void.	Clauses in a mortgage that have been obtained unconscionably will be struck out as void.
Fairclough v Swan Brewery Co Ltd [1912] AC 565	A clause in a mortgage over leasehold property postponed redemption until the final 6 weeks of the lease. Held void.	A clause postponing the ability to redeem must not have the effect of rendering the right illusory.
Jones v Morgan [2001] EWCA Civ 995	A mortgage was created and 3 years later the parties entered into a second agreement giving the mortgagee the right to purchase some of the mortgaged property. The right was deemed invalid. The second agreement was seen as a reconstruction of the initial mortgage entered into 3 years previously. The mortgage and the option to purchase were therefore not truly independent transactions.	Where a right to purchase some or all of the mortgaged property can be seen as part of the mortgage transaction, that right will be held void.

Case	Facts	Principle
Knightsbridge Estates Trust Ltd v Byrne [1939] Ch 441	A clause in a mortgage over freehold property postponed the ability to redeem for 40 years. The clause was held valid.	As per *Fairclough* above.
Kreglinger v New Patagonia Meat & Cold Storage Co Ltd [1914] AC 25	The mortgage contained a right of first refusal for the benefit of the mortgagee to buy sheepskins produced by the mortgagor. The right could extend beyond the duration of the mortgage. The clause was upheld.	Parties to a mortgage can agree for the mortgage to contain a collateral advantage which is to last beyond the duration of the mortgage itself, provided they have acted freely and the clause itself is reasonable.
Multiservice Bookbinding Co Ltd v Marden [1979] Ch 84	Linking the interest rate to the Swiss franc, leading to large interest payments when currency values fluctuated, was upheld as valid.	A clause will not be struck out of a mortgage agreement for being unreasonable. It must have been imposed in a morally reprehensible way.
Noakes & Co Ltd v Rice [1902] AC 24	Mortgage created over a public house contained a clause tying the mortgagor into selling the mortgagee's liquor for the entire duration of the lease, not just for the duration of the mortgage. The clause was held void.	Upon redemption, the mortgagor should get back his property in virtually the same state as when the mortgage was created, unencumbered by any collateral advantages in favour of the mortgagee.
Palk v Mortgage Services Funding plc [1993] Ch 330	The mortgagee wished to lease the mortgaged property, despite the fact that rent acquired would cover no more than a third of the mortgage interest payments. Realizing that the effect of this would be to increase their debt, the mortgagors requested a sale which was granted by the Court of Appeal.	Under s 91 LPA 1925 the court has a jurisdiction to sell mortgaged property independent of the mortgagee's right to do so.
Reeve v Lisle [1902] AC 461	A mortgage of a ship was created and 12 days later the mortgagee was granted an option to purchase the ship. The option was held valid.	An option created independently of mortgage transaction, even where the option relates to purchasing the mortgaged property, can be upheld as valid.
Royal Bank of Scotland v Etridge (No 2) [2002] 2 AC 773	Eight conjoined appeals by wives seeking to have mortgages held void as against them on the basis they were obtained by undue influence. In each case, the mortgages appeared to be for the principal benefit of the husbands.	Established key steps a lender must take to avoid being affected by undue influence asserted over the borrower.

Exam questions

Case	Facts	Principle
Samuel v Jarrah Timber and Wood Paving Corporation Ltd [1904] AC 323	A mortgage of stock gave the mortgagee an option to buy the stock within 12 months of the date of the mortgage. The option was held void.	A mortgage should not include clauses which prevent a mortgagor from ever being able to repay the loan and get his property back.

(?) Exam questions

Problem question

In January 2007, Karl purchased two pubs. The first pub, the Fox and Hounds, is a freehold prop-erty and in order to raise cash to purchase it, Karl mortgaged the premises to Erinsborough Bank plc. The mortgage is a repayment mortgage over a period of 20 years and contains a clause stipulating that the mortgage cannot be redeemed before 1 January 2022. Since Erinsborough Bank plc was uncertain about the commercial viability of the business, it insisted upon an inter-est rate 10% above current market values. In a separate agreement, completed the day after the mortgage agreement, Karl entered into an option to purchase in favour of Erinsborough Bank plc that stipulated 'the mortgagee reserves for itself the right to purchase the property up to the date of redemption of the mortgage at a price that is equivalent to its then current market value assuming vacant possession at a discount of 4%'.

The second pub that Karl purchased, The White Hart, was a leasehold property. He purchased a 21 year lease from the vendor, King Brewery Ltd. To help raise finance for this purchase, he mort-gaged the property to King Brewery Ltd. The mortgage agreement stipulates the earliest date for redemption as 1 January 2024. As part of the agreement, King Brewery Ltd insisted upon the inclusion of a clause that Karl only purchase and retail beer and ale products from the mortgagee for the duration of the lease term.

The pub trade has recently been in decline and Karl now founds himself in three months arrears with his mortgage payments to King Brewery Ltd. King Brewery have recently written to Karl stating that it wishes to seek possession of the property so that it may lease it to another tenant. Karl is unhappy about this; not only has he been living above The White Hart but he is also due to receive a substantial cash inheritance from his Aunt who has just died.

Advise Karl:

1. as to the legality or otherwise of the clauses contained in both mortgage agreements; and

2. as to the likelihood of King Brewery Ltd securing a possession order in respect of The White Hart pub.

An outline answer is available at the end of the book

Essay question

To what extent does the law strike a fair balance between the interests of the mortgagor and those of the mortgagee in respect of:

1. ascertaining the validity of clauses within a mortgage; and
2. enforcing the mortgagee's remedies of possession and sale?

An outline answer is available online at www.oxfordtextbooks.co.uk/orc/concentrate/

Outline answers

Chapter 1

Problem answer

1. Determine whether the items are fixtures, and therefore should be returned to Tim, or chattels and therefore have been validly removed.

- Explain the two keys tests: degree of annexation and purpose of annexation: *Holland v Hodgson* (1872); *Hamp v Bygrave* (1983).

- Apply the tests to the items and assess their status using case law to support arguments.

- Key cases include *Elitestone Ltd v Morris* [1997]; *Leigh v Taylor [1902]*; *D'Eyncourt v Gregory* (1866); *Botham v TSB Bank plc* [1997].

- Arguments may include looking at whether the items rested on their own weight; if attached, what was the purpose of that attachment; whether any evidence can be produced that the items enhanced the overall architectural design of the property; how much damage, if any, has been caused to the property by the removal of the items etc.

2. Since the true owner of the necklace cannot be found, to determine who can keep it:

- Assess whether it is treasure trove and thus belongs to the Crown. Apply rules in **Treasure Act 1996** and **Treasure (Designation) Order 2002**.

- If not treasure determine whether the object was found embedded in the ground or lying on the surface. Here, under a bush which the postman could see suggests lying on the surface of the ground. Apply rule in *Parker v British Airways Board* [1982].

3. Does this amount to a trespass of Tim's lower airspace?

- Determine what amounts to the lower airspace: *Anchor Brewhouse Developments v Berkley House (Docklands Developments) Ltd* (1987).

- Assess whether overhanging branches invade this space: *Lemon v Webb* (1895).

- If yes, identify whether Tim can keep the branches to make a basket.

Chapter 3

Problem answer

1. Auntie Vera

She has a beneficial interest under a trust.

- Consider whether a restriction has been entered on the proprietorship register (**s 40 LRA 2002**) which will lead to overreaching (**ss 2** and **27 LPA 1925**; *City of London Building Society v Flegg* [1988]) and purchaser taking free from the interest.

- If not entered and purchaser deals with one trustee only, as may be the case here, beneficial interest will bind as an overriding interest if conditions under **Sch 3 para 2** are met. Key consideration here will be whether Auntie Vera can establish that she is in actual occupation of the land.

2. Malcolm

Appears to have a lease created by deed as required for one over 3 years in duration (**s 52 LPA 1925; s 1 LP(MP)A 1989**). Consider whether additional formality of registration has been complied with (**s 27 LRA 2002**):

- if yes, legal lease and notice would have been entered on register to make it binding upon all (**s 38 LRA 2002**);

- if no, lease could only be equitable.

  - Would bind all if entered as a notice on charges register (**s 32 LRA 2002; s 29(2) LRA 2002**).

  - If not entered, would not bind purchaser for valuable consideration (**s 29(1) LRA 2002**) unless binding as an overriding interest under **Sch 3 para 2**. So would bind Rory as inherited the property but possible enforcement against Natural Farming Ltd would require assessing whether conditions under **Sch 3 para 2** are met.

3. Peter

Appears to have an easement of access. Although made by deed it is not equivalent in duration to a legal estate (**s 1(2) LPA 1925**) and

Outline answers

✱✱✱✱✱✱✱✱✱✱

therefore could only be equitable. Consider if entered as a notice on charges register:

- if yes, binds all (**s 29(2) LRA 2002**);
- if no, will not bind a purchaser for valuable consideration (**s 29(1)** and **s 132 LRA 2002**) unless established as overriding interest under **Sch 3 para 2**. So would bind Rory as inherited the property but enforcement against Natural Farming Ltd would depend upon whether conditions under **Sch 3 para 2** are met.

4. Larry

Appears mere licence as lacks requirements/ formalities of lease/easement. Revocable at will.

Chapter 4

Problem answer

Marian

- Potential beneficial interest under a trust by virtue of her contribution to the purchase. Identify this as an equitable interest (**s 1(3) LPA 1925**) incapable of registration as a land charge (**s 2(4) LCA 1972**, but capable of being overreached. Explain requirements of overreaching under **ss 2** and **27 LPA 1925**; apply to the facts. Appears not overreached as only one trustee, Guy (**William's & Glyn's Bank Ltd v Boland** [1981]). Therefore, whether enforceable against Josh depends upon the doctrine of notice. Explain and apply. Here the surveyor is likely to have acquired constructive notice of her rights and thus Josh acquired imputed notice thus Josh would be bound. Key cases include **Hunt v Luck** [1901]; **Kingsnorth Trust Ltd v Tizard** [1986]. If a giftee, Josh is not a purchaser for value under the doctrine thus bound by the right.
- Potential statutory right to occupy the matrimonial home under **Family Law Act 1996**, enforceable against Josh if registered as a Class F land charge (**s 198 LPA 1925**). No information therefore explain whether Josh would be bound if not registered (**s 4(5)** and **4(8) LCA 1972**). If a giftee, Josh would be bound as not a purchaser (**s 17 LCA 1972**).

Susie

- Identify potential easement of access. Consider whether legal or equitable by looking

at **s 52 LPA 1925, s 1 LP(MP)A 1989**. Told by deed so probably legal. Legal rights bind whole world. No difference if Josh had been a giftee.

Pete

- Potential lease. Identify whether legal: **s 52 LPA 1925; s 1 LP(MP)A 1989**. Whilst signed by grantor other deed requirements not apparent. Assess whether equitable instead: **s 2 LP(MP) A 1989**; **Walsh v Lonsdale** (1882). Explain enforcement of equitable lease against Josh depends upon whether registered as a Class C(iv) land charge. Discuss **s 198 LPA 1925** and **s 4(6) LCA 1972**; **Midland Bank Trust Co Ltd v Green** [1981]. Explain operation of **s 4(6) LCA 1972** means that it would bind Josh if a mere giftee as not a purchaser for money/money's worth.

Chapter 6

Problem answer

Identify the issue: are Raj and Sally tenants or licencees? Explain the significance of the distinction.

Distinguish a lease from a licence. Explain the essential characteristics of a lease. Explain substance not form is important. Key authorities include **Street v Mountford** [1985]; **s 205 LPA 1925**; **Ashburn Anstalt v Arnold** [1989]. Here, fact called 'licence' agreements is not conclusive.

Assess whether there is certainty of term. Key authorities include **Lace v Chantler** (1944); **Prudential Assurance v London Residuary Body** [1992].

Assess whether there is exclusive possession. Key points to consider include:

- Landlord reserves right to introduce one other to share. Is this realistic? Look to the number of people that could be introduced to share with Raj and Sally and nature of the accommodation when making this assessment. Look to the relationship between Raj and Sally. Is it feasible others share with them? Has this clause ever been acted upon? Key authorities include **Antoniades v Villiers** [1990]; **AG Securities v Vaughan** [1990]; **Aslan v Murphy** [1990].
- Retention of keys and provision of laundry services. In assessing whether this is real

and precludes exclusive possession consider the purpose for which the keys were retained and whether such purpose was ever acted upon. Key authorities include *Aslan v Murphy* [1990]; *Facchini v Bryson* [1952]; *Marchant v Charters* [1977].

Assess whether, if tenants, they occupy as individual or joint tenants. Do they have the four unities to be joint tenants? Key points to consider include the fact they have individual bedrooms, signed separate agreements and pay £200 each. Key authorities include *AG Securities v Vaughan* [1990]; *Antoniades v Villiers* [1990]; *Mikeover Ltd v Brady* [1989].

Draw appropriate conclusions.

Assess difference if points to consider include:

• whether it is more realistic to introduce others to share if strangers and applied separately;

• whether no unity of title exists if signed on different days.

Chapter 7

Problem answer

This questions concerns issues regarding covenants in leases.

First establish whether Patrick is bound the covenants originally entered into by Miriam. As a new lease, governed by the **Landlord and Tenant (Covenants) Act 1995**, the burden of the covenants probably passed to Patrick upon assignment of the lease under **s 3**. (If granted originally in 1994, whether the burden of covenants passed to Patrick upon assignment would depend upon satisfaction of the requirements from *Spencer's Case* (1583)).

Assess whether Patrick is liable for the disrepair. Explain how an express tenant covenant to repair can be overridden by an implied landlord obligation to repair under **LTA 1985**. As a lease of 6 years, the **LTA 1985** applies. (Had the lease been for 25 years, it would not and liability would fall to Patrick under his express covenant assuming the disrepair falls within the ambit of the covenant. Case law discussion of the boundaries of such express covenants should be analysed including *Lister v Lane* (1893); *Ravenseft Properties Ltd v Davstone (Holdings) Ltd* [1980]; *Pembury v Lamdin* [1940]; *Post Office v Aquarius Property Ltd*.)

Assess whether the disrepair in question falls into the **LTA 1985**. Key authorities include **s 11(1)** and **(2)(a) LTA 1985**; *Quick v Taff-Ely BC* [1986]; *Re Irvine's Estate v Moran* (1992); *O'Brien v Robinson* [1983]. Constance may be liable to repair the window but possibly not the damp as Patrick didn't take steps to mitigate his loss.

Identify remedies available for breach of a repair covenant, including forfeiture and damages. (Remember that if a 25 years lease, the **Leasehold Property (Repairs) Act 1938** would apply.)

Finally assess whether Constance can withhold consent to the sub-letting to George. Explain **s 19(1)(a) LTA 1927** and utilize case law to determine whether she has any grounds upon which consent could be refused. In particular consider *International Drilling Fluids Ltd v Louisville Investments (Uxbridge) Ltd* [1986]; *Ashworth Frazer Ltd v Gloucester CC* [2001].

Chapter 8

Problem answer

Is there adverse possession: *Pye (JA) (Oxford) Ltd v Graham* [2003].

• Is Fred dispossessed of the wooded area? He seems to be given that there is no presence on the property. But not using the property is clearly not enough. It is more arguable that he is dispossessed of the wooded area given that George and Hilly seem to be here on a permanent basis. Remember, Fred need not know of their presence to be dispossessed but they do need to be discoverable.

• Do George and Hilly have factual possession? The test is one which involves a sufficient degree of control (*Powell v McFarlane* (1977)). There are different points when George and Hilly might have factual possession. The tent may be too impermanent, but it could be argued that they are on the land the whole time and the nature of the structure is not relevant. It is certainly not trivial. Fitting the padlock is similar to *Buckinghamshire CC v Moran* [1990] and seems to suggest factual possession.

• Intention to possess. George and Hilly need an intention to possess they do not need to intend to own it. The intention needs to be for the time being not forever: *Buckinghamshire CC v Moran* [1990].

Outline answers
✳✳✳✳✳✳✳✳✳✳✳

- The possession must be adverse/unauthorized.

You may also mention **Sch 1 para 8(4) LA 1980**.

Identify registered land and the potential claim is post 2003, so **LRA 2002** applies.

Consider the point that Ian and John have only resided since 1999. There must be ten years adverse possession before applying to be registered as proprietor: **Sch 6 para 1(1) LRA 2002**. However, consider the possibility of establishing continuous adverse possession albeit through different people (George and Hilly) from 1996 (arguably) and certainly from 1997. It is not relevant that the registered proprietor differs at the time adverse possession begins.

Examine procedure under **LRA 2002**, noting specifically an inability to be registered as proprietor unless one of the exceptions in **Sch 6** applies. Explain how, upon notification by the Land Registry, Town and Country Hotels Ltd need to take steps to evict Ian and John within two years and the consequences under **Sch 6** if they fail.

Chapter 9

Problem answer

The purpose of this question is for you to think about the nature of landholding, **TLATA 1996** and overreaching.

Perhaps begin by explaining that Alan holds the property on trust for himself and Bill and Claire as beneficiaries. They are all tenants in common in equity. Alan is the sole trustee under a trust of land.

The starting point is that Alan, as a trustee, has the powers of absolute owner: **s 6(1) TLATA 1996**.

1. The relevant provision is **s 11 TLATA 1996**. Apply the wording of this section to the facts, drawing attention to the fact that Bill and Claire are of full age and beneficially entitled to an interest in possession. Alan need only act according to their wishes in so far as it is consistent with the general interest of the trusts. There is a dispute between the parties but Alan seems to be in the majority according to the value of his interests. There is no provision excluding the right to be consulted: **s 11(2) TLATA 1996**.

2. The general position is that Bill and Claire have a right to occupy under **s 12 TLATA 1996** but the conditions in **s 12(1)** and **(2)** must be met.

3. There is no express provision as to consent but Bill and Claire, as persons with an interest in the property, could make an application under **s 14 TLATA 1996** given that Alan's power of sale is one of the trustee's functions. They would then need to consider the matters relevant in **s 15 TLATA 1996**.

4. The question here is whether there is overreaching (**ss 2** and **27 LPA 1925**). The land is registered but it is unclear if any attempt has been made to protect the beneficial interests, for example as a restriction (**s 40 LRA 2002**). In any event there is only payment to one trustee and so overreaching cannot occur (*William's & Glyn's Bank Ltd v Boland* [1981]). The normal rules then apply and in essence Bill and Claire would need to rely on **Sch 3 para 2** overriding interests.

Chapter 10

Problem answer

In chase

- Identify property held by way of a trust of land and explain how legal and equitable title respectively is held.

- Key authorities regarding legal title include **s 1(6) LPA 1925**; **s 34(2) TA 1925**. Remember, Bobby could not hold legal title at this time as only 17 years old.

- Key authorities regarding equitable title include: *AG Securities v Vaughan* [1990]; *Lake v Craddock* (1732); *Bull v Bull* [1955]; *Pink v Lawrence* (1977). Remember, where four unities are present to allow a joint tenancy, an express declaration to this effect will trump presumptions of a tenancy in common based upon business/unequal contributions.

Carl mortgages his share

- Consider possible severance under act operating on your own share, specifically partial alienation.

- Key authorities include *Williams v Hensman* (1861); *First National Securities v Hegarty* [1985]; **s 36(2) LPA 1925**; *Goodman v Gallant* [1986].

- Here, severance probably effective. Carl remains joint tenant at law but tenant in common as to ¼ in equity. In equity, others remain joint tenants between themselves.

Bobby offers to sell his interest

• Consider possible severance under mutual agreement.

• Key authorities include *Williams v Hensman* (1861); *Burgess v Rawnsley* [1975]; *Hunter v Babbage* [1994]; *Neilson Jones v Fedden* [1975]; *Gore and Snell v Carpenter* (1990).

• Here, probably effective based upon all now seeing Bobby as having a distinct share in the property. Lack of agreement regarding price may not be an obstacle. Bobby becomes tenant in common as to ¼ in equity.

Bobby dies

• If effectively severed (above), Bobby died as tenant in common, so follow instructions in the will.

• Remember, a person (here David) may be both a joint tenant and a tenant in common in equity at the same time.

Alex's letter

• Consider possible severance by notice in writing.

• Key authorities include s 36(2) LPA 1925; *Re Drapers Conveyance* [1969]; *Kinch v Bullard* [1999].

• Remember all intended recipients need not see the notice for it to be effective if it has been effectively delivered.

Alex's desire to sell

• Discuss application under s 14 TLATA 1996 and the s 15 TLATA 1996 criteria.

• Continuing purpose and interests of creditors may be significant.

Chapter 11

Problem answer

This question requires you to think about the consequences of licences and third parties.

Brian

It is suggested that you focus upon considering whether this is a licence coupled with an interest. Explain the circumstance in which such licences arise. Has Brian been granted an 'interest'? What is an interest for the purpose of this licence? Consider key authorities such as *Hurst v Picture Theatres Ltd* [1915] and *Hounslow LBC v Twickenham Garden Developments Ltd* [1971]. It seems this may be unlikely – there appears to be more of an informal arrangement between himself and Albert rather than having been granted a proprietary interest by Albert. A *profit à prendre*, for example, would need to be created by a deed or prescription.

If it is a licence coupled with an interest then it should bind Eric as long as the interest to which it is attached continues.

If not a licence coupled with an interest then it should be considered whether it could be an implied contractual licence with the sculpture acting as consideration. Generally, such licences do not bind third parties (*Ashburn Anstalt v Arnold* (1989)) and since Eric does not know of Brian's existence, it is difficult to see how a constructive trust could arise to make Eric bound by the licence.

Colin

This looks like a bare licence which would not be binding on Eric.

David

This looks like a contractual licence. (You might also consider whether it could be a lease or an easement.) Discuss the issue of whether a contractual licence binds a third party. The starting point would be that they do not automatically bind a third party (*Ashburn Anstalt v Arnold* [1989]) but that they might if there is a constructive trust (*Binions v Evans* [1972]). It would seem, for example, that a mere notice of a contractual licence is not in itself enough; there must be something else to attach to the purchasers conscience (*Ashburn Anstalt v Arnold* [1989]).

Chapter 12

Problem answer

Introduction

• Identify issue: does Shirley have a right to use the internal stairs, the parking space for a flower stall and to put a sign on the house? Did she acquire these rights as easements from Danielle? If so, could they now be enforced against Roger?

Main body

- Consider whether rights sought are capable of being easements.

- Identify the requirements under *Re Ellenborough Park* [1956] and assess whether the rights being sought satisfy these requirements. Further, consider whether anything else prevents the rights from being capable of being easements.

- Particular points to discuss here would include whether the placing of an advert on the side of the house actually accommodates the dominant land or rather just the business of the dominant land owner (analyse and apply *Hill v Tupper* (1863) and *Moody v Steggles* (1879). On the facts, it may be the latter); whether the right to use the parking space amounts to exclusive possession (analyse and apply *Copeland v Greenhalf* [1952]; *Hair v Gillman* (2000); *Batchelor v Marlow* [2003]).

Upon determining those rights claimed that have capability to be easements (possibly all except right to place sign on house), assess whether they have been appropriately acquired:

- Regarding the right to use internal stairs: identify no formal express grant of the right in the lease. Granted a licence which may have elevated into an easement upon lease renewal. Explain and apply acquisition by **s 62 LPA 1925**.

- Regarding the right to use the parking space: identify formally granted in both leases. However, issue that right was presumably to park a car, not place a flower stall. How strictly will courts interpret expressly granted easements?

If acquired by Shirley from Danielle, could she now enforce the easements against Roger? Determine the status of the easements ie legal or equitable, and apply appropriate enforcement rules for such easements in registered land.

Conclude

Chapter 13

Problem answer

Introduction

- Identify the issue: can Gillian enforce the covenants breached by Eric against him?

- Identify the original covenantor and covenantee/the dominant and servient land.

- Identify that as successors to the land, enforcement against Eric by Gillian will only be possible if the burden and benefit of the covenants have passed to them respectively.

Have the burden of the covenants passed to Eric?

- Consider common law position that generally burden will not pass: *Austerberry v Corporation of Oldham* (1885).

- Will equity pass the burden to Eric? Identify, explain and apply the *Tulk v Moxhay* (1848) requirements.

- Particular discussion points here include the fact that only covenant a) is negative (*Haywood v Brunswick Permanent Benefit BS* (1881)); whilst you do not know whether the covenants were appropriately entered on the register to give notice to Eric, as the land was gifted to him he would be deemed to have notice anyway (**s 29 LRA 2002**).

Has the benefit of covenant a) passed to Gillian in equity?

- Appropriate method to explain and apply on the facts is probably statutory annexation (s 78 LPA 1925; *Federated Homes Ltd v Mill Lodge Properties Ltd* [1980]). Consider whether successful annexation is problematic where the dominant land is a large estate (*Re Ballards Conveyance* [1937]; Brightman LJ in *Federated Homes Ltd*).

What about enforcement of the positive covenants b) and c)?

- Explain ability to enforce against original covenantor: **s 79 LPA 1925**. Note that John was seriously ill and therefore may be difficult to pursue him / his estate.

- No evidence of indemnity covenant between John and Eric that might exert pressure upon Eric to stop the breaches.

• Explain possibility of using the rule in *Halsall v Brizell* [1957] as regards enforcing covenant b). Identify requirements and apply.

• Remember to show benefit of these covenants passing to Gillian using common law methods; here likely to be implied if satisfy requirements under *P&A Swift Investments v Combined English Stores Group plc* [1989].

Conclude and identify possible remedies.

Chapter 14

Problem answer

1. Clauses attempting to postpone ability to redeem.

Consider whether they render right to redeem illusory/imposed in a morally reprehensible manner.

• Key case law to analyse and apply includes *Fairclough v Swan Brewery Co Ltd* [1912]; *Knightsbridge Estates Trust Ltd v Byrne* [1939].

• Relevant points to consider include whether property is leasehold or freehold and the equality of bargaining power between the parties.

High interest rate

Consider whether oppressive/unconscionable.

• Key case law to analyse and apply includes *Multiservice Bookbinding Co. Ltd v Marden* [1979]; *Cityland & Property (Holdings) Ltd v Dabrah* [1968]. Consider relevant legislation protecting consumers against unfair terms.

• Relevant points to consider include the equality of bargaining power between the parties; reason for purchase of pub; commercial and not residential property.

Option to purchase

Consider whether truly independent of mortgage transaction.

• Key case law to analyse and apply includes *Samuel v Jarrah Timber and Wood Paving Corporation Ltd* [1904]; *Reeve v Lisle* (1902); *Jones v Morgan* [2001].

• Relevant points to consider include fact it was a separate agreement and 4% discount.

Collateral advantage re purchase of beer and ale

• Key case law to analyse and apply includes *Kreglinger v New Patagonia Meat & Cold Storage Co Ltd* [1914]; *Jones v Morgan* [2001].

• Key points to consider include fact only for duration of mortgage; equality of bargaining power between the parties; no apparent discounts apply.

2. This requires detailed analysis of the ability for a mortgagee to repossess the property. Of particular importance will be the fact that Karl resides at the property. Consider the impact of **Administration of Justice Act 1970 / 1973** and how far a court would be influenced by the fact that Karl is expecting to inherit a large sum of money when exercising its discretion under the Act.

Essay outline answers are available online at www.oxfordtextbooks.co.uk/orc/concentrate/

Glossary

adverse possession a process by which title to land can be acquired through acts of possessing land of another (i) until such time as the real owner is statute barred from recovering the land (at which point his title to land will be extinguished) or (ii) until such time as the adverse possessor is registered as owner

assignment a transfer of a proprietary interest (used, for example, in relation to a transfer of a lease or reversionary interest or in relation to the transfer of a benefit of a restrictive covenant)

beneficiary a person who holds a beneficial interest in property held by way of a trust

chattel a thing usually not fixed to the land and not regarded as forming part of the land (as opposed to a fixture)

commonhold a form of freehold estate applicable to blocks of flats where unit holders hold the freehold of their flat (unit) and a commonhold association, of which unit holders are members, holds the freehold of the common parts

conveyance the deed used to transfer the legal estate where title is unregistered

covenant a promise made by deed (either requiring someone to do something ie positive, or not to do something ie negative)

covenantee the person in whose favour a covenant is made and thus who has the benefit of a covenant and may enforce it if breached

covenantor the person from whom a covenant is extracted and thus who has the burden of the obligation

deed a document compliant with s 1 LP(MP) A 1989 and normally required to create a legal estate or interest in land

disposition a dealing with land (for example sale of a freehold estate)

dominant tenement the piece of land that is benefited by a proprietary right

easement a proprietary right exercised over one piece of land (the servient tenement) for the benefit of another piece of land (the dominant tenement); can be positive or negative in nature

equity of redemption the mortgagor's interest in the mortgaged property

estate a type of proprietary right entitling the holder to possess, use, and enjoy land for a period of time, be it unlimited (freehold) or fixed (leasehold) to the exclusion of others

estate contract a contract to grant an estate in land (includes options to purchase and rights of pre-emption)

fee simple absolute in possession the technical title for a freehold estate

fixture a thing that has become fixed to land so that it becomes part of the land (as opposed to chattel)

freehold estate the largest of the two estates in land that have legal capacity; lasts indefinitely until such time as the owner dies without heirs

headlease the lease out of which the sub-lease has been granted

incorporeal hereditaments inheritable rights that are intangible and which benefit land

in gross where a right exists in gross, it is not for the benefit of a dominant piece of land but merely for the benefit of an individual (for example, *profits à prendre* can exist in gross, easements cannot)

injunction an equitable remedy that forbids someone from doing something (for example erecting a fence that would obstruct a right of way)

interest a type of proprietary right entitling the holder to use and enjoy land of another

inter vivos a disposition which takes place during the lifetime of the grantor (rather than by operation of his will upon his death)

joint tenancy a way of holding co-owned property, where co-owners are seen as a single legal entity holding the whole of the property as a single owner (contrast tenant in common).

The right of survivorship operates between joint tenants.

lease a leasehold estate (also known as 'tenancy')

leasehold estate the second largest of the estates in land that have legal capacity; has a fixed and certain maximum duration

licence permission given by a land owner (the licensor) to another (the licensee) to use his land

mortgage the grant of an interest in property as security for a loan

mortgagee the person to whom a mortgage is granted and who acquires an interest in the property of the mortgagor as security for money lent

mortgagor the person who creates the mortgage and grants an interest in his property to the mortgagee as security for a loan

negative equity where the value of a mortgaged property is worth less than the debt

notice (i) knowledge of an interest: actual (real knowledge); constructive (knowledge of things you could have found out about if you had made reasonable enquiries; imputed (knowledge acquired by an agent is deemed in the knowledge of his agent); (ii) a type of entry that appears in the charges section of the register of title protecting certain interests in registered land

overreaching a procedure by which a purchaser of a legal estate can take that estate free from certain equitable interests, notably beneficial interests under a trust, provided purchase monies are paid to at least two trustees or a trust corporation

overriding interest an interest in registered land that bind third parties coming to the land without any need to be protected by being entered on to the register

personal right a right not exercised against the land itself (as opposed to a proprietary right) and (generally) can only be enforced against the person who gave it to you

prescription a method by which easements and profits can be acquired by evidence of long use

privity of contract the existence of a contractual relationship between the parties

privity of estate a direct relationship of landlord and tenant between the parties

profit à prendre a proprietary right that allows a person to go on the land of another and take something from that land, be it natural produce of the land or animals

proprietary right a right governing a person's ability to use and enjoy land that is potentially enforceable against third parties (as opposed to a personal right)

puisne **mortgage** a legal mortgage of unregistered land that is not secured by the deposit of title deeds. Usually a second or subsequent mortgage

purchaser when used in its technical sense, a person who acquires an estate or interest in land through the action of another, rather than automatically by operation of law

quasi easement a right exercised over, and for the benefit of, your own land which has the potential to develop into a proper easement should that land be divided into two plots that are separately owned and/or occupied

registered land land where title has been registered at the Land Registry

registered proprietor the person registered as owner of a legal estate in registered land

remainder an interest in land granted under a settlement which takes effect after some previous interest has expired

rentcharge similar to rent paid in respect of a lease but rather it relates to a freehold estate

restriction a type of entry that appears in the proprietorship section of the register of title limiting the way in which the registered proprietor can deal with the land

reversion the right remaining in a grantor after he has granted some interest to another that is shorter in duration to his own (for example landlord retains a reversionary interest upon granting a lease)

right of survivorship a process which occurs automatically upon the death of a joint tenant of co-owned property whereby his entitlement

Glossary

✱✱✱✱✱✱✱✱✱✱

to the property extinguishes and the co-owned estate survives to the remaining joint tenants

servient tenement the piece of land that is burdened by a proprietary right

settlement a disposition of land which creates successive interests in that land

severance a procedure whereby a joint tenant becomes a tenant in common

specific performance an equitable remedy that requires someone to do something (for example perform a contract for the transfer of a freehold estate)

sub-let creation of a sub-lease, a lease granted by a landlord who is himself a tenant of another lease (the headlease)

tenancy in common a way of holding co-owned property where each co-owner holds a distinct, individual but as yet undivided share in the property (contrast joint tenancy). The right of survivorship does not operate between tenants in common.

tenure services provided by a tenant in return for holding land from his feudal lord

term of years absolute the technical title for a leasehold estate

title a person's proof of ownership of property

transfer the deed used to transfer the legal estate where title is registered

trust a way of holding property whereby legal title vests in the trustee(s) and the beneficial interest vests in the beneficiaries

trustee a person who holds legal title to property which is held by way of a trust

trust for sale a trust whereby the trustees have a duty to sell. Since TLATA 1996, now takes effect as a trust of land

trust of land a trust whereby trustees have a power to sell. Introduced by TLATA 1996. Any trust with land as trust property will be a trust of land

unregistered land land where title has not been registered at the Land Registry

Table of cases

88 Berkley Road, Re [1971] Ch 648...159, 169

Abbey National BS v Cann [1991] 1 AC 56, HL...43, 44, 45

AG Securities Ltd v Vaughan [1990] 1 AC 417...73, 74, 77, 78, 80, 90, 151, 152

Akici v LR Butlin [2006] 1 WLR 201...90

Ali v Hussein (1974) 231 EG 372...165

Anchor Brewhouse Developments v Berkley House (Docklands Developments) Ltd (1987) 38 BLR 82...5

Antoniades v Villiers [1990] 1 AC 417...78, 80, 91

Appleby v UK (2003) 37 EHRR 783...176

Arlesford Trading Co Ltd v Servansingh [1971] 1 WLR 1080...108

Ashburn Anstalt v Arnold [1989] Ch 1...74, 79, 174, 175, 179–180, 181, 183

Ashworth Frazer Ltd v Gloucester CC [2001] 1 WLR 2180...100

Aslan v Murphy [1990] 1 WLR 766...78, 79, 91

Austerberry v Corporation of Oldham (1885) 29 Ch D 750...214

Bailey v Stephens (1862) 12 CB (NS) 91...190

Ballards Conveyance, Re [1937] Ch 473...217, 219–220, 227

Banco Exterior International v Mann [1995] 1 All ER 936...240

Bank of Baroda v Rayerel [1995] 2 HLR 387...240

Bank of Ireland Home Mortgages Ltd v Bell [2001] 2 FLR 809...165, 167

Bannister v Bannister [1948] 2 All ER 133...140, 147

Barca v Mears [2005] BPIR 15...151, 167

Barclay v Barclay [1970] 2 QB 677...144

Barclays Bank Ltd v Bird [1954] Ch 274...243

Barclays Bank Ltd v Taylor [1974] Ch 137...85

Barclays Bank plc v O'Brien [1994] 1 AC 180...239

Barclays Bank plc v Thomson [1997] 4 All ER 816...240

Batchelor v Marlow [2003] 1 WLR 764...193, 205

Beaulane Properties Ltd v Palmer [2005] 4 All ER 461...119, 129

Bernstein of Leigh (Baron) v Skyviews & General Ltd [1978] QB 479...3, 6, 11

BHP Petroleum GB Ltd v Chesterfield Properties Ltd [2000] Ch 234...103, 107

Biggs v Hoddinott [1898] 2 Ch 307...236

Billson v Residential Apartments Ltd [1992] 1 AC 494...89, 90

Binions v Evans [1972] Ch 359...181, 184

Borman v Griffith [1930] 1 Ch 493...198

Botham v TSB Bank plc [1997] 73 P&CRD 1...7, 11

Breams Property Investment Co Ltd v Stroulger [1948] 2 KB 1...105

Bremner, Re [1999] 1 FLR 912...167

Brew Brothers v Snax (Ross) Ltd [1970] 1 QB 612...97, 109

Bridges v Mees [1957] Ch 475...124

British & Benningtons Ltd v NW Cachar Tea Co [1923] AC 48...68

Brown v Raindle (1796) 3 Ves 256...160

Bruton v London & Quadrant Housing Trust [2000] 1 AC 406...74, 75, 82, 91, 180

Buchanan-Wollaston's Conveyance, Re [1939] Ch 738...164, 169, 170

Buckinghamshire CC v Moran [1990] Ch 623, CA...114, 115, 117, 119, 120, 129

Bull v Bull [1955] 1 QB 234...155

Burgess v Rawnsley [1975] Ch 429...161, 162, 168

Burns v Burns [1984] Ch 317...141

Caines, Re [1978] 1 WLR 540...157

Campbell v Holyland (1877) 7 Ch D 166...247

Central Estates (Belgravia) Ltd v Woolgar (No 2) [1972] 1 WLR 1048...88

Table of cases

✳✳✳✳✳✳✳✳✳✳

Central London Commercial Estates Ltd v Kato Kagaku Ltd [1998] 4 All ER 948...126

Chaffe v Kingsley [2000] 1 EGLR 104...191

Chandler v Clark [2003] 1 P&CR 15...155

Chandless-Chandless v Nicholson [1942] 1 KB 321...89

Cheltenham & Gloucester BS v Norgan [1996] 1 WLR 343...242, 248

Cheltenham & Gloucester plc v Krauz [1997] 1 WLR 1558...242

Chhokar v Chhokar [1984] FLR 313, CA...43, 46

Citro, Re [1991] Ch 132...167

City & Metropolitan Properties Ltd v Greycroft Ltd [1987] 1 WLR 1085...103, 106

City of London Building Society v Flegg [1988] AC 54...40, 46, 57

City of London Corporation v Fell [1994] 1 AC 458...103, 106

Cityland & Property (Holdings) Ltd v Dabrah [1968] Ch 166...232, 237, 248

Claughton v Charalambous [1999] 1 FLR 740...167

Cleaver v Mutual Reserve Fund [1892] 1 QB 147...162

Clore v Theatrical Properties [1936] 2 All Er 483...175

Coatsworth v Johnson (1885) 55 LJQB 220...20, 26, 84, 85

Commission for the New Towns v Cooper (GB) Ltd [1995] Ch 259...68, 70

Copeland v Greenhalf [1952] Ch 488...192, 205

Cottage Holiday Associates v Customs & Excise Commissioners [1983] QB 735...75

Courage Ltd v Crehan [2002] QB 507...237

Cowcher v Cowcher [1972] 1 WLR 425...155

Crabb v Arun DC [1976] Ch 179...182

Crago v Julian [1992] 1 All ER 744...86

Credit Suisse v Beegas Nominees Ltd [1994] 4 All ER 805...96

Crest Nicholson Residential (South) Ltd v McAllister [2004] 1 WLR 2409...221

Crow v Wood [1971] 1 QB 77...191

Cuckmere Brick Co Ltd v Mutual Finance Ltd [1971] Ch 949...244

David v LB Lewisham (1977) 34 P&CR 112...79

Dean v Andrews [1986] 1 EGLR 262...7

Dennis v McDonald [1981] 1 WLR 810; [1982] Fam 63...145, 165

D'Eyncourt v Gregory (1866) LR 3 Eq 382...7, 11

Diligent Finance Co Ltd v Alleyne [1972] 23 P&CR 346...55, 58

Dodsworth v Dodsworth [1973] EGD 233...181, 182

Dolphin's Conveyance, Re [1970] Ch 654...223

Donohoe v Ingram [2006] EWHC 282...151, 167

Draper's Conveyance, Re [1969] 1 Ch 486...158, 161, 169

Duncliffe v Caerfelin Properties Ltd [1989] 2 EGLR 38...107

Dyce v Lady James Hay (1852) 1 Macq 305...191

Dyer v Dyer (1788) 2 Cox 92...133, 139

Eastern Telegraph Co Ltd v Dent [1899] 1 QB 835...101

Ecclesiastical Commissioners for England's Conveyance, Re [1936] Ch 430...211

Elitestone Ltd v Morris [1997] 1 WLR 687...7, 12

Ellenborough Park, Re [1956] Ch 131...175, 186, 187, 188, 189, 190, 191, 206

Errington v Errington & Woods [1952] 1 KB 90...179, 180

Esso Petroleum Co Ltd v Harper's Garage (Stourport) Ltd [1968] AC 269...237

Estates Gazette Ltd v Benjamin Restaurants Ltd [1994] 1 WLR 1528...105

Evers Trust, Re [1980] 1 WLR 1327...164, 170

Expert Clothing Service & Sales Ltd v Hillgate House Ltd [1986] Ch 340...90

Facchini v Bryson [1952] 1 TLR 1386...73, 74, 79

Fairclough v Swan Brewery Co Ltd [1912] AC 565...232, 236, 248

Federated Homes Ltd v Mill Lodge Properties Ltd [1980] 1 WLR 594…208, 209, 220, 221, 222, 227, 228

Ferrishurst Ltd v Wallcite Ltd [1999] Ch 355…42

First National Bank v Achampang [2004] 1 FLR 18…163

First National Bank v Syed [1991] 2 All ER 250…242

First National Securities Ltd v Hegarty [1985] QB 850…161

Firstpost Homes Ltd v Johnson [1995] 1 WLR 1567…68, 71

Flight v Thomas (1841) 8 Cl & Fin 231…201

Four Maids Ltd v Dudley Marshall (Properties) Ltd [1957] Ch 317…241

Fullers Contract, Re (1933) Ch 652…155

Gadd's Land Transfer, Re [1966] Ch 56…216

George Wimpey & Co Ltd v Sohn [1967] Ch 487…117

Gissing v Gissing [1971] AC 866…140, 147

Goldberg v Edwards [1950] Ch 247…198

Goodman v Gallant [1986] Fam 106…151, 158, 166

Gore and Snell v Carpenter (1990) 60 P&CR 456…161

Greater London Council v Jenkins [1975] 1 All ER 354…176

Greenfield v Greenfield (1970) 38 P&CR 570…162

Grescot v Green (1700) 91 ER 179…105

Grigsby v Melville [1974] 1 WLR 80…192

Grossman v Hooper [2001] 3 EGLR 662…67

Hair v Gillman (2000) 80 P&CR 108…192, 205

Hall v Ewin (1887) 37 Ch D 74…109

Halsall v Brizell [1957] 1 All ER 371…210, 225, 227

Hammersmith & Fulham LBC v Monk [1992] 1 AC 478…88

Hamp v Bygrave [1983] EGD 1000…7

Hansford v Jago [1921] 1 Ch 322…197

Harris v Goddard [1983] 1 WLR 1203…158, 159, 169

Haywood v Brunswick Permanent Benefit Building Society (1881) 8 QBD 403…215

Hill v Tupper (1863) 2 H&C 121…190, 205

Hodgson v Marks [1971] Ch 892…42

Holland v Hodgson (1872) LR 7 CP 328…6

Hollington Brothers Ltd v Rhodes [1951] 2 All ER 487…53, 58

Hollins v Verney (1884) 13 QBD 304…199

Hooper v Sherman [1994] NPC 153…68

Hounslow LBC v Minchinton (1997) 74 P&CR 221, CA…116, 118, 129

Hounslow LBC v Twickenham Garden Developments Ltd [1971] Ch 233…177, 178

Hua Chiao Commercial Bank Ltd v Chiaphua Industries Ltd [1987] AC 99…107

Hughes v Cork [1994] EGCS 25…120

Hunt v Luck [1901] 1 Ch 45…25, 27

Hunter v Babbage [1994] 2 FLR 806…161

Hunter v Canary Wharf Ltd [1997] AC 655…191

Hurst v Picture Theatres Ltd [1915] 1 KB 1…177

Hussein v Mehlman [1992] 2 EGLR 87…88

Hypo-Mortgage Services v Robinson [1997] 2 FLR 422…44

International Drilling Fluids Ltd v Louisville Investments (Uxbridge) Ltd [1986] Ch 513…100

Inwards v Baker [1965] 2 QB 29…181

Irvine's Estate, Re v Moran (1992) 24 HLR 1, QBD…98

Ives v High [1967] 2 QB 379…183

Jackson v Jackson [1971] 1 WLR 1539…165

Javad v Aqil [1991] 1 All ER 243…76

Jeune v Queens Cross Properties [1974] Ch 97…99

Jones v Challenger [1961] 1 QB 176…164

Jones v Morgan [2001] EWCA Civ 995…232, 235, 237, 248

Jones v Pritchard [1908] 1 Ch 630…192

Joyce v Barker Bros (1980) 40 P&CR 512…155

Table of cases

✳✳✳✳✳✳✳✳✳✳

Kelsey v Dodd (1881) 52 LJ Ch 34...211

Kinch v Bullard [1999] 1 WLR 423...159

King, Re [1963] Ch 459...108

King v David Allen & Sons [1916] 2 AC 54...179, 184

Kingsnorth Trust Ltd v Tizard [1986] 1 WLR 783...25, 27

Knightsbridge Estates Trust Ltd v Byrne [1939] Ch 441...236, 249

Kreglinger v New Patagonia Meat & Cold Storage Co Ltd [1914] AC 25...237, 249

Kumar v Dunning [1989] QB 193...223

Lace v Chantler [1944] KB 368...74, 75

Lake v Craddock (1732) 3 P Wms 157...155

Lambeth LBC v Blackburn [2001] 92 P&CR 494...120

LCC v Allen [1914] 3 KB 642...216, 227

Lee v Leeds CC [2002] EWCA Civ 6...98

Leigh v Jack (1879) 5 Ex D 264...118, 119, 129

Leigh v Taylor [1902] AC 157...7, 12

Lister v Lane [1893] 2 QB 212...96, 109

Liverpool City Council v Irwin [1977] AC 239...192

Lloyds Bank plc v Rosset [1991] 1 AC 107...43, 133, 140, 147

London & Blenheim Estates v Ladbroke Retail Parks Ltd [1994] 1 WLR 31...189

London Borough Council of Islington v Green [2005] EWCA Civ 56...82

Long v Tower Hamlets LBC [1998] Ch 197...84

Lyus v Prowsa Developments Ltd [1982] 1 WLR 1044...38

McClausland v Duncan Lawrie Ltd [1997] 1 WLR 38...68, 71

McDonald v Morley (1940) 101 P2d 690...161

Manjang v Drammah [1990] 61 P&CR 194...194

Marchant v Charters [1977] 1 WLR 1181...79

Marcroft Wagons Ltd v Smith [1951] 2 KB 496...79

Marquess of Zetland v Driver (1939) Ch 1...220, 221

Marten v Flight Refuelling Ltd [1962] Ch 115...222

Martin v Martin (1987) 54 P&CR 238...155

Martin v Smith (1874) LR 9 Ex 50...76

Martinson v Clowes (1882) 21 Ch D 857...244

Mayes v Mayes (1969) 210 EG 935...165

Medforth v Blake [2000] Ch 86...246

Melluish v BMI (No 3) Ltd [1996] AC 454...6

Mercantile Credit Co v Clarke [1996] 71 P&CR D18...245

Midland Bank Trust Co Ltd v Green [1981] AC 513...26, 38, 56, 58, 59

Mikeover Ltd v Brady [1989] 3 All ER 618...80

Miles v Easter [1933] Ch 611...219, 222

Miller v Emcer Products [1956] Ch 304...193

Mills v Silver [1991] Ch 271...199

Mirror Group (Holdings) Ltd, Re (1993) 65 C&PR 252...104

Moffat v Kazana [1969] 2 QB 152...8

Moody v Steggles (1879) 12 Ch D 261...190, 205

Morley v Bird (1798) 3 Ves 628...155

Morrells of Oxford Ltd v Oxford United Football Club [2001] 1 Ch 459...217

Mortgage Corporation v Shaire [2001] Ch 743...164, 167

Moule v Garret (1872) LR 7 Ex 101...104, 107

Multiservice Bookbinding Co Ltd v Marden [1979] Ch 84...237, 249

National & Provincial Building Society v Lloyd [1996] 1 All ER 630...242

National Car Parks Ltd v Trinity Development Co (Banbury) Ltd [2002] 2 P & CR 18...77

National Provincial Bank Ltd v Ainsworth [1965] AC 1175...179

Nickerson v Barraclough [1981] Ch 426...195

Nielson-Jones v Fedden [1975] Ch 222...159, 161

Noakes & Co Ltd v Rice [1902] AC 24...236, 249

Norris v Checksfield [1991] 1 WLR 1241...79

Nunn v Dalrymple (1990) 59 P&CR 231...79

Oakley v Boston [1976] QB 270...200

O'Brien v Robinson [1973] AC 912...98

Old Grovebury Manor Farm Ltd v W Seymour Plant Sales & Hire Ltd (No 2) [1979] 1 WLR 1397...101

Oxley v Hiscock [2005] QB 211...140, 148

P&A Swift Investments v Combined English Stores Group plc [1989] AC 632...210, 213, 214, 227

P&S Platt v Crouch [2004] 1 P&CR 242...196

Palk v Mortgage Services Funding plc [1993] Ch 330...244, 245, 249

Parker v British Airways Board [1982] QB 1004...8, 12

Parker-Tweedale v Dunbar Bank plc [1991] Ch 12...244

Pascoe v Turner [1979] 1 WLR 431...182, 184

Pavlou (A Bankrupt), Re [1993] 1 WLR 1046...155, 161, 165

Payne v Inwood (1996) 74 P&CR 42...197

Payne v Webb (1874) LR 19 Eq 26...155

Peffer v Rigg [1977] 1 WLR 285...38

Pembury v Lamdin [1940] 2 All ER 434...97

Penn v Wilkins (1974) 236 EG 203...196

J Pereira Fernades SA v Mehta [2006] EWHC 813...67

Pettitt v Pettitt [1970] AC 777...139

Phipps v Pears [1965] 1 QB 76...191, 206

Pink v Lawrence (1977) 36 P&CR 98...155

Polden v Bastard (1865) LR 1 QB...197

Post Office v Aquarius Property Ltd [1987] 1 All ER 1055...97, 109

Powell v Hemsley [1909] 2 Ch 252...216

Powell v McFarlane (1977) 38 P&CR 452...116, 120, 129

Pritchard v Briggs [1980] Ch 338...37, 53

Proudfoot v Hart (1890) 25 QBD 42...95, 97

Prudential Assurance v London Residuary Body [1992] 2 AC 386...76, 84, 91

Pryce v McGuiness [1966] Qd R 591...194

Pugh v Savage [1970] 2 QB 273...190, 200

Purchase v Lichfield Brewery Co [1915] 1 KB 184...105

Pye (JA) (Oxford) Ltd v Graham [2003] 1 AC 347...114, 116, 119, 120, 127, 129, 130

Quick v Taff-Ely BC [1986] QB 821...98, 110

Rainbow Estates Ltd v Tokenhold Ltd [1999] Ch 64...99

Raval, Re [1998] 2 FLR 718...167

Ravenseft Properties Ltd v Davstone (Holdings) Ltd [1980] QB 12...97, 110

Record v Bell [1991] 1 WLR 853...67, 71

Reeve v Lisle [1902] AC 461...235, 249

Regis Property Co Ltd v Dudley [1959] AC 370...95, 97

Regis Property Co Ltd v Redman [1956] 2 QB 612...191, 206

Renals v Cowlishaw (1878) 9 Ch D 125...219

Rhone v Stephens [1994] 2 AC 310...210, 214, 216, 227

Roake v Chadha [1984] Ch 40...221, 223, 228

Rodway v Landy [2001] Ch 703...145

Roe v Siddons (1888) 22 QBD 224...190

Rogers v Hosegood [1900] 2 Ch 388...217, 219

Ropaigealach v Barclays Bank plc [1999] 1 QB 263...241

Ropemaker Properties Ltd v Noonhaven Ltd [1989] 2 EGLR 50...90

Royal Bank of Scotland plc v Etridge (No 2) [2002] 2 AC 773...230, 231, 232, 239, 240, 249

Rugby School (Governors) v Tannahill [1935] 1 KB 87...90

Russell v Archdale [1964] Ch 38...220, 221

Rye v Rye [1962] AC 496...196

St Marylebone Property Co v Tesco Stores (1988) 2 Ch 40...89

Samuel v Jarrah Timber and Wood Paving Corporation Ltd [1904] AC 323...235, 250

Scala House District Properties v Forbes [1974] QB 575...90

Shelfer v City of London Electric Lighting Co [1895] 1 Ch 287...224

Shepherd Homes v Sandham (No 2) [1971] 2 All ER 1267...216

Table of cases

✳✳✳✳✳✳✳✳✳✳

Silven Properties Ltd v Royal Bank of Scotland plc [2004] 1 WLR 997...244

Smith & Snipes Hall Farm Ltd v River Douglas Catchment Board [1949] 2 KB 500...213–214, 228

Smith v Lawson (1997) 74 P&CR 34...118

Smith v Marrable (1843) 11 M & W 5...95, 97

Sookraj v Samaroo [2004] UKPC 50...66

South of England Dairies Ltd v Baker [1906] 2 Ch 631...108

Sovmots Investments v Secretary of State for the Environment [1979] AC 144...196, 197

Spencer's Case (1583) 5 Co Rep 16a...104, 106, 107

Spiro v Glencrown Properties Ltd [1991] Ch 237...69

Stanhope v Haworth (1886) 3 TLR 34...89

Staves & Staves v Leeds CC (1990) 23 HLR 107...98

Strand Securities v Caswell [1965] Ch 958, CA...43, 46

Street v Mountford [1985] AC 809...73, 74, 75, 77, 79, 91

Stribling v Wickham (1989) 2 EGLR 35...77

Stuart v Joy [1904] 1 KB 362...106

Swansborough v Coventry (1832) 9 Bing 305...197

Techbild Ltd v Chamberlain (1969) 20 P&CR 633, CA...116, 117, 130

Tehidy Minerals v Norman [1971] 2 QB 528...200

Thamesmead Town Ltd v Allotey [1998] 37 EG 161...225

Thomas v Sorrell (1673) Vaugh 330...173, 175

Thursby v Plant [1668] 1 Wms Saund 237...103

Toomes v Consent (1745) 3 Atk 261...235

Tophams Ltd v Earl of Sefton [1967] 1 AC 50...215

Tse Kwok Lam v Kwong Chit Sen [1983] 1 WLR 1349...244

Tulk v Moxhay (1848) 2 Ph 774...108, 109, 209, 210, 215, 228

Union of London & Smith's Bank Ltd's Conveyance, Re [1933] Ch 611...222

United Bank of Kuwait plc v Sahib [1997] Ch 107...84

Verrall v Great Yarmouth BC [1981] QB 202...178, 184

Wallis's Cayton Bay v Shell-Mex and BP [1975] QB 94...118

Walsh v Lonsdale (1882) 21 Ch D 9...66, 73, 74, 83, 84, 91, 202

Ward v Kirkland [1967] Ch 194...198

Warnborough Ltd v Garmite Ltd [2004] 1 P&CR D18...235

Waverley BC v Fletcher [1996] QB 334...8, 12

Webb v Paternoster (1619) 2 Rolle 143...177

Webbs Lease, Re [1951] Ch 808...194

Weston v Lawrence Weaver Ltd [1961] 1 QB 402...204

Wheeldon v Burrows (1879) 12 Ch 31...187, 188, 190, 194, 196, 197, 198, 199, 206

Wheeler v JJ Saunders Ltd [1996] Ch 19...198

White v City of London Brewery Co (1889) 42 Ch D 237...242

Wilford's Estate, Re (1879) 1 Ch D 267...162

Wilkes v Spooner [1911] 2 KB 473...26, 27

William Aldred's Case (1610) 77 ER 816...191

William's & Glyn's Bank Ltd v Boland [1981] AC 487, HL...40, 46

Williams v Hensman (1861) 1 J&H 546...150, 156

Wilson v Martin's Executors [1993] 1 EGLR 178...118

Wilson v Rosenthal (1906) 22 TLR 233...95, 100

Winter Garden Theatre (London) Ltd v Millennium Productions Ltd [1948] AC 173...174, 178, 184

Wong v Beaumont Property Trust Ltd [1965] 1 QB 173...195, 206

Wood v Leadbitter (1845) 13 M&W 838...178

Wright v Gibbons (1949) 78 CLR 313...160, 161

Wright v Macadam [1949] 2 KB 744...196, 206

Wright v Robert Leonard Developments Ltd [1994] NPC 49...67, 71

Wrotham Park Estate Co Ltd v Parkside Homes Ltd [1974] 1 WLR 798...217, 220, 227, 228

Yaxley v Gotts [2000] Ch 162...69, 71

Table of statutes

Access of Neighbouring Land Act 1992...192

Administration of Justice Act 1970...231, 232
s 36...241

Administration of Justice Act 1973...231, 232, 241
s 8...242

Civil Aviation Act 1982...6

Civil Partnership Act 2004...54

Coal Industry Act 1994...6

Common Law Procedure Act 1852
s 210...89

Commonhold and Leasehold Reform Act 2002...64, 226

Consumer Credit Act 1974...238

Consumer Credit Act 2006...238

Contracts (Rights of Third Parties) Act 1999...53, 210, 212, 215
s 1(1)...212

Criminal Law Act 1977...241
s 6...89

Electronic Communications Act 2000...68

Enterprise Act 2002...166

Family Law Act 1996...37, 54

Financial Services and Markets Act 2000...238

Housing Act 2004...65

Human Rights Act 1998...126, 129, 176
s 3...129

Insolvency Act 1986
s 283A...166
s 305(2)...166
s 335A...150, 151, 166
s 335A(3)...166, 167

Land Charges Act 1972...35, 49, 50, 52, 53, 54, 56, 57, 122
s 2...53
s 2(5)(ii)...218
s 3(1)...54
s 4...50, 55, 57, 247
s 4(5)...56
s 4(6)...56, 87, 203, 218
s 4(8)...56
s 17(1)...55

Land Registration Act 1925...44, 45, 128, 129

Land Registration Act 2002...31, 32, 41, 45, 74, 112, 113, 115, 122, 123, 127, 129
s 1...32
ss 2–3...33
s 4...29, 30, 33, 61, 70, 87
s 4(1)(a)...86
s 4(1)(c)...84
s 4(8)...33
s 6...29, 33, 61, 70
s 7...29, 34, 70
s 9...34
ss 10–12...34
s 23(1)(a)...232, 233
s 26...133, 146
s 27...21, 29, 30, 61, 87, 247
s 27(1)...34, 70
s 27(1)(a)...86
s 27(2)...34
s 27(2)(a)...70
s 27(2)(b)(i)...84
s 27(2)(d)...202
s 27(2)(f)...233, 234
s 29...87, 202
s 29(1)–(2)...30, 38, 218
s 32...30, 38, 42, 45, 87, 202, 218
s 33...37

Table of statutes

s 37...37
s 38...36, 42, 45, 202
s 40...30, 39
s 48...248
s 62...35
s 65...45
s 66...32
s 71...34
s 96...123
s 103...31, 45
s 115...37
s 116...183
s 132...38
Sch 1...35, 41
   para 1...30, 41
   para 3...30, 42
Sch 3...34, 35, 42
   para 1...29, 30, 42, 87
   para 2...29, 30, 38, 41, 42, 43, 44, 46, 87,
      183, 202, 218
   para 3...29, 30, 44, 202
Sch 4...45
Sch 6
   para 1...126
   para 1(1)...123
   para 1(4)...123
   para 2...123, 125
   para 5...124
   para 6...123
   para 8...123
   para 9...126
   para 11...123
Sch 8...45
Sch 12...45
   para 20...104
Landlord and Tenant Act 1927...100
s 18...99
s 19(1)(a)...94, 95, 100
Landlord and Tenant Act 1985...94, 95
s 8...98
ss 11–14...98, 99
s 17...99
Landlord and Tenant Act 1988
s 1(6)...101
Landlord and Tenant (Covenants) Act
   1995...94, 95, 102
s 3...105, 107
s 3(1)...106
s 3(5)...108
s 3(6)...105, 107

s 5...102
s 6...106, 108
s 8...106
s 11...103, 106
s 16...103
s 17...95, 102, 103, 104
s 18...95, 102, 103
s 19...95, 102, 104
s 20...95, 102
s 22...101
s 23...105, 106, 107, 108
s 24...103, 106, 107
s 24(4)...108
Law of Property Act 1925...95, 102, 133, 134
s 1...10, 11, 64, 134
s 1(1)...3, 23, 62, 214
s 1(1)(a)...61, 62, 63
s 1(1)(b)...73, 74, 75
s 1(2)...3, 15, 16, 20, 21, 23, 36, 189
s 1(2)(a)...20, 201
s 1(2)(b)...20
s 1(2)(c)...20, 232, 233
s 1(2)(d)–(e)...20
s 1(3)...15, 23
s 1(6)...151, 154
s 2...30, 39, 50, 52, 136
s 14...144
s 27...30, 39, 50, 52, 57, 136
s 30...137, 163, 164
s 34...153, 154
s 36...150, 151, 153, 156, 158
s 36(2)...156, 157, 158
s 40...66
s 52...15, 21, 61, 69, 84, 86, 201
s 52(1)(b)...139
s 52(2)(d)...84
s 53(1)(a)...201, 234
s 53(1)(b)...133, 141
s 53(1)(c)...86, 142, 160, 234
s 53(2)...133, 141
s 54(2)...84
s 56...210, 211
s 62...175, 187, 188, 194, 195, 196,
   197, 198, 199, 203, 223
s 62(4)...197
s 77...104
s 78...214, 220, 221, 228
s 79...103, 106, 215, 217
s 84(1)...226
ss 85–86...232, 233

s 87…25
s 91…245, 249
s 91(2)…245
s 101…232, 243, 245, 246
s 103…232, 243, 245
s 104…243
s 105…232, 244
s 109…232, 246
s 136…210, 213
s 141…108
s 142…107
s 146…89
s 146(2)…90
s 146(4)…89
s 153…225
s 196(3)–(4)…159
s 198…50, 53, 87, 203, 218
s 199(1)…53
s 205…196
s 205(1)(ix)…5
s 205(1)(xix)…63, 84
s 205(1)(xxix)…137
s 205(1)(xxvii)…75, 79
s 205(1)(xxxi)…56
Law of Property Act 1969
  s 23…25
  s 23…51
  s 24…54
  s 25…55
  s 28…226
  s 78…227
Law of Property Amendment Act 1926…63
Law of Property (Miscellaneous Provisions)
  Act 1989…61
  s 1…21, 61, 86, 201
  s 1(2)…69
  s 2…22, 61, 66, 67, 68, 69, 71, 83,
    84, 202, 234
  s 2(2)…67
  s 2(4)…67
  s 2(5)…22, 66, 83
Leasehold Property (Repairs) Act 1938…90,
99
Limitation Act 1980…8, 126, 127, 128, 129
  s 15…114, 121
  s 15(1)…121
  s 17…114, 121
  s 32(1)…117
  Sch 1
    para 8(4)…119

Matrimonial Proceedings and Property Act
  1970…141

Prescription Act 1832…187, 188, 194, 199, 200,
  201
  s 3…201
Protection from Eviction Act 1977…81
  s 2…88

Rentcharges Act 1977…32, 226
Rights to Light Act 1959…201

Settled Land Act 1925…131, 133, 134, 135
  s 4…133
  s 4(1)…135
  s 18…136
  s 39…136
  s 41…136
  s 71…136
  s 101…136
  s 106(1)…136
  s 109…136
Supreme Court Act 1981
  s 37…246
  s 50…224

Treasure Act 1996…8
Trustee Act 1925
  s 34…151, 153
  s 36(1)…141
  s 36(6)…141
  s 36(a)–(b)…141
  s 39…157
  s 40…142, 157
  s 41…141
Trustee Act 2000
  s 1(1)…143
Trusts of Land and Appointment of Trustees
  Act 1996…62, 131, 133, 134, 135, 137, 138,
  144, 146, 147, 149, 150, 153, 164
  s 1…134, 138
  s 2…134
  s 3…137
  ss 4–5…138
  s 6…132
  s 6(1)…142, 143
  s 6(3)…143
  s 6(5)–(6)…143
  s 7…132, 168
  s 8…132

Table of statutes

s 8(1)...143
s 9...143
s 9(1)...143
s 11...132, 133, 144
s 11(1)...143, 153
s 12...132, 133, 144, 145
s 13...132, 133, 144
s 13(1)...143
s 13(4)...145
s 13(7)...145
s 14...132, 133, 145, 150, 151, 163, 164, 166, 169, 170
s 15...132, 133, 150, 151, 163, 164, 166, 167, 169, 170
s 15(3)...163
s 15(4)...166
s 16...133, 146
s 19...141, 142, 157

s 21...142
Sch 2...138

UK secondary legislation
Treasure (Designation) Order 2002 (SI 2002/2666)...8
Unfair Terms in Consumer Contracts Regulations 1999 (SI 1999/2083)...238

European legislation
EC Treaty
Art 81...237

International legislation
European Convention on Human Rights 1950...123
Art 1...167
Art 8...98, 167
Protocol 1
Art 1...41, 114, 126, 127, 128

Index

abatement
easement remedy 204
acquisition of easements
express 194
implied 194–199
necessity 194–195
prescription 199–201
statute 201
*Wheeldon v
Burrows* 197–199
actual occupation
establishing 44
occupation by
another 43–44
physical presence
on land 43
registrable equitable
interest 54
see also **overriding
interests**
adverse possession 112
discontinuance 116
dispossession 116
establishment of 115–116
principle 121, 123
registered land 122–125
subsequent dealings 122,
124
successful claims
121–122, 124–125
ten years 123–124
twelve years 121
unregistered
land 121–122
exam questions 130
exclusive possession 117
factual possession 116–118
human rights
and 126–129
intention to possess 120
key cases 129–130
key facts 113
leasehold estate
by tenant 125
by third party 125
occupation licence 118

permission of paper
owner 118–120
physical control 116–117
Pye 127–129
registered land 122–125
rent, willingness to pay 119
unregistered land 121–122
**agreement to grant
lease** 82–83
airspace 5–6
alteration of register 45
annexation of fixtures 6–7
**applications for sale
(co-ownership)**
by co-owners in
dispute 163–165
by trustee in
bankruptcy 165–168
exceptional
circumstances 167
human rights
issues 167–168
trusts of land 162
trusts for sale 162
appointment of receiver
mortgagee's
remedy 245–246
assignment of lease
covenant against 99–101
enforcement of
covenant 102–106
assignment of reversion
enforcement of
covenant 106–109

beneficial interest
overriding interest 43
under trust 17–18, 43
**beneficiaries under
trust** 144–146
application to
court 145–146
capital proceeds 146
consent 144
consultation 144
dispute resolution 145
occupation 144–145

*bona fide purchaser for
value* 24

charges register 32
notices 32, 38
chivalry 8–9
co-ownership 149
applications for sale
by co-owners in
dispute 163–165
by trustee in
bankruptcy 165–168
exceptional
circumstances 167
human rights
issues 167–168
trusts of land 162
trusts for sale 162
equitable title 154–156
exam questions 170
imposition of trust 153–156
joint tenancy 152
key cases 168–170
key facts 150
legal title 153–154
severance 156–162
homicide 162
methods 156, 158–162
mutual
agreement 161–162
mutual conduct 162
operating on own
share 160–161
reasons for 156
result of 157–158
timing 156–157
written notice 158–160
survivorship 152, 156, 162
tenancy in common 152
termination
conveyance to single
purchaser 168
partition 168
union in sole
ownership 168
trust of land 153
trust for sale 153

Index

✳✳✳✳✳✳✳✳✳✳✳

commonhold 64–65, 226
constructive trust 140–141
licences protected
by 180–181
covenants
freehold *see* **freehold covenants**
covenants in leases 93
assignment or
subletting 99–101
absolute 100
consequences of
breach 101
qualified 100
enforcement
assignment of
lease 102–106
assignment of
reversion 106–109
between original
parties 101–102
between
successors 102–109
privity of
contract 101–109
exam questions 110–111
fair wear and tear 97
forfeiture for breach 98–99
key cases 109–110
key facts 94
repair
damages for breach 99
design fault
correction 97
express covenants 96–97
extent of liability 96–97
fit for human
habitation 97–98
forfeiture for
breach 98–99
good and substantial
repair 96
implied covenants 97–98
notice of disrepair 97
remedies 98–99
specific performance 99
standard of repair 97
structure 98
when liability
arises 97

Crown
ownership of land 5
customary tenure 9

damages
breach of repair covenant
remedy 99
easement remedy 204
freehold covenant
remedy 224
deed
legal interest granted by 21

easements 20, 21, 53, 186
acquisition
express 194
implied 194–199
necessity 194–195
prescription 199–201
statute 201
*Wheeldon v
Burrows* 197–199
capability 189–193
capable definition 191
capable of grant 190
definition 191
diversity of ownership 190
dominant tenement 189
right to
accommodate 189–190
enforcement against third
parties
registered land 202
unregistered land 203
exam questions 207
exercised as of right 193
grantor and grantee 190
key cases 205–206
key facts 197
licence compared 175
no exclusive possession of
servient land 192–193
no expenditure by servient
owner 191–192
overriding interest 44–45
prescription
acquisition by 199–201
common law 200
lost modern grant 200
Prescription Act 1832
200–201

remedies
abatement 204
damages 204
injunction 204
servient tenement 189
status of easement
acquired 201–202
termination
merger 203
release
express 203
implied 204
traditionally
recognised 191
equitable interests 10–11
agreements to grant
interests 22–23
beneficial interests under
trust 17–18
*bona fide purchaser for
value* 24
distinction between legal
and 24–26
easements 54
enforcement 24–25
estate contract 18–19, 54
exam question 27
failed attempt to grant
legal interests 22
failure to register as land
charge 55–57
freehold estate
transfer 65–66
key cases 26–27
key facts 14–15
notice 25, 57–58
occupation rights 54
overreaching 57
recognition 17–19
registrable as land
charge 53–57
remedies 24
restrictive covenants 18,
54
unregistered land 53–58
equitable lease 84–85, 87
equitable mortgages
appointment of
receiver 246
creation 234

foreclosure 247
possession 243
sale 245
equitable remedies
characteristics 19–20
injunctions 19, 204, 224
right to redeem 18,
234–236
specific performance 19, 99
equitable title
co-ownership 154–156
estate contracts 18–19, 54
estates 9–11
see also **freehold estate;**
leasehold estate
estoppel
licences protected by an
enforcement against
third parties 183
termination 182
when arise 181–182
tenancy by 91
exclusive possession 76–79
adverse possession
claim 117
attempts to exclude 77–78
easements and servient
owner 191–192
exceptions 79
licences and 76–77

fair wear and tear 97
fee absolute 62
fee simple 62–63
on condition precedent 63
on condition subsequent 63
determinable 63
fee tail 62
first registration 33–34
caution against 33
trigger events 33
voluntary 33
fixed term lease 80–81
fixtures 6–7
annexation 6–7
foreclosure
mortgagee's
remedy 246–247
forfeiture of lease 88–90
breach of covenant 89–90

breach of repair covenant
remedy 98–99
non-payment of rent 89
freehold covenants 208
at common law
passing of
benefit 213–214
passing of
burden 214–215
benefit of covenant
enforcement 212
passing *see* passing of
benefit
burden of covenant
enforcement 212–213
passing *see* passing of
burden
commonhold creation 226
discharge
by court 226
by parties affected 226
enforcement
between original
parties 211–212
between successors in
title 212–213
enlargement of long lease
into freehold 225
in equity
accommodate dominant
land 216
intention of original
parties 217
negative covenant 215
notice to purchaser 217
passing of
benefit 218–224
passing of
burden 215–217
exam questions 228–229
extinguishment 226
Halsall v Brizell rule 225
indemnity
covenants 224–225
key cases 227–228
key facts 209
meaning 211
passing of benefit
annexation 219
at common law 213–214

in equity 218–224
express 213, 219–220,
222–223
implied 213–214, 222
scheme of
development 223
statutory 220–222
passing of burden
accommodate dominant
land 216
at common law 214–215
in equity 215–217
negative covenant 215
notice to purchaser 217
positive covenants 224–226
remedies
damages in lieu of
injunction 224
injunction 224
rentcharges 225–226
freehold estate 5, 9–10
characteristics 62–65
commonhold 64–65
fee absolute 62
fee simple 62–63
on condition
precedent 63
on condition
subsequent 63
determinable 63
fee tail 62
key facts 60–61
in possession 63–64
in remainder 64
in reversion 64
transfer *see* **freehold**
estate transfer
freehold estate transfer
completion stage 69–70
formalities 69–70
contract
arising out of
correspondence 68–69
containing all terms 67
equitable rights and 69
omissions 67
options to
purchase 68–69
signed by both
parties 68

Index

✶✶✶✶✶✶✶✶✶✶

freehold estate transfer
(*Cont.*)
variation of terms 68
in writing 67
contract stage 65–66
deed 69
estoppel intervention 69
failure to register title 70
formalities 66
home information pack 65
key cases 70–71
pre-contract stage 65
registration of title 70
transfer of equitable
interest 65–66
transfer of legal
interest 69

glossary A8–A10
good root of title 51
guarantor
lease creation 81–82

hereditaments, incorporeal 6
home information pack 65
homicide
right of survivorship
and 162
human rights
adverse possession
and 126–129
peaceful enjoyment of
possessions 127
Pye 127–129
trustee in bankruptcy
sale 167–168

incidents of tenure 9
incorporeal hereditaments 6
indemnities
covenants 224–225
mistakes in register 45
injunction 19
easement remedy 204
freehold covenant
remedy 224
insurance principle 31
interests 9–11
entered in register
see **register**

equitable *see* **equitable**
interests
exam question 27
identification of
status 20–23
key cases 26–27
legal *see* **legal interests**
overriding *see* **overriding**
interests

joint tenancy 80, 152
severance 156–158
see also **co-ownership**

land
airspace 5–6
animals 6
buildings 6
fixtures *see* **fixtures**
incorporeal
hereditaments 6
meaning 5–6
mines and minerals 6
ownership *see* **ownership**
of land
registered
see **registered land**
river beds 6
trusts *see* **trusts**
unregistered *see*
unregistered land
wild plants 6
land charge
equitable interests
registrable as 53–57
land charges register
searches 54–55
lease
agreement to grant 82–83
assignment of
existing 85–86
certainty of term 75–76
covenants *see* **covenants in**
leases
creation 81
enforcement against third
parties 86–87
equitable 84–85, 87
exam questions 92
exclusive possession 76–79

exceptions 79
exclusion of 77–78
licences and 76–77
family members 79
fixed term 80–81
formalities
agreement to
grant 82–83
assignment of existing
lease 85–86
creation 81
grant of lease 83–85
grant 83–85
guarantor 81–82
implied period 76
individual leases 80
joint tenancy 80
key cases 90–91
legal 84–85, 87
licences and 76–77
lodgers 79
multiple occupancy 79–80
periodic 91
rent 79
service occupancy 79
sub-lease 99–101
tenancy at sufferance 91
tenancy at will 91
tenancy by estoppel 91
termination
expiry 87
forfeiture 88–90
merger of estates 88
notice to quit 88
repudiatory breach 88
surrender 88
uncertain term 76
leasehold estate 5, 9–10,
72–73
adverse possession
by tenant 125
by third party 125
contractual agreement *see*
lease
key facts 73
slice of time 75
term of years absolute 75
legal estate
purchaser 25
legal interests 10–11

deeds 21
distinction between
    equitable and 24–26
easements 20, 21, 53
enforcement 24
exam question 27
failed attempt to grant 22
formalities 21
freehold estate transfer 69
identification of
    status 20–22
key cases 26–27
key facts 15
mortgage 20
    puisne 53, 54
registration 21
remedies 24
rentcharge 20, 21, 225–226
rights of entry 20
unregistered land 52–53
legal lease 84–85, 87
legal title
co-ownership 153–154
licences 172
bare 176
    enforcement against
        third parties 176
    termination 176
    when arise 176
contractual
    enforcement against
        third parties 179–180
    termination 178–179
    when arise 177
coupled with interest
    enforcement against
        third parties 177
    termination 177
    when arise 176–177
description 175
easements compared 175
exam questions 185
key cases 183–184
key facts 173
personal right 175
protected by constructive
    trusts
    enforcement against
        third parties 181
    when arise 180

protected by estoppel
    enforcement against
        third parties 183
    termination 182
    when arise 181–182
lodgers 79

mines and minerals 6
mirror principle 31
mistakes in register 45
mortgagee's remedies
appointment of receiver
    duty of receiver 246
    equitable mortgage 246
    reasons for 245
foreclosure 246–247
    equitable mortgage 247
possession 241–243
    duty of mortgagee 242
    equitable mortgage 243
sale 243–245
    duty of
        mortgagee 244–245
    equitable mortgage 245
    purchaser 244
    requested by
        mortgagor 245
    timing 243
sue on personal
    covenant 241
mortgages 230
equitable
    appointment of
        receiver 246
    creation 234
    foreclosure 247
    possession 243
    sale 245
exam questions 251
formalities of creation
    equitable mortgages 233
    legal mortgages 233
key cases 248–250
key facts 231
legal, creation 233
legal interest 20
oppressive or unconscion-
    able terms 237–238
priorities
    registered land 247–248

unregistered land 247
puisne 53, 54
remedies *see* **mortgagee's
    remedies**
rights *see* **mortgagor's
    rights**
undue influence 238–240
    actual 239
    effect of finding 239
    evidence of 239
    lenders and 239–240
    presumed 239
mortgagor's rights
collateral advantages for
    mortgagee 236–237
principle 234
redemption right
    clauses attempting to
        postpone 235
    clauses attempting to
        remove 235
    equitable 234–236
    striking out oppressive
        or unconscionable
        terms 237–238

notice doctrine 25, 57–58
notice to quit 88
notices on register 25, 32,
    57–58
on charges register 32, 38
consequences 38
entered by holder of
    interest 37–38
entered by registrar 36–37

options to purchase
freehold estate
    transfer 68–69
overreaching 39–40, 57
overriding interests 31–32,
    41–45
binding upon purchaser 42
disclosure of
    interest 42–43
on first registration 41–42
impliedly created legal
    easements 44–45
leases of seven years or
    less 42

Index

****

overriding interests (*Cont.*)
occupation *see* **actual
occupation**
Sch 3 para 1 42
Sch 3 para 2 42
Sch 3 para 3 44–45
subsequent transactions 42
transitional provisions 45
see also **actual occupation**
ownership of land 5–8
Crown 5
doctrine of tenures *see*
tenures
estates
freehold *see* **freehold
estate**
leasehold *see* **lease; leasehold estate**
land, meaning 5–6
see also **co-ownership**

periodic tenancy 91
personal rights 4, 5
possession
adverse *see* **adverse
possession**
exclusive *see* **exclusive
possession**
mortgagee's
remedy 241–243
pre-emption right 37, 53
**prescription, acquisition of
easement** 199–201
common law 200
lost modern grant 200
Prescription Act 1832
200–201
privity of contract
enforcement of lease
covenants 101
profit à prendre 177, 204
property register 32
proprietary rights 1, 4–5
equitable 10–11
estates *see* **estates; freehold estate; leasehold
estate**
exam question 12
interests *see* **interests**
key cases 11–12

key facts 2
legal 10–11
ownership of land 5–8
proprietorship register 32
restrictions 39–40

redemption right
clauses attempting to
postpone 235
clauses attempting to
remove 235
equitable right to
redeem 18,
234–236
register
alteration 45
charges register 32, 38
exam questions 46–47
indemnities 45
interests entered
onto 36–45
interests which override
register *see* **overriding
interests**
key cases 45–46
mistakes in 45
notice
on charges register 32,
38
consequences 38
entered by holder of
interest 37–38
entered by
registrar 36–37
notices 32
overreaching 39–40
property register 32
proprietorship register 32,
39–40
restriction
limitation of dealing 38
overreaching 39–40
proprietorship
register 39–40
protection of interest 41
third party interests 31,
35–45
transitional provisions 45
registered land 28–47
adverse possession 122–125

enforcement against third
parties
of easement 202
of lease 87
insurance principle 31
key facts 29
legislation 31
mirror principle 31
mortgage priority 247–248
purchase of trust land 146
register *see* **register**
registration *see*
registration of title
registration of title
exam questions 46–47
failure to register 70
first registration 33–34
caution against 33
trigger events 33
voluntary 33
freehold estate transfer 70
key cases 45–46
substantive
registration 32–33
upgrading title 35
see also **title**
rent 79
adverse possession
claim 119
rentcharge 20, 21, 225–226
repairing covenant
damages for breach 99
design fault correction 97
express covenants 96–97
extent of liability 96–97
fit for human
habitation 97–98
forfeiture for breach 98–99
good and substantial
repair 96
implied covenants 97–98
notice of disrepair 97
remedies 98–99
specific performance 99
standard of repair 97
structure 98
when liability arises 97
restriction
consequences of entry or
failure to enter 40

restriction (*Cont.*)
overreaching 39–40
on proprietorship
register 39–40
protection of interest 41
purpose 39
restrictive covenants
equitable rights and 18, 54
unregistered land 54
right of entry
legal interest 20
right of survivorship 152,
156, 162
river beds 6

sale
co-ownership *see*
**applications for sale
(co-ownership)**
mortgagee's
remedy 243–245
service occupancy 79
**severance of
co-ownership** 156–162
homicide 162
methods 156, 158–162
mutual agreement 161–162
content 161–162
form 161
mutual conduct 162
operating on own
share 160–161
reasons for 156
result of 157–158
timing 156–157
written notice 158–160
slice of time 10, 75
socage 9
specific performance 19
breach of repair covenant
remedy 99
spiritual tenures 9
strict settlements 135–137
tenant for life 135–136
trust instrument 135
trustees 136–137
vesting deed 135
sub-leases
covenant not to
sub-let 99–101

surrender of lease 88
survivorship 152, 156, 162

tenancy at sufferance 91
tenancy at will 91
tenancy by estoppel 91
tenant for life
powers 136
strict settlements 135–136
successive interests 136
tenants in common 152
severance and 156–158
see also **co-ownership**
tenures
aids 9
chivalry 8–9
customary 9
doctrine of 8–9
free tenure 8–9
incidents of tenure 9
relief 9
socage 9
spiritual 9
unfree 9
villeinage 9
term of years absolute 75
**termination of
co-ownership**
conveyance to single
purchaser 168
partition 168
union in sole ownership 168
termination of easement
merger 203
release
express 203
implied 204
termination of lease
expiry 87
forfeiture 88–90
breaches of
covenants 89–90
non-payment of rent 89
merger 88
merger of estates 88
notice to quit 88
repudiatory breach 88
surrender 88
third party interests 31,
35–45

occupation *see* **actual
occupation**
overriding register
see **overriding
interests**
transitional provisions 45
see also **register**
title
co-ownership 153–156
equitable 154–156
good leasehold 35
good root of title 51
legal 153–154
possessory 35
qualified 35
registration *see*
registration of title
upgrading 35
trustee in bankruptcy
application for sale
by 165–168
trustees of land
appointment 141–142
duties 143
powers 142–143
delegation 143
restrictions 143
removal 142
trustee as beneficiary 142
trusts
beneficial interests
under 17–18
co-ownership
see **co-ownership**
concurrent interests 134,
137–138
constructive 140–141
licences protected
by 180–181
key facts 131
resulting 139–140
role 137–138
strict settlements 135–137
successive
interests 134–137
TLATA 134
trustees *see* **trustees of
land**
trusts for
sale 137–138

Index

✳✳✳✳✳✳✳✳✳✳

trusts of land 138–140
  beneficiaries
    application to
      court 145–146
    capital proceeds 146
    consent 144
    consultation 144
    dispute resolution 145
    occupation 144–145
  co-ownership 153
  exam question 148
  express
    declaration of trust
      effect 139
    formalities for
      creation 139
    when arise 138
  implied
    constructive 140–141
    formalities for
      creation 141
    resulting trust 139–140
    when arises 139
  key cases 147–148
  protection for purchaser
    registered land 146
    unregistered land 146
trusts for sale 137–138
  co-ownership 153
  TLATA and 138

undue influence
  actual 239
  effect of finding 239
  evidence of 239
  lenders and 239–240
  mortgages 238–240
  presumed 239
unregistered land 48–59
  adverse possession 121–122
  brought into registered
    system 29
  conveyancing procedure 51
  enforcement against third
    parties
    of easement 203
    of lease 87
  equitable easements 54
  equitable interests 53–58
    failure to register 55–57
    notice doctrine 57–58
    overreaching 57
    registrable as land
      charge 53–57
  estate contract 54
  exam questions 59
  examination of title
    deeds 51
  good root of title 51
  key cases 58–59
  key facts 49
  land charges register
    search 54–55
  legal interests 52–53
  mortgage priority 247
  occupation rights 54
  proof of title 31, 51
  proprietary interests 51–58
  puisne mortgage 53, 54
  purchase of trust land 146
  restrictive covenants 54

vesting deed 135
villeinage 9

wild animals 6
wild plants 6